THE PARADOX OF MAUPASSANT

Guy de Maupassant
(Photo-Nadar) by courtesy of Editions Albin Michel, Paris

THE PARADOX OF
MAUPASSANT

Paul Ignotus

FUNK & WAGNALLS

Funk & Wagnalls, *A Division of* Reader's Digest Books, Inc.

CONTENTS

PART TWO

THE MADNESS OF LACKING ILLUSIONS

PREFACE

It was a stipend granted by the Congress for Cultural Freedom, on the initiative of the Secretary to its International Council, Mr Michael Josselson, that enabled me to concentrate for years on this book. In addition I am indebted to the Society of Authors through the Crompton Bequest Fund for its most generous help.

I did most of the research in the reading rooms of the British Museum, including its Newspaper Library in Colindale, and am grateful for the helpfulness of its officials. The same applies to the staffs of the Bibliothèque Nationale in Paris, and public libraries in Dieppe, Fécamp and Rouen, of which I had an opportunity of making use when on a visit to France, together with my wife who greatly assisted me. During my stay in Normandy I had an interesting talk with the guardian of the Flaubert museum, Croisset, near Rouen; with M. Dubuc of 'Les Amis de Gustave Flaubert', Landrieu, near Rouen; with the distinguished historian, Mme de Payer, occupier of the house which used to belong to Mme de Maupassant in Etretat; and with the keepers of *La Guillette*, the house built and inhabited in Etretat by Guy de Maupassant himself.

In and from Paris, I have been supplied with extremely precious material by my friend (and translator of my former English book, *Political Prisoner*), M. Michel Chrestien, who was kind and patient enough to read my text carefully and comment on it in detail. I am indebted to him for his pertinent criticism and interesting suggestions – most of which I was delighted to accept.

I am unable to enumerate all friends to whom I owe gratitude for information, encouragement and criticism of some chapter seen by them, but I must mention Arthur Koestler, whose help at a critical stage proved decisive. The friend who worked most on the manuscript is Mrs Mary Sur, who, at my request, undertook the job of improving my English. The French fragments quoted, except when otherwise stated, are her translations or, less frequently, my own with her improvements. I also had the benefit of her advice on certain aspects of the subject matter. In the preparation of the Index I was assisted by my sister, Charlotte.

In Chapter 10 I quote some paragraphs of *Une Vie* ('A Woman's Life', translated by Antonia White, Hamish Hamilton), and in Chapter 20, one of *Boule de Suif* (translated by H. N. P. Sloman, Penguin Books, 1946), with the kind permission of the copyright owners.

In the course of my correspondence with French colleagues, M. Dumesnil was kind enough to present me with a copy of his important book, *Guy de Maupassant*, and M. Borel with one of his curious publications in *Les Œuvres libres*.

I had been planning to reduce the use of footnotes in this book to the minimum, but, in the course of writing, was unable to resist the temptation to prove that my points on controversial matters were, if not necessarily true, at any rate tenable. For this reason, it was not possible to adopt a completely uniform procedure in footnote references; on doubtful points, it seemed to me necessary to give page references, whereas on other occasions this practice may have appeared artificial and overdone.

As I have very frequently upset the chronology in my narrative so as to cover a particular subject more coherently, I felt an unusually long chronology indicated and, let me hope, useful. On the other hand, I did not think it necessary to add a special chapter on 'Literature'; my references in the text, footnotes and Index represent my tribute to the Maupassant biographers, critics and commentators by whose works I was profiting, and also serve as a guide for anyone interested in Maupassant, his works, his surroundings, his ancestry, his epoch. Amongst writings on Maupassant which I found helpful, but had no opportunity to quote in my text, were the Introduction by J. H. Matthews to his *Selected Short Stories* (University of London Press, 1959), and the relevant chapters in *Histoire du Naturalisme Français* by Charles Beuchat (Editions Corea, Paris, 1949).

There are certainly many moot points in the book – starting with trivialities such as questions of spelling names and titles of books. Nothing can be so trivial as to warrant neglect about it; but as the sources themselves are conflicting, one has just to accept one of them and drop the other. Whether Maupassant's lady friends were Mesdames Kann, Straus and Lecomte du Nouÿ, as I put it, or Kahn, Strauss and Le Conte du Nouÿ, as spelt in a minority of documents I saw, will not, in the final analysis, matter very much. Conflicting information, for instance, on whether Maupassant did revisit England in 1890, and other such details occasionally pointed out in my footnotes, may I feel also be left undecided.

An omission that may be held against me consists of having skipped in my analyses of Maupassant's works his very famous, successful, and in a way typical, short story, *La Parure*, to which I only refer briefly in the Introduction and the Chronology. But frankly I could add nothing to the brilliant chapter on the story of that story – and its merits and the limitation of its merits – in Mr Steegmuller's *Maupassant*, which I quote on other occasions and recommend to any English reader interested in French literature. Besides, I had naturally to make some selection deciding on which of Maupassant's writings to dwell at some length, and I thought it permissible to choose (*a*) those which impressed me most, and (*b*) those most markedly illustrating Maupassant's mental development as I saw it. Although Maupassant lived not long ago and his career was of interest to many of his contemporaries, not a few of the details we know about his life appear to be contradictory. It is possible to question the authenticity of important documents attributed to him. Here already, however, we tread on delicate ground and whilst I discuss some such points, others I have preferred to leave open to further research. Certainly there is much yet to be clarified about this champion of clarity.

P. I.

INTRODUCTION

The puzzling thing about Guy de Maupassant is his fantastic mixture of greatness and mediocrity. He did what seems most obvious for any author to do. He described people as they were, as they appeared to him in everyday life, on the seashore, in the streets, at the table or by the fireside. His sources were the sights he saw, or the stories he overheard, or read in the *faits-divers*. These he sometimes combined, but often did not, and he either rounded them off with a neat little twist in the tail, or left them as they were, his main contribution to the ready-made material being to stop where carrying on would have been tedious. He told his stories in the style of 'small talk', with a light touch that could more often than not be mistaken for that of a clever but unimportant chronicler, using devices which became obvious as soon as he had applied them, and indeed had often been regarded as hackneyed before him – for often he simply made use of some well-known *clichés* which had been employed by his elders and even by some eighteenth-century story-tellers. Yet with these simple instruments he succeeded in digging up depths of existence only hazily suspected by visionary poets and profound philosophers, in projecting the hidden conflicts within individual souls, as well as in partnerships in bed and business, in family homes and social classes, in fact in depicting life with alarming and amusing reality. This he did mainly in his short stories – *Boule de Suif* which established his fame; *Le Père Milon, Pierrot, Le Mal d'André, L'Armoire, Amour, Miss Harriet, L'Héritage, Le Petit Fût* and others; *Le Champ d'Oliviers* ('Aeschylean' as Taine called it) which showed his elegance in tragedy; *La Maison Tellier* and *Yvette* which illustrate his genius for frivolity; *La Parure*, one of his most brilliant, though now hackneyed stories, with the characteristic twist in the tail – but also in parts of his novels, especially in *Bel-Ami*, in *Pierre et Jean* and in *Une Vie*; and in his meditative travel diary, *Sur l'Eau*.

His greatness has often been questioned in his own lifetime and since, on the grounds that it is, after all, his *short* stories in which he was at his best – a ludicrous objection, I feel, though it may appeal to many a believer in monumentality. There is more to be said for those who feel some coarseness in the texture of his writing, smooth and polished coarseness, verging on that psychical climate of mediocrity that is inseparable from his brilliance. But even this objection is demolished by his stature which can, so to speak, be measured. If the greatness of an author consists in his knowing much about people and in his ability to convey that knowledge in an easily readable and impressive way to others, then Maupassant was one of the greatest ever born – second only, in my view, to Tolstoy.

The Maupassant puzzle has teased the literary critics both in and outside France ever since he emerged and captured the reading masses in 1880. He has never been a 'writer's writer' like his master, Flaubert; never one destined for highbrow admiration – rather the opposite. It was the general public that acclaimed him, not the initiated few. But the power of his gifts overwhelmed even those who, rightly or wrongly, imagined that the road of a genius must lead through incomprehension and hostility to triumph. A new genius is indeed non-conformist by definition, even if conservative in one respect or another; he usually needs sophisticated exegetists to explain, even to vulgarize, his hidden meanings, and to demolish those bastions of conventionality that bar him from general appreciation. Genius, before being recognized, bores or staggers or even paradoxically does both, whereas Maupassant did neither. He now and then shocked, partly because it was *chic* to do so and it was a fashion he rather enjoyed; partly because he belonged, after all, to the school of realists or naturalists whose very *raison d'être* was to some extent questioned at that time by traditionalists, mystics and the common prude. But even his way of shocking was conventional and mild when compared with that of his elders such as Hugo, Flaubert, Baudelaire and, particularly, Zola. He was reprimanded rather as a schoolboy hoaxer than as an innovator or a rebel. And what could be found to require elucidation or popularization in his works? There were no hidden meanings, no strange symbols, no new ideas or unusual adjectives – his most open-minded contemporary reviewers, Lemaître and Anatole France, for instance, confessed to being quite embarrassed at finding nothing. It was just a natural phenomenon, to be taken or left, and since it was enjoyable, as well as frighteningly truthful, it was taken. The only problem was how to pin the problem down; it was the mystery of clarity, the originality of the obvious.

The puzzling contrast in Guy de Maupassant, then, was not that of the madman or the savage capable of producing master-pieces, though this too comes into the picture. Thanks mainly to Lombroso, we are nowadays anything but surprised to learn of a great man that he was a lunatic; nor would anybody be surprised to hear of a barbarous genius that outshone the light of libraries and universities. Maupassant's madness – of syphilitic origin – was a medical fact; and there was also some savagery in him, a rough-hewn rock of power, manifest not in visions or melodies, but in his sensuality, his familiarity with nature, his manner of hunting, sailing, love-making. As one of his mistresses, Gisèle d'Estoc, said, there was in him, or in both of them, something primordial – '*pré-social*'. All this would come under the heading of 'high and low', a contrast to which we are accustomed. But as a literary figure he showed the more unusual contrast of high and mediocre, or a miracle very near the pedestrian average.

He was so strikingly 'upper middle' in practically everything! Coming from a typical upper middle-class family in France – a mixture of lower aristocracy and higher *bourgeoisie*, with much riches in the background and yet not actually rich, with deep roots in Normandy and yet not entirely Norman, neither entirely urban nor entirely rural – he grew up a handsome, lively, light-witted boy, bright and pleasant, reasonably good at everything, not outstanding in anything – except practical jokes and amateur navigation – and not suspected of great gifts by anyone save his mother. He learned easily and often well, he versified well but conventionally. He then became a good soldier in the war, a good civil servant in peace, companionable as a rowing and drinking fellow and helpful as a sort of voluntary research assistant to Flaubert – who loved him for reasons of his own, but was most doubtful about his gifts. He was nice, well-read, polished, but second-rate. Turgenev, who knew him from Flaubert's entourage and rather liked him, regretted that that charming young fellow would never become a real writer. The young fellow was thirty, too old to show the first signs of originality, but too young to reach perfection. Yet suddenly, as a sign of originality, he did reach perfection. 'The little blighter has surpassed us,' Flaubert triumphed, and Turgenev hastened to admit that he had been wrong.

Maupassant called his own career 'meteoric', and so it was; when he was forty it was over. From the first three decades and the last three years of his short life there remain various literary materials, sometimes fascinating, sometimes poetic, but nothing that shows any mastery. In a span of ten years, then, he poured out a lava of writing, very uneven in quality, impeccable at its best, cheap and shallow at its worst, mediocre more often than not, but never unsuitable for sale. 'Je suis un industriel des lettres,' he said, in a provocative air of self-irony of course, but not without foundation. As he matured, after his literary apprenticeship, he grew into an obsessed mass-producer, a cross between a meteor and a conveyor belt. Success does not improve manners, nor does diligence; he turned less kind, less pleasant as he gained in fame and fortune, and even the responsiveness of his mind shrank in breadth, though not in depth and sharpness, as he concentrated only on what he could make use of in his writing. Fundamentally, however, he never changed; not, at any rate, his spiritual level. In his intellect, his curiosities, his philosophy, his tastes, his whole outlook, he remained strikingly 'upper middle'. Not the vulgar snob whom Edmond de Goncourt would have liked to see in him, nor the generous mind and profound thinker who, according to some of his admirers, had been hidden behind the crude and mundane mask – no, he was definitely above the average, but only just. And he was just clever enough to be more piercing, more concise, more cruelly sincere, more disarmingly elegant than anyone else in a genre cultivated by many, very many, before, during and particularly after his lifetime. For he had thousands of disciples and imitators all over the world, quite a number of them brilliant – in English literature Somerset Maugham is the textbook example. But I have not come across a similar meteor; I am sure there was and is nobody to match him. In what seems straightforward routine, like composing a multiplication table, he was unique.

It is the magic of the obvious feat that could only be performed once. Is there any explanation as to why it happened when it did? Of so many 'upper middle' intellects of the upper middle class interested in mirroring people through anecdotes, why should it have been just this one who succeeded? And, of so many theatres of intellectual and artistic life, why should it have been just the Paris of 1880–90 where it could succeed?

This is the question I have set myself to answer. I wish Maupassant's genius for simplicity could assist me in presenting the results of my research. But I am afraid, even if I shared his genius, this would be a hopeless task. Maupassant himself conspicuously failed whenever he tried to explain anything of his own literary background and ideas. In this field his Preface to *Pierre et Jean* was his most momentous achievement, an attempt to outline his opinions on writing. This essay is highly thought of, amongst others, by René Dumesnil whose judgment can certainly not be dismissed on such matters; yet I would rather agree with Anatole France who felt it was like the performance of a lion expounding the theory of courage. One of the reasons is that Maupassant was far more gifted in representing and narrating things than in analysing them. And he seemed strangely inhibited on this subject. He was notorious for becoming quite panic-stricken when people started talking literature in his presence or when journalists tried to make him say something about himself as a writer. During his meteoric decade he wrote incessantly, as if obsessed; when it was not stories, plays, articles, travel accounts, it was private letters, many of them still unpublished. But from what has been published one does not find a clue to the obsession itself. One may come across smart remarks such as 'I only write for money', or 'if you are interested in the money you earn, do anything you like but keep off literature'. As confessions they were equally valid, however contradictory; but it is no good consulting *him* about the nature of such contradictions. He discloses everything powerfully, except the key to his power to disclose.

Not only his style was strikingly simple; his outlook, his philosophy was so also. 'Pessimism' is the catchword for it. It was not, however, the pessimism springing from a metaphysical system such as Schopenhauer's (though, incidentally, he professed to be Schopenhauer's admirer), but simply that of a man who sees things dark and who only believes what he sees. It was, in a word, lack of illusions. His shrewd observation of people, his ubiquitous familiarity with souls and surroundings, his vivid reactions to the phenomena of the sea, of rivers, fields, streets, cemeteries and dining-rooms, his ability to extract the poetic or the humorous as well as the depressing, the tragic and the hopelessly drab, out of them, even his struggles with weird ghosts and visions of the supernatural related in the straightforward manner of a single-track mind – all this can be reduced to the negative virtue of not going beyond that which his senses revealed to him. This attitude was, in any case, his frame of mind as well as the frame of his writing. Nothing could be simpler than that. And nothing, I am afraid, could be more complicated than that which distinguishes *his* simplicity from that of other comparable writers – whether predecessors, contemporaries or successors.

The reason, as his great contemporary, Ernest Renan, said, is that 'complexity is anterior to simplicity'; and if this applies to the ordinary streams of simple thought, which only look limpid because their shallowness makes them transparent, however polluted they may be, it applies even more to the simplicity of a Maupassant, which turns the ocean into a transparent medium teeming with live creatures under our very eyes – creatures as familiar as the greengrocer on the next corner and as exciting as any greengrocer can be if stripped of the haze of conventionality usually surrounding him. Maupassant's utterly limpid medium was in reality an enormously rich solution, distilled from all the experience, social conflict and intellectual endeavour of his background and environment, both actual and historical.

Though Maupassant was a chronicler of his own time *par excellence*, he himself was strikingly the product of his ancestors, biologically and spiritually. The memories of his paternal and, even more, of his maternal ancestry were decisive in his approach to people and to the arts from his early childhood onwards. To understand the nature of the apparent simplicity of his method of observing and writing, one has to trace the past of those two families and of their friends, such as Dr Flaubert of the *Hôtel-Dieu* hospital and his son, Gustave, for it was the complex strands of their experiences which met in him and which he was able to weave together in such a deceptive way. The exchanges

which took place several years before his birth between his
uncle, Alfred Le Poittevin, and his 'spiritual father', Gustave
Flaubert, foreshadowed the conflicts which he was to face; and
the psychical climate of their adolescent gang was to influence
young Guy's family surroundings and appear again and again
in varying settings until his character fully developed and his
meteoric career started.

Even if all these threads of past history can be traced, the
secret of his ability to weave them remains, and, as far as the
secret of creative genius can be probed at all, the obsessions
revealed in his lunacy may provide some clue – although, needless to say, they must not be allowed to overshadow his work
which, at its best, was as un-lunatic as a work of art can be.

Jules Lemaître thought Maupassant's distinctive mark was his
'deep sensuality', and he struggled hard to explain what he meant
by this. I feel it can only be approached by going through the
stages of history that led up to it. To be sensual is really a lion's
virtue, as well as a rabbit's, but to make it 'deep', the memories
of generations were needed, some of whom grew up in a discipline that banned sensuality, others in the striving for its libera-
tion, but all adding new shades to its manifestations until it took
the shape in which Maupassant projected it, exuberant as the
male *pré-social*, and sophisticated as the *haute-bourgeoisie* of
Faubourg Saint-Honoré A.D. 1880. It was the sensuality of
illusions lost and of wealth and artistry reconquered after so
many revolutions and counter-revolutions – economic, spiritual,
social and political – since the Enlightenment. It stemmed from
the history of the rising French middle class and, even more,
from the protests against the morality represented by that middle
class, the cry 'épater les bourgeois', first Romantic and then
anti-Romantic; and all embodied in a shy and decent middle-
class man, Gustave Flaubert, Maupassant's mentor and master.
It was for Maupassant to carry Flaubert's ideas into practice.
His personality, his intellect, his style were of a poor quality
when compared with those of his master; but so, necessarily, is
practice when compared with ideas. It was in Maupassant, and
in his Paris of the 1880s, that the mixture of self-asserting pride
and self-debasing scepticism, of money-seeking, pleasure-seeking and liberality characteristic of the wealthy Republican

ruling classes, showed itself in its full splendour. That moment, like Maupassant's meteoric career, was unique in history.

Almost as soon as Maupassant died that moment came to an end. It may seem trite to consider the coincidence as symbolic, but it was indeed the fact. With the *affaire Dreyfus* a new chapter started, and the heyday of the liberal *haute-bourgeoisie* had gone. To find careless pleasure in mirroring the miseries of life became a psychical, almost a physical, impossibility. One could carry on with pleasure, without naked mirrors; or with naked mirrors, without careless pleasure; or else seek comfort in God or socialism or the secular religion of national intolerance; and the further alternative of an ostentatious *danse macabre* also survived. Some germs of these attitudes could be traced in Maupassant; especially the macabre heritage of Flaubert's surroundings. But this, together with likes or dislikes for tyrants, masses, Saints, wars, Jews, universal suffrage and theosophy, could at that time be presented with the detached casualness of jovial after-dinner chatter, introduced in the way Maupassant was so fond of: 'It won't be an amusing story, ladies . . .', but with a view to amusing them all the same. That sort of detachment has since been irretrievably lost, its cult sunk into that mediocrity which swamped Maupassant's genius without defeating it. A society turned inside out can no longer be faithfully pictured without an analytical view of its entrails. Faithful picturing of society is not everything; nor is snappy and detached story-telling; but there is something fascinating in the memory of the *milieu* that united the two in a perfect compound.

To discover the components of that perfection one has to risk lengthy historical divagations; and at the moment of its fading, one will have to face the uncanny fluorescence of a disintegrating mind. Not long before Maupassant's early death Goncourt noted in his diary – without the hypocrisy of trying to hide his satisfaction – 'il est en train de *s'animaliser*'. This was true; all the same the 'animal', in its unsavoury agony, groped its way towards revealing some realities on which the 'meteor' had failed to throw light. Maupassant's end was tragic, without a moral for consolation. 'It won't be an amusing story, ladies.'

PART ONE

THE MAKING OF A GENIUS: FLAUBERT AND HIS DISCIPLE

1 · Guy's birth

Amongst the fertile fields of Normandy, her mild slopes, winding lanes, tidy yellow haystacks and herds of lazy brown cows, in a vast greenness speckled with flowers of brilliant colours under a faintly misty sky, not far from the coast leading from the fisheries of Fécamp to the architectural fancies of that much-advertised holiday resort, Etretat, there stands near the pretty village of Tourville-sur-Arques, a stately castle in a huge park, named after its erstwhile master, the Marquis of Miromesnil, a distinguished statesman of the French monarchy on the eve of the Great Revolution.

It is a showpiece of well-groomed archaism. Occasionally it is inhabited by its present owner, the Marquis de Vogüé and his family, but it is always open to visitors, for an entrance fee. It is under the care of an Italian farming family, whose elder daughter shows visitors round and recites the guide-book which, like guide-books in general, illustrates the history of past centuries by pointing to the good deeds of deceased nobles and to the beauties of the trees grown and the walls built under their auspices. The origins of the estate date back to the late middle ages, and its main attractions, besides the château, are a majestic alley of beeches and a little Renaissance chapel built in flint and representing in its stained-glass windows the humiliation of Jesus Christ and the glory of the Miromesnil family. The château has been made ageless through innumerable refittings and additions even up to recent times, but its general character still reflects, as it did a hundred or two hundred years ago, the dignified splendour of the *roi soleil* and his courtiers. It breathes an air of polished, outdated and yet powerful feudality, in its elegant harmony of pink and grey.

It was in this château, in the room under its western great turret, that on 5 August 1850 Henri-René-Albert Guy de Maupassant was born, if his mother's word is to be trusted.[1] But most of those who knew her in Fécamp, in Etretat, in Tourville, agreed that it could not be trusted.

This scepticism is justifiable. Mme Gustave de Maupassant, *née* Laure Le Poittevin, was a fine woman, of spiritual beauty and intelligence, highly educated, sensitive, tender-hearted, but whimsical, self-centred and ambitious to an extent that often drove her into vulgar outbursts. A neurotic soul, torn between insomnia and daydreams, she was only too ready to believe, and to have others believe, what she wished to be true; and her imagination, fired by Shakespeare and the current fashion, made her prone to the appeals of lordliness, even to its hackneyed ornaments. This snobbery she shared with her husband; as Dumesnil says,[2] it was the only thing on which the two of them agreed in their unhappy partnership.

Not that Gustave de Maupassant was a believer in aristocratic superiority or privilege; he was far too cynical to be so. He was, at any rate on the surface, a happy-go-lucky fellow, fond of easy money, easy love affairs, smart clothes, heavily laid tables, with painting as a hobby that evoked most of what he was too dandified to put into words, and with no attachment to any social creed, either aristocratic or democratic. But, for this very reason, he gladly accepted the conventions of common snobbery, particularly when able to share in their benefits.

When his wife was pregnant, in the summer of 1850, they were residing in Fécamp, tenants of a sordid apartment in a house inhabited by petty traders in the Rue Sous-les-Bois – today Quai Guy de Maupassant. They could not bear the idea that this should be the birthplace of their heir. They rented a summer residence at Miromesnil castle, with a view to moving in before the baby was born. But Guy was actually born before the date foreseen in the Fécamp street that bears his name today. Mme de

---

[1] Her letter to Henri Gadeau de Kerville, 5 July 1894; *Souvenirs sur Maupassant*, edited by Albert Lumbroso; Rocca, Rome, 1905. Edouard Maynial, *La vie et l'œuvre de Guy de Maupassant*, Mercure de France, Paris, 1906.

[2] René Dumesnil, *Guy de Maupassant*, Tallandier, Paris, 1947.

Maupassant, in a hurry, moved into the castle and when, on the day foreseen, the midwife who had been ordered turned up, put on an act pretending that, for some nervous whim not surprising in her condition, she was unable to accept the care of that particular midwife and dismissed her. Some weeks later, on 23 August, the baby was privately baptized, *ondoyé*, by the special permission of the Archbishop, in the dim light filtering through the stained glass windows of the Miromesnil chapel. He was given his baptism proper one year later, on 17 August 1851.

This is, apparently, the more credible story as against Mme de Maupassant's own version, a story thoroughly elaborated on by the writer Georges Normandy,[1] himself a native of Fécamp. But there are other versions as well; some put Guy's birthplace in another Tourville, near Le Havre; some in Rouen; some, including his death certificate, in Sotteville, near Yvetot. In any case, says Georges Dubosc,[2] learned and charming chronicler of everything Norman, Guy de Maupassant was born *en pays cauchois* in the most Norman, most sea-ridden province of Normandy; and, even if this were not so, we may ask, what would it matter? The background atmosphere of the stories is more significant in this case than their foundation in fact. Guy de Maupassant was born in a cloud of gossip, wrapped in high ambitions ridiculed by the very people who indulged in them, surrounded by a rich gamut of perfumes ranging from that of the fishmarket to that of the beech alleys.

The most typical part of the gossip surrounding his birth and origins relates to his family links with Gustave Flaubert. In a number of writings, as well as in conversation, he was referred to as Flaubert's nephew, and later as his godson, though he was neither. Meanwhile, rumour had it that he was really Flaubert's natural son, a conjecture that fluttered all the time above the guesses about his birthplace. All serious writers who have been into the matter thoroughly, including René Dumesnil, the greatest living authority on the literary circle that included

[1] *La vie anecdotique et pittoresque des grands écrivains: Guy de Maupassant*, Vald, Rasmussen, Paris, 1926.

[2] Georges Dubosc, *Trois Normands* (Corneille, Flaubert, Maupassant), Defontaine, Rouen, 1917.

them both,[1] dismiss this story as absurd, and do so with full reason. It is most unlikely that Flaubert and Laure de Maupassant ever had a love affair or even met about nine months before Guy's birth. Besides, despite all the links of literature and friendship, there was no similarity between the characters of the two great novelists; nothing, at any rate, that would strike one as inherited. There was, on the other hand, despite their violent contrasts, a great deal of similarity between Gustave de Maupassant and Guy – a bit even in their looks, as far as can be seen from their pictures. They themselves were aware of their resemblance. 'Guy owes me his powers,' his father said to a friend,[2] meaning by *puissance* his sexual potency as well as his talent; 'to his mother he owes only what is worst in him, that is, his *développement*'. This was, of course, a jocular remark about one who had by then developed into a famous author and who was known to be, by his upbringing and education as well as by his affections, much more a mother's than a father's son. But in a way, Gustave was right; and so, in a different way, were those who insisted on links as intimate as blood relationship between his son and Flaubert. Guy de Maupassant was, spiritually, the offspring of a 'gang' – a kind of juvenile and parochial free-masonry, a sect united by common sensual and artistic experiences – a gang founded in the nurseries, colleges and playrooms *en pays cauchois*, and principally in Rouen, by a set of languid and sensitive *enfants terribles* of the upper middle class, in the twenties and thirties of the last century.

By the fifties, when the infant Guy first opened his eyes on the world, there were only two persons left to keep up the gang's rituals and to transpose its visions of puberty into mature literature; Gustave Flaubert and his 'brother in spirit', the poet, Louis Bouilhet. The founder and erstwhile chief of the gang, Laure de Maupassant's brother, Alfred Le Poittevin, had died young before Guy was born.

[1] René Dumesnil, *Le Réalisme et le Naturalisme; Gustave Flaubert;* and *Guy de Maupassant.*

[2] Jean de La Varende, *Grands Normands* (Flaubert, Barbey d'Aurevilly, Maupassant), Defontaine, Rouen, 1939.

2 · The upper middle classes of Rouen

For a moment, however, let us take a step farther back in time in order to trace the antecedents of this gang.

At the cradle of everything modern on the Continent of Europe there had been the Great Revolution. In France, its birthplace, which it had transformed for some one hundred and twenty years into the guinea-pig country of the world, it was the source of unforeseen developments, of Liberty culminating in butchery, of despotism exporting civic rights, of heroism, treachery, *gloire* and nausea. It was a *Romantic* period if ever there was one; but it was only later to give itself that name. As long as it lasted, it cherished the idea of a lofty Reason. Its gods wore togas, irrespective of their religious and political denominations. As Anatole France was to point out in *Les Dieux ont soif*, Enlightenment was not only the cry of the *sans-culottes* but also the all-pervading hobby of the aristocrats, and the Enlightened vision of a rational and dignified discipline continued to determine the style of the legal codes, as well as the shape of chairs and tables, under the spell of Napoleon's eagle. When eventually the eagle fell, a host of more colourful, more erratic, more emotional birds swarmed in and carried on the revolution in style and the counter-revolution in longings known as Romanticism.

The laws of lasting success were not, however, so romantic. Throughout the whole period of rapid change it was characteristic *bourgeois* abilities that paid the highest dividends: eyes steadily kept on the exchange rate, hearts never committed to anything but the family fortunes; the Voltairian advice, 'Cultivate your garden', translated into industrial terms and only qualified by a tempered homage to celestial powers which required attendance at Sunday services and the like. Shrines and thrones collapsed, but stocks rose steadily. By the time the Bourbons came back middle-class ideals had been eclipsed, but the middle classes had established themselves irrevocably as the new ruling class. Marx, some thirty or forty years later, in his analysis of recent French history, went so far as to say that there had, in fact, been no aristocracy or nobility of importance since the beginning of the century; that what had survived the Republic and the Empire and was called back to notoriety by the Restoration, was simply the *agrarian bourgeoisie*. This may be an exaggeration. By a natural reaction to both Robespierre's and Bonaparte's failures, the mystic cult of hereditary privileges shone brighter under the restored Bourbons than it had under those princes who had been ready to share their own glory with plebeian philosophers. Certainly it was no longer the old aristocracy, no longer the flippant and generous patrons of art and letters, no longer the worldly ladies and gentlemen highly amused by the wit of their would-be executioners. Their successors were both more modest and more die-hard. Those unwilling to melt into the new aristocracy created by bayonets and the stock exchange, withdrew into a parochial ritualism which, as time marched on, grew into its own parody, as touching and impressive occasionally as it was on the whole ludicrous. These pathetic relics can be encountered in many a Maupassant story, from *Une Vie* to *A cheval*.

Between the lords of the land and those of the banks, but largely outside both, there was the old *bourgeoisie*. As to their heritage, they were as old as the aristocracy; but in their capacity as a ruling class, as new as the upstart millionaires. They had their own protagonists under the Republic and their own martyrs under its guillotines, they had been decimated and robbed by all the revolutions and counter-revolutions, but they weathered them all. They had thrived and flourished in Paris, as well as in the small towns and villages, but nowhere so intensely perhaps as in the old provincial centre of Rouen, the Norman capital.

For Rouen is an impressive city, a *cité*, a *civitas*, in both the traditional and the modern sense. 'She seems to be the privileged town of France,' Edouard Herriot wrote:[1] 'it is the Seine that has made her great.' Situated on the river, though near enough to the sea to act as a maritime harbour, she is rather like the Port of London; but her Gothic spires, the ancient schools and lawcourts in her heart, surrounded by narrow, tottering houses, with the patterns of brown timbers on their walls, would rather remind an English onlooker of Oxford, or Salisbury. To Mau-

[1] *La Porte Océane*, Hachette, Paris, 1932.

24

passant's Bel-Ami 'it appeared as if soaked in the morning mist, with flashes of sunlight reflected from her roofs, and her thousand fragile steeples, pointed or squat, frail and wrought like giant jewels, her square or round towers capped with heraldic coronets, her belfries, her bell-turrets, the whole Gothic population of the church summits, dominated by the sharp arrow of the cathedral, that surprising bronze needle, ugly, strange, out of proportion, and the highest in the world'. A city where religion, commerce, craftsmanship, sailing, learned professions, bohemian licence and virtuous rituals all had equally deep roots, where Joan of Arc had been burnt and Maître Corneille had pleaded at the bar, Rouen was the most imposing abode of that respectable *bourgeoisie* which, after the bankruptcy of the blue-blooded and the downfall of those standing for *hoi polloi*, had asserted itself as the backbone of the nation.

But a rather bowed backbone it was. It accepted its own power with resignation rather than in a state of triumph. It owed everything to its caution and its opportunism, to its willingness to put up with the *terreur* of the rabble as well as with that of the vindictive gentry, with the privileges of the Imperial swashbucklers as much as with those of the restored Royal parasites. Its faith in Catholicism battered, its faith in Reason compromised, it diluted the two in the practical wisdom of making the best of both worlds. The gardens its members cultivated were often apple orchards, Normandy being renowned for its cider; or vineyards, for though their wine would never be a match for those produced in other provinces, their wine trade ranked with the first. Gardens yielding even more lucrative crops were the shipping trade and the textile industry, with their various ramifications. The members of the legal and medical professions, intermarried with the merchants and industrialists, maintained a high standard of life and social behaviour. The Flauberts, Le Poittevins, Fleuriots, Thurins, Chevaliers, possibly also the fierce Republican middle-class family of the Cord'hommes, and that of the less prosperous Dr Bouilhet, appear to have belonged to this same group of people, sharing similar experiences and developing similar patterns of conduct. Though with differing emphasis, they all tried to combine liberalism with conformism and *bon ton* under a monarchy which was itself trying to combine constitutional proceedings with hereditary authoritarianism. Tutored by *abbés*, used to looking up for guidance to agnostic philosophers, versed in antique as well as medieval Latin, they did their best to pass their education, as well as their wealth, on to their children and grandchildren.

M. Paul Le Poittevin, owner of important spinning mills in Caux, was one of the outstanding members of the Rouen *bourgeoisie*; the distinguished surgeon, Dr Achille-Cléophas Flaubert, head of the large *Hôtel-Dieu* hospital, was another. One of Le Poittevin's grandmothers, Mme Bérigny, had been a famous letter-writer in the eighteenth century, peak period of that literary genre, and had also been known as a clever versifier; interest in poetry and painting was hereditary in the family. The Flauberts, on the whole, were more interested in science and philosophy; they had been keen botanists and zoologists for generations. M. Le Poittevin and Dr Flaubert were great friends, godfathers of each other's children. M. Le Poittevin had a son, Alfred, born in 1816, and two daughters, one of whom, Laure, was born in 1821. Dr Flaubert also had a daughter, Caroline, and two sons, of whom the elder, Achille, was to become his father's assistant and successor at the *Hôtel-Dieu*, and the younger, Gustave, born in 1821, the novelist.

By the time these children started to grow up the Bourbon monarchy had once again collapsed. It was superseded by that *bourgeois* institution *par excellence*, the constitutional monarchy, with the Protestant scholar, Guizot, at its helm. Guizot was a puritanical and self-denying believer in racketeering as the most efficient instrument of sound government. 'Liberty, Equality, Fraternity' were re-enshrined, with the proviso that they must be 'limited by a limited number of enfranchised citizens'; the national colours were hoisted with the cry 'enrichissez-vous!' — get rich as fast as you can. It was reasonable advice, but falling far short of Reason. It was the enthronement of the middle class, and the frustration of those who had looked forward to their ascendance as to a millennium of superhuman virtues and undiluted intellectual delights.

3 · Hôtel-Dieu

The *Hôtel-Dieu* is a vast and bulky building, a monument of unpoetical solidity, a place, therefore, where poetic minds could most suitably and comfortably take stock of the beauties and horrors of existence. It was in its billiard-room that the Flaubert children, Gustave, then eight or nine years of age, and Caroline, three years his younger, started playing life, death, poetry, drama and unhappiness. They were accomplices as well as playmates. By climbing the grating and hanging on to the bars, they could clandestinely peep through the garden into the dissecting chamber and gaze at the dead bodies prepared for the scalpel and the microscope. 'The sun shone on the corpses, and the flies were buzzing to and fro between them and the flowers, and ourselves,' as Gustave nostalgically recalled many years later.[1] When caught and chased away by their father, they consoled themselves with play-acting in the billiard-room, in the company of their pal, Ernest Chevalier. Their repertory consisted mainly of historical dramas by Gustave Flaubert. How Gustave had become the prolific author which he then was (though never in later life) is rather a mystery. In his earlier childhood – to use the words of Guy de Maupassant in his essay written on Flaubert after his death – he was 'the very opposite of an infant prodigy'; it was only with the greatest difficulty that he learned to read and write. But when he reached the threshold of his ninth year, he seems to have dived from backwardness right into precocity. He was not yet ten when, in a letter to Ernest Chevalier, he complained, somewhat in the style of an adult platform speaker, about the scandal caused by the Citizen King, Louis Philippe, in sacking the hero of Liberty, Lafayette, and he promised his friend to send him the text of 'my liberal political and constitutional speeches', as well as 'some of my comedies'.

This little stage company was joined by others, among them Alfred and Laure Le Poittevin. Laure helped Caroline in sewing costumes for the performances, whereas Alfred, already well in

[1] In a letter to Louise Colet.

27

his teens, quite naturally became their spiritual leader. He was, at that early age, an accomplished classical philologist, a brilliant Latin scholar, versed in history and philosophy, tormented by metaphysics, interested in science as well as in politics, and intrigued by modern French, English and German poetry no less than by the classics. Though an eminent pupil of his college, and a multiple prize-winner, he hated school discipline and preferred scholarship in the nursery, or in the billiard-room. He taught Laure English so that she could read Shakespeare in the original. He taught Gustave epistemology and popular swearwords. He set the pace for the whole gang both in gobbling down culture and in defying Tyranny – the tyranny of Richard III, of the Holy Inquisition, of Napoleon the Great, of the Russian Czar, of all oppressors, villains and blood-thirsty war-lords, as well as of decent, dutiful, loving parents. The era of *épater les bourgeois* (literally 'shock the middle class') was dawning.

Alfred and Gustave were simply bewitched with each other. They talked incessantly about boredom and disgust – *ennui*, *dégoût*, both more spleenish in French than in their literal English translation – but they seem never to have been bored or disgusted with each other's company. They would go boating on the Seine together, rambling across the harbours and the cliffs together, slim, dark, delicate Alfred, fragile and visibly susceptible to illness, and his sturdy-looking young friend, tall, blond, blue-eyed Gustave, conspicuous for his beauty but also for his physical laziness, his reluctance to use his limbs more than necessary. Together they would call on grown-up friends whose stories they particularly enjoyed, such as Gustave's Uncle Parain, the goldsmith notorious for his bawdy geniality, or the boss at the swimming pool who fascinated them with his racy idioms and his style in rum-drinking. Then they would mix with their contemporaries or withdraw into the melancholy bliss of their dual solitude, Alfred reciting his poems to Gustave, Gustave reading his plays to Alfred, both raving over Victor Hugo, analysing Hegel, talking literature for five or six hours without a stop.

This friendship, always at boiling point, was to last till death. In childhood or boyhood, it mainly consisted in persuading each other how wicked, how stupid, how drab, filthy and futile life was; in manhood, it consisted in reminding each other of how hilarious it had been to come to those depressing conclusions. Their favourite spot had been by the fireplace, 'that hearth now probably embellished in my memory', Le Poittevin wrote, 'for I know we shall never have such balls as we used to have there . . .'. Yes, Flaubert echoed, 'there was never anything like our chats in the dirty chimney corner'. And the walks, too, despite Flaubert's conviction that only a sedentary posture befitted a philosopher. 'I have a stroll on the pier every evening,' Le Poittevin wrote to him. 'It is fine, and I think of you as much as Calypso thought of Ulysses. Do you remember the story I told you when we were climbing the sea wall? . . . Do you still see the gleams of sunlight falling on our faces?'

In fact, of the two, it was Alfred who should have been compared to Ulysses. It is he who committed the acts of desertion. Though he was more provocative, more inventive and revolutionary than his friend in challenging *bourgeois* rules of conduct, it was he who capitulated to them. Not only because he agreed to read Law – as did Gustave, under paternal pressure – but because he succeeded in it. Whilst Flaubert, under the sheer weight of his clumsiness and heaviness in everything outside his art and intellectual interest, was hopeless at it, Le Poittevin became a most gifted lawyer, who took revenge for his own success, in his letters to his old friend, by making bitter fun of the Justice he served. Still Flaubert forgave him for deserting Art, the more so as Le Poittevin later, to his own surprise, was overwhelmed once again by *rage littéraire* and towards the end of his short life, produced the only few fragments in which as a writer he rose above the mediocre. But he committed a more dramatic act of desertion when he married. In Flaubert's view, which is likely to have stemmed from Le Poittevin's original attitude, marriage for a man of letters was 'apostasy'. The marriage of his closest friend, his master and comrade in artistic and slightly lecherous celibacy, struck him as 'une rupture, un arrachement', as a sudden and treacherous separation from someone he could never hope to replace in his affection, and he underwent a terrific *chagrin de jalousie*, as he confided many years later in a letter, incidentally, to Alfred's sister, Laure.

Their mutual affection, however, outlived even this apostasy.

Flaubert stood by Le Poittevin's death-bed. He died in 1848, just after the further revolution, which removed the Citizen King. Le Poittevin had foreseen it and was interested in its development, but was too weak to move when it came. His heart was failing, but he stuck to his pipe, defying doctor's advice. With morbid passion, he smoked himself to death, when only thirty-two years of age. Or was it just the logical conclusion of his – of *their* philosophy? In a way, perhaps; for if Flaubert took Art more seriously, Le Poittevin took *dégoût* more seriously. The expressions of his disgust with life were to echo, some thirty-five and forty years later, in the despairing outcries of his nephew, Guy de Maupassant, also ensnared in lethal attachment to narcotics.

In a letter to Maxime Du Camp, Flaubert described how Alfred in his bed read Spinoza until late at night so long as he was able to, and when, in daylight, the beams of sunlight fell in through the open window, he shouted: 'Shut it, it's too beautiful, *too* beautiful.' Flaubert could never forget his friend. He had never been fascinated by anyone as by him, he said; he had never come across 'a mind as transcendental as his'; he had never loved anybody, 'either man or woman', so much as he loved Alfred. That childhood spent together haunted him in sensual images: 'we were beautiful'. It was beautiful even to suffer with him: 'The *ennuis*, the *ennuis*! all those souvenirs appear to me in vermilion.'

4 · The spell of 'Don Juan'

The nature of the friendship between Alfred Le Poittevin and Gustave Flaubert, in the light of their letters, seems obvious; but reality was less than obvious. Neither of them was a homosexual. But their genius consisted (as perhaps genius always does) in daring to be a child while knowing everything an adult does. In our post-Freudian epoch, it is no secret that children are, by nature, first, pan-sexual, thirsty for protective love, inclined to indulge in reveries about carnal fairies and to play with excrement; in a later stage, homosexual, boys despising, girls hating the opposite sex; and then, in adolescence, bisexual, in both their lewd and ethereal fancies, boys obsessed with all sorts of women, girls with all sorts of men, but boys as well as girls still in reality finding a more intimate pleasure, a more intense satisfaction, in sharing their fantasies with their fellow boys or girls rather than in seeing them materialize. In the adult stage, much of this survives; though the way it does survive differs enormously, from person to person, from country to country, and one of the determining factors is the spiritual fashion of the epoch. The styles of the Renaissance and the early Baroque provided a suitable setting for men infatuated by the beauty of men; think of Leonardo's life, Michelangelo's statues, Shakespeare's sonnets. There are similar aesthetic trends, though more criss-crossed with self-tormenting and self-asserting literature in our own epoch which, from this point of view, may be classified as starting with Paul Verlaine and Oscar Wilde. In the interval, men either liked women or liked to be virtuous; Western culture from 1620 to 1870 was non-homosexual.

It was not, however, more ascetic or more puritanical for that; not, at any rate, in all countries and epochs. There was the French Rococo period of embroidered and polygamous sensualism, with its sophisticated flippancy, often nauseating, often charming, which was to beguile some of the most important writers in the second half of the nineteenth century, such as Edmond de Goncourt, who in a way rediscovered its beauties, and Guy de Maupassant, who revived its graceful and libertine chattiness in his style. Its last breath before the Revolution was the novel, *Les Liaisons dangereuses*, by Laclos, which in the subsequent decades of Republican *vertu* was dismissed simply as 'obscene', but was vindicated as a work of art in the second half of the nineteenth century. Maupassant loved it and took one of his early pen-names – Guy de Valmont – partly from its hero. This should be pointed out at this juncture to show those waves of sensual imagery and style that led up to him; but actually in the years of the children's stage in the *Hôtel-Dieu*, the magnetism of Rococo erotics was at its lowest ebb. Both the restorers of royal authority and the spokesmen for liberal reform despised ostentatious frivolity. The drive for more sensual liberty was almost driven underground – in any case, into new and more tortuous channels. The Romantic wave of sensualism, which superseded that of the Rococo was less polygamous but all the more passionate, often incestuous in character; it fed on Rousseau's cult of emotions and was best personified perhaps in Byron, who held the young highbrows on the Continent more strongly under his spell than he did in England.

The circle of Le Poittevin and Flaubert was profoundly devoted to Byron. 'Don Juan' haunted the minds of the nineteenth century; first as seen by Byron, and later again as seen by Molière or Mozart, with his psychical qualms only lightly touched upon in the comedy, and only expressed in the music of the opera. Flaubert, halfway between Romanticism and the reaction against it, was intrigued by 'Don Juan' in both ways. Amongst the scraps left behind by him was the draft of a novel he had been planning: *Une Nuit de Don Juan*. It is rather a set of notes made by the author for his own use, in crackling short sentences but showing a tortuous trend of thought, barely understandable. Maupassant first published it in his essay on Flaubert in order to give an idea of how he had 'conceived and prepared his works', without, however, trying to get at its meaning. What it does illustrate is man's obsession with the manhood of the one who makes love more often, and to more women, than do other men.

This fanciful and nostalgic Don Juanism is the homosexuality of the heterosexual. And Don Juan, obsessed with the arithmetical projection of his own conquests, must have been, in this paradoxical way, a homosexual himself. To impress his fellow men was to him more important than the physiological pleasures that he got out of the innumerable – or perhaps one should say numerable – conquests of his 'Register Aria'. Alfred Le Poittevin and Gustave Flaubert were no more and no less homosexual (though with Registers very different) than he was.

Their friendship was a love affair in so far as it was a passionate partnership in each other's love affairs. The language in which they communicated was enthusiastic, exhibitionist, sophisticated, facetious, aphoristic, intuitively lofty and wilfully foul, a constant mental shuttling between Olympus and the poetry of the stews. In their words, written or spoken, they made each other constantly *voyeurs*, whether it concerned spiritual or carnal love.

Need this distinction between 'spiritual' and 'carnal' be made? The fact is *they* made it. On the grounds of their philosophy, they ought not to have done so; neither of them believed in a moral law separating the soul from the flesh. Le Poittevin was, in his flashes of insight, a forerunner of Freud as well as of Baudelaire, and an advocate of what would be called Scientism today; Flaubert, in his views on the composition of the universe (if not in those on Art) was a positivist and materialist. But in their emotions they were incurably romantic, and their experiences revealed quite a melodramatic simultaneity.

Each had his own great romantic and idealistic love of his life; each fell in love at first sight, in very similar circumstances, on the seashore under the cliffs of Caux.

Alfred, when about twenty, saw a young girl, 'Flora', with her mother; they only met two or three times, and hardly spoke to each other; but his infatuation with her was to last throughout his life. One day, in Le Havre, he imagined he saw her, again with her mother, at a hotel window, and when this turned out to be a mirage, he avenged himself on reality, as was his way, by running to prostitutes. He wrote poems to her, somewhat in the vein of Musset and Lamartine, sentimental, rhetorical poems, with touches of sensual diabolism – uninteresting poems to a name rather than a woman by an interesting man who offers his Angel the pleasure of flying to Hell with him, via copulation. The Angel was never given a chance to learn of the heaven or hell she had been missing; he raved about her, and about the disappearance of his very will to be happy in love, but he raved to himself or to Gustave (as in 1845):

> . . . I was brought up in this country, Le Havre and Honfleur . . . their sight still makes my heart soft. It is here that I used to dream of love when I was very young, of that love which I would refuse today, wherever it came from, whatever it were like. Today I have *le mot de cette bouffonnerie, exquise entre toutes*, but I like to return into the past when I believed! . . . A strange thing, I've got a bitter taste in my mouth; I am unable to give a kiss without its being ironic. I wonder what you think of my plan which I am going to carry out as soon as I get a chance: I shall spend three days in Le Havre

or Honfleur with a whore whom I shall pick out *ad hoc*. I'll have her drink, eat, walk and sleep together with me. I shall have great pleasure in showing her round, in the country where I used to believe when I was young . . . Then, I shall dismiss her.[1]

'Je ne peux donner un baiser qui ne soit ironique' is a strikingly neat formula; the rest is a pathetically outdated piece of literature, not in spite of but because of its repressed idealism, the self-pity clad in *blasé* 'buffoonery'. Le Poittevin's letters to Flaubert, in general, teem with detailed and obscene descriptions of his (and not only his) sex adventures, for which the conscientious editor of his works and correspondence, M. Descharmes, was at great pains to substitute dotted lines. There may be some information of interest hidden in those intimate reports, but they are unlikely to modify the psychical portrait of Alfred Le Poittevin, a man at his best when analytical and at his worst when lyrical.

His young friend, Gustave, was fourteen when on the beach one day he saw a lady's coat left on the sand and in danger of being washed away by the rising tide. He politely took it to a safer place. Then occurred the romantic moments quoted in the form of a dialogue in his first approximately mature (in any case, poetical) novel, *Mémoires d'un Fou*. At lunch-time that very day he heard in the inn:

'Thank you very much, sir, for your courtesy.'
I turned round; it was a young woman, sitting with her husband by the table.
'Why do you thank me?' I asked her absent-mindedly.
'For moving my coat away. Or wasn't it you?'
'O yes, madame,' I answered, embarrassed.
She looked at me.
I lowered my eyes and blushed. My word, what a glance! How beautiful she was, that woman! I still see her glowing eyes under black brows like sunshine fixed on me. She was tall and dark, her magnificent black hair falling in plaits over her shoulders; . . . her Greek nose, her flashing eyes, her high

---

[1] Alfred Le Poittevin, *Une promenade de Bélial, et Œuvres inédites*, edited and introduced by René Descharmes, Les Presses, Paris, 1924.

eyebrows admirably arched, her skin glowing and as if vel-
veted with gold; she was slender and delicate, with azure veins
serpenting on that flushed brown throat. Add to that the fine
down that cast a brown shadow on her upper lip and gave a
virile and energetic expression to her appearance, making
blonde beauties pale beside her . . .

Every morning, I went to see her bathing; I gazed at her
from a distance; I envied the soft and peaceful waves that
stroked her thighs and covered her heaving breast with
foam . . .

He went on envying those waves for decades to come, without
ever making an attempt to join them in embracing her; the story
is well known, mainly from *L'Education sentimentale*. The
lifelong idyll of Fréderic Moreau and Madame Arnoux is really
the most beautiful story of non-consummated love ever written.
It ends with a scene in which the picturesque dark lady, now
white at the temples, goes to see her old friend and admirer.
They press each other's hands: 'The very sight of your feet dis-
concerts me,' he says courting her. 'Fréderic! at my age!' she
protests; he is overwhelmed by 'the horror of incest' that numbs
his limbs; then, they do not know what to say; and she, with a
sudden and 'brutal' gesture, cuts a tress from her hair and leaves
it with him as a souvenir.

What can be guessed from the novel, and taken for granted
from the information available about Elisa Foucault-Schlésinger,
the woman on whom Mme Arnoux was modelled, is that it was
not she, even before her hair had turned grey, who insisted on the
spirituality of their connections. She would, presumably, have
been quite willing to become Gustave's mistress; and M.
Arnoux (or Maurice Schlésinger, as he was in real life) was both
too tolerant and too concerned with his own fleeting love affairs
to mind very much about what she did. But Gustave's love, like
Alfred's, was calculated to be its own frustration.

5 · 'The horror of incest'

What was at the root of that reluctance to see one's own desire achieved? Flaubert described it as 'the horror of incest', and, as this was some fifty years before the 'Oedipus complex' came into fashion, his insight may be trusted. All we know about his relations with women confirms this. Elisa Foucault-Schlésinger was substantially older than he was, and a mother of two children already when they first met. He ran after his mother's image when he fell in love with her and, in his search for a substitute home, made friends not only with herself but also with her second husband, Maurice, a rather Bohemian music publisher of German-Jewish extraction, with whom she lived in a loyal and lukewarm partnership. It was a lifelong friendship, undisturbed by the novelist's lyrical passion, undisturbed even by the publication of *L'Education sentimentale*.

Another substitute mother, with a record richer but more painful in his life, was Louise Colet, poet, novelist and thirteen years his elder. The trouble with her was that the desire *had* to be achieved. His contribution was that of giving way to what others had decided for him. There he was, that handsome, pleasant young man, already twenty-five and still without a mistress; something must be done about it, his artist friends in Paris felt; and Mme Colet, with her literary gifts and feminine vividness, experienced and a bit overripe but still attractive, and without any serious attachment, seemed the ideal choice. For Flaubert, as he later said, it was the *fatalité*, the 'abyss', and he gave in.

In the little pavilion which he used as his rest room – it is still intact today, although the house in Croisset has been pulled down – a little dagger in a leather sheath can be seen amongst the long rows of books and other relics; it was with this dagger that Louise Colet tried to kill him. Then she left it with him as a souvenir! Theirs was a disharmonious but most inspiring relationship which lasted, with one long and several short gaps, for some eight or nine years. Flaubert's letters to her were heart-rending, as spirited in expressing his tenderness as in providing excuses for its limitations. He was sincere in his declarations of love, but burdened from the outset with alarmed qualifications.

He was not really interested in sex; he had gone three years without feeling such desires at all, and even when it had been different, 'the women I chose I chose merely for the purpose of satisfying desire aroused in me by others'. 'As to what ordinarily touches men most closely, and for me is secondary – I mean physical love – I have always kept it separate from the other.' Now it had changed: 'You are the only woman I have loved *and* possessed.' This for Flaubert was much indeed, but not enough to make Louise feel that she had a lover, rather than an analyst of love. Flaubert feared he would ultimately disappoint her: 'You may be grateful to me for having the courage not to be more tender to you now,' he warned her, in 1846, the first year of their affair. But she could not reconcile herself with a lover who only talked Art to her. 'Is there anything more interesting to talk about?' he pleaded; and this, only a year later.

Flaubert had since his twenty-second year suffered from epileptic fits which he painfully concealed; this may have been one reason for his inhibitions. Apart from that, to 'talk Art' was really his life; he lived in a dreamland like a child, dreamy in mood even when observant in mind, obsessed with the magic of words as a child is with its toys – words printed, written or spoken. When he sought relaxation from writing works of art he wrote letters; when he was not writing he was reading; when he was not reading he talked about writing and reading. Skies and forests were beautiful to look at because they could be described in well-balanced, well-cadenced sentences, and an orgasm got its reality through the articulate reminiscences of it. He was noted for rattling out obscene words with delight, getting into trouble with shockable ladies when he forgot to curb his tongue. Loving Rabelais and Byron, he loved to talk sex, but for the sake of talk, 'for Art's sake'. Everything he said was true; he was so movingly honest that Louise Colet deserves all our sympathy for being incensed against him. We are also indebted to her for some of the scathing observations on the feminine nature in *Madame Bovary*.[1]

[1] 'Emma Bovary had begun, perhaps, as young Madame Delamare, and there was no question but that she had subsequently taken on a resemblance to Louise Colet.' Francis Steegmuller, *Flaubert and Madame Bovary*, Collins, 1947 edition, p. 253.

Then there was the Romantic, Republican and enthusiastic novelist, George Sand, Flaubert's most reassuring, most soothing mother-figure; his correspondence with her surpassed in beauty even that with Louise Colet, in its uninhibited philosophizing, the ostentatious lack of illusions and the declaration that gave *his* illusions away: 'L'homme n'est rien, l'œuvre est tout.'

'The horror of incest' is noticeable in the love adventures of Alfred Le Poittevin, too, but in a strikingly different way. He was running all the time after the image of the *jeune fille*, hunting and fleeing it in that mirage, 'Flora', wilfully debasing it in his savage debaucheries which are supposed to have precipitated his death, and ultimately still trying to find it in the girl he married, who was a close friend of one of his two younger sisters. He only survived his marriage by two years, leaving a one-year-old boy, Louis. We cannot know how his married life would have developed later, but the pattern of his emotions, in comparison with Flaubert's, seems clear; Flaubert had a mother complex, and Alfred Le Poittevin a younger sister complex.

The girl whom Alfred married was Louise de Maupassant, Guy's aunt. And it was Alfred's sister Laure, Gustave Flaubert's childhood friend at the *Hôtel-Dieu*, who was to become Guy's mother, for in the year that Alfred married Louise – 1846 – Laure married Louise's brother Gustave de Maupassant.

6 · Protests against the 'bourgeois'

The contrasts, then, of almost complementary character, between Alfred Le Poittevin and Gustave Flaubert were no less significant than their emotional and intellectual kinship. Whereas Le Poittevin's dominating vision was adolescent, Flaubert's was juvenile; they both seem to have stuck, at the bottom of their hearts, in the billiard-room of the *Hôtel-Dieu*, with Alfred fourteen and Gustave nine years old.

Their philosophy even then was 'pessimism', a pessimism sincerely felt but also indulged in as a pastime. Practically all literary historians agree that theirs was the pessimism of disappointed dreamers and idealists, of illusions lost and converted into what they called *dégoût*. Such was, indeed, their state of mind, their style of language and behaviour. But that there was any actual experience of disenchantment behind it seems an invention. When *had* they ever held those high illusions? What had they been? When and how did they come to realize that these 'illusions' could not be achieved? There is no answer either in their works or in what we know from other sources of their 'sentimental education'. Indeed, Flaubert himself said that he really had never had any illusions. Flora (Elisa) did not, after all, do anything to disenchant her admirer, except in so far as she appeared to him too fairy-like to be seduced. It was not *her* wish, it was *his* imagination; whether her own leanings fitted that image was never tested. And her willingness to be seduced might have disenchanted the romantic seducer even more than would her unwillingness. One cannot help thinking that he simply *liked* the attitude of disenchantment, from the outset, partly because it provided his neurotic depressions with a rational excuse, and partly because he was impressed by the poets and thinkers of disenchantment. Flaubert, when seventeen, said the two writers who impressed him most were Rabelais and Byron because 'only these two set out to write with the intention of harming mankind and laughing in its face'. He knew as well as we do that neither Rabelais nor Byron had, in the final analysis, written 'to harm'; and Flaubert himself was a thoroughly *good* man, extraordinarily sympathetic and generous, as all who knew him recognized. But it may have been precisely his embarrassment with his own goodness which drove him in his fits of misanthropy into longings for superior wickedness.

In political and social matters, the disillusioned attitude of the two young men was of a no less sentimental *a priori* character than it was in love. If there were in Alfred's and Gustave's environment people who had suffered definable disenchantment of political hopes, they belonged to the generations of their parents and grandparents, who had been believers in Roman Catholicism and Royal authority, or in Reason and the Republic, or in the Noble Savage or in Imperial Glory. To the audience of the billiard-room under the Citizen King, all this was past history; Alfred and Gustave were unable to lose their belief either in God or in human nature because they had never had any. They had a natural sense of justice, love of truth and neighbourly love, and this humanitarian idealism, coupled with the scepticism of their brains, moulded them politically into liberals.

At this point, however, the contrast emerges. Alfred Le Poittevin was a radical. He owed this both to the adolescent in him, eager to protest against the established order, and to his responsive and imaginative mind, open to mythical fancies and scientific findings alike. He made a point of not signing a letter *votre serviteur*, for 'I am nobody's servant'; and neither pessimism nor his *blasé* mood prevented him from composing an *Ode to Poland*, very rhetorical in style, attacking 'Monstrous Russia' with crusading hatred, and invoking 'the banner of Liberty' in adoration. His approval of Republicanism and democratic progress, was expounded in his short *Essay on the French Revolution*, an abortive piece of writing – unintentional mirror of his whole career – the first part of which contains a most lucid and far-sighted general introduction to the subject whilst the second part heaps together factual material in noticeable haste, almost in panic. The interest of this essay lies in his effort to vindicate the defeated Revolution, even its violence, except for that wave of Republican fratricide when 'the sword that ought to strike at the criminals defeats its purpose by hitting the good citizens'.

Though an unbeliever in God, Le Poittevin was a believer in the purposefulness of change. The only work of literary importance left by him is a curious phantasmagoria, a philosophical novel, or rather dramatized soliloquy, *Une Promenade de Bélial*, written, and rewritten, in his renewed *rage littéraire*, in a frenzy (only outstripped by Flaubert's own) to find the right word and the right cadences everywhere. The work, though it has an ending, has not really been finished – and M. René Descharmes[1] must have toiled harder even in deciphering, comparing and juxtaposing its variants than in deleting the obscenities from his letters. In this piece of writing, inconclusive and somewhat confused, but thought-inspiring even today, Le Poittevin gave an idea of that mixture of materialistic agnosticism and spiritualism

[1] See footnote on p. 34.

which dominated his vision and which was to haunt the mind of many an important writer in later epochs, including, as will be seen, his nephew, Guy de Maupassant.

The chief characters in that strange novel are: a duke, eclectic owing to his education; his duchess, Catholic owing to her upbringing in a convent; and a witty and likeable Devil, claiming to some extent Amor's myth-honoured powers. 'It is about me that Milton was talking when he mentioned that Belial, the god of impure love,' he says; 'but he calumniated the Devil as all Christians do.' The ideas of this Belial, however, are more Hegelian than diabolical. He conceives evolution as starting with the rule of Matter, instincts and brute force; continuing with the Spirit ridding itself of their tyranny; and reaching its peak in a synthesis, the scientific mind growing impartial in its own struggle with matter, the Spirit finding its union with Nature. Clearly this Belial had read Darwin's early publications and Strauss's *Jesus*, as well as ancient mystics and pantheists. He says:

> The child, in his mother's womb . . . takes on with the new body the typical forms of inferior species; the long work of whole centuries is accomplished again in a short time. Ultimately, the human form supersedes the animal forms, and the embryo, by this work, seems to reveal the entire secret of the past . . .
>
> . . . Outside mankind, there are the superior regions which will some day be penetrated by men of wonderful genius . . . New needs will open a whole world of new emotions. But, even in those higher spheres, the Spirit will have to pass through the three phases we know: overwhelmed by the abundance of unknown marvels furnished by Nature, the Spirit will first become its slave again, then it will deny Nature so as to liberate itself, and, finally, by returning to Nature the Spirit will conquer it for its own empire.

Le Poittevin, had he lived longer, might have grown into a representative thinker of the century, the greatest perhaps of all, somewhat of an amalgam of Renan, Heine and Herbert Spencer, with sparks of Schopenhauer and Kierkegaard, and even more of Ferdinand Lassalle in him; ill-health alone seems to have prevented him. But, then, without ill-health, without his morbid over-sensibility, would he have been Alfred Le Poittevin at all?

Flaubert in his turn, was a liberal and humanitarian anti-democrat. He did not, in his opinions, differ substantially from his friend, but their approach was different. When he argued, in the 1870s, that Republican ideas should in the last analysis be treated as part of a scientific discipline he might be said to be following his friend who, in the 1830s, argued that the human past, including the French Revolution, should be dissected and studied in the service of the future just as were cadavers in the service of life. But whereas Le Poittevin wrote this as a challenge to the monarchist vilifiers of Republicanism, Flaubert wrote in a mood of irritation against the rhetoric of Republican self-glorification. This difference is partly due, of course, to the times when these statements were made; the categories of the *bourgeois* to be pilloried had changed since the end of the royal power. But there were differences of temperament as well. Unlike the rebellious adolescent, Alfred, Gustave was a child, a *good* child, very much attached to his parents and willing to do anything to please them, except respectable work that would distract him from his favourite playthings, verbs, nouns, adjectives. His sickish idiosyncrasies were also different from Alfred's: he feared any contact with 'physical reality', any change, and felt that, at any rate for himself, 'if happiness is to be found anywhere, it is in stagnation'. He was, by nature, much more of a conservative than was his friend.

As to progress, he said, 'I am sick of those phrases'; as to patriotism, 'it means nothing to me'; as to mankind, 'people nowadays are so concerned with it as to forget about man'. Authority was a good thing because it kept order, and a bad thing because it pestered artists, authors, thinkers, by trying to impose its own moral code upon them and because it failed in its duty of enabling the poor and the underprivileged to enjoy the blessings of higher education. He hated 'modern tyrannies', mainly on account of their 'pettiness', but could not help admiring some of the 'old tyrannies' (even Nero!) for their 'magnificent manifestations'. He was indignant about any infringement of civic rights and full of admiration, for instance, for Victor Hugo's courage and eloquence in standing up against

'Napoleon the Little', but he trusted the judgment of the common voters even less than that of their oppressors. 'Give the people every freedom but no power!' was his panacea. Who, then, should wield power? He who succeeds in being more liberal and, at the same time, more businesslike than others are. Distrusting the wisdom of the few selected by inheritance or military *coups* as well as the instincts of the masses, he favoured a cautious Republican government, 'positivist, without *blague* or metaphysics', that is, the rule of the *bourgeoisie*.

He was, as will be remembered, the most cruel dissector of the *bourgeois*, of characters such as the pompous free-thinker, M. Homais, the village apothecary, or those blunderers in science, the clerks Bouvard and Pécuchet. Flaubert certainly did not spare his own class, nor, within that class, the category he might have relied upon as his prospective readers. In this respect, he was very much a son of his time, or rather the protagonist of the time that was just coming. The second half of the nineteenth century was the golden age of the vilification of the *bourgeois* as it was that of his consolidation in wealth and power. Good artists treated the *bourgeoisie* with irritated contempt; as did Courbet, on behalf of a proletariat imbued with Proudhon's ideas; Goncourt, on behalf of an aristocracy moulded in nostalgia for the *salons* of the eighteenth century; Baudelaire, on behalf of an artistically minded Satan who hesitated between the proletariat and the aristocracy until he decided for a Negro hetaera. Flaubert differed from them in so far as he challenged the *bourgeois* on behalf of the *bourgeois*, and pilloried liberal sloganology as a thoroughbred liberal. His vision of things was static. Public affairs interested him, but, unlike Le Poittevin, he did not see them *evolving* anywhere. Guy de Maupassant took after his uncle in his ecstasies over sex and drugs, but he followed Flaubert in his political views.

7 · Intermarriage

If the upper middle classes of Rouen and Caux were a club, the Maupassants were its associate members. They were noblemen, with vague claims on aristocratic links and symbols but, on the whole, not of higher standing than their friends from the 'third estate' with whom they readily mixed. If they added anything to the atmosphere of *bourgeois* respectability that permeated the intermarried circle of lawyers, doctors, ship-owners, wine-traders, cotton manufacturers, it was the instability of the knight errant rather than the stability of a feudal estate. Quite well-bred but far from lordly, they could have been looked upon as *parvenus* no less than *ci-devants*. In Normandy, at any rate, they were newcomers, but they had settled down without difficulty, by the beginning of the nineteenth century, and when some of them later left their native land to make and spend money in Paris, like Gustave, or in a frenzy of incessant journeys like Guy, they attributed their restlessness to their Viking heritage rather than to lacking roots in the Viking soil. To all intents and purposes, they were Norman.

Theirs was an ancient family in the sense that there had been records of Maupassants from the end of the sixteenth century onwards. The first of the Maupassants referred to in documents was a blacksmith in Lorraine. He and his dependants intermarried with other artisans' families. An apothecary, a notary royal cropped up in their family tree somewhat later, helping them to the fringes of the professional classes; and, about a hundred years later, the bravery and adventurous spirit of a soldier Maupassant made them almost gentlemen. They started being referred to as *sieurs*; and in 1752 a Maupassant was properly ennobled by the Austrian Emperor in Vienna.

The Maupassants of the nineteenth century seem to have had one thing in common with their forefathers: the pleasure of mystifying their own, or one another's, origins. In the eighteenth century two Maupassant brothers, or allegedly brothers, figured in a public row, accusing each other of stealing birth certificates and birth rights, of pretending to be what they were not. Were they genuine noblemen at all? The coronet of *merquisat* appeared on their coat of arms. For some, however, that coronet only provided an additional reason to doubt the authenticity of the coat of arms itself; could it be imagined that the Maupassants had been entitled to so high a distinction without making use of it? The pattern of the blazon, ridiculed by some as 'German', by others as 'absurd', was in Guy de Maupassant's lifetime, and has been since his death, a headache to the students of heraldry, and the subject of several essays.[1] The particle *de* was the subject of similar doubts; Guy's father was registered on his birth certificate simply as 'Gustave Maupassant', but his nobility was later officially acknowledged, and the legitimacy of his use of the particle made incontestable.

All this is of interest to the reader only in so far as it affected Guy de Maupassant; that is, not very much. He made fun of ranks and titles, of the solemnity surrounding them in *Une Vie*, of their phoney manipulation in *Bel-Ami* or *Yvette*, but he liked to parade in archaic splendour. In a letter to his mother, when he was twenty-four, he reported on 'old papers' he had just been reading about his paternal ancestors and enumerated somewhat facetiously but with noticeable enjoyment the sonorous names and titles of some of the highest aristocrats with whom his forefathers had been associated through marriage or otherwise. But he did not make any serious study of his family history. The person whose memory he most cherished in the Maupassant family tree – and whose portrait faced visitors from the wall in his Paris flat, 10 rue Montchanin – was a legendary Mlle de Maupassant, who became Mme Chadron, of the Rococo period, beautiful, coy and foolhardy. The famous lady-killer, the Duke of Lauzun, is supposed to have fallen madly in love with her, first for resisting him, then for yielding to him with extraordinary tact and devotion, and finally for risking her life in a battle to save him. When he reprimanded her for that *bravura*, she answered, 'Do you think the child-bed is the only place where a woman can risk her life?'[2] It was a snappy story, and unauthentic.

The authentic Maupassant chronicle starts after the Great Revolution, with Guy's grandfather, Pierre Jules, an exemplary middle-class character, modest, businesslike, good humoured, hospitable. Born in Paris, he first served in the meagre government post of finance inspector. He later settled in Normandy. In Rouen he worked as a tobacco warehouse-keeper, was known

---

[1] Deffeux et Zavie, Georges Maurebert, 'J.G.P.', quoted in *Guy de Maupassant* by R. Dumesnil; several references in Goncourt's *Journal*; in *Souvenirs sur Maupassant*, ed. Lumbroso, etc.

[2] Dubosc, *Trois Normands*; Dumesnil, *Guy de Maupassant*, p. 62.

to be a staunch opponent of the (Bonaparte) Empire, and died when Guy was about twenty-five. The most prosperous years of his life seem to have been those before Guy's birth, between 1840 and 1846, when he owned and assiduously cultivated a farm in Neuville-Champ-d'Oisel, which, however, had later to be sold on account of financial difficulties. Whilst he was prosperous, he was a kind and generous host in his cosy country house; he was fond of artists and men of letters, and often entertained them.

There was one great and much talked-of romance in his life – his marriage. As a young man, he had fallen in love with a girl famous for her beauty, Aglaé-Françoise-Joseph Pluchard, daughter of a tax-collector in Berney. The parents opposed the match; and the wedding was held in secret, at midnight, in a forsaken little village church. A torrent of rain contributed to the dramatic background; the young couple had to ford a swollen brook to get home, and they started their honeymoon drenched to the bone. A picture of Jules de Maupassant, attributed to the painter of maritime scenes, Eugène Le Poittevin, represents him less romantically, squatting behind a haystack, his breeches pulled down, ready to relieve himself whilst, at the same time, aiming with his shotgun at a hare that is running across the field. This Rabelaisian sense of humour, combined with a passion for hunting, fitted in with the traditions of the Maupassants as well as of the Flauberts and Le Poittevins.

The ties amongst these families multiplied all the time. But the most important took place in 1846 when Jules de Maupassant's two children married Paul Le Poittevin's two children: Louise de Maupassant became Mme Alfred Le Poittevin, and Laure Le Poittevin became Mme Gustave de Maupassant.

These bonds of love and convenience turned out to be unhappy, though for different reasons: Le Poittevin's because of his lassitude, and heart trouble, followed by his early death; and Gustave de Maupassant's because he was too fond of lovemaking – at any rate, for his wife's liking.

8 · Gustave and Laure

Gustave de Maupassant was an *amateur* in several senses. Though by profession a stock-broker, associated with the Stolz firm, in Paris, he seems to have been an agreeable outsider in business life just as he was in the artistic world, on account of his cultivating painting as a pastime. He was indeed fond of many things, especially women. But his fickleness and promiscuity, which started almost immediately after his marriage, were a result rather than the cause of the lack of understanding between him and his wife. At the root of the trouble lay Laure's frigidity in ordinary sex life, aggravated by her insatiability in everything else. It was a common enough tragedy of the nineteenth-century *incomprise*, depicted with elegant and tender cruelty by her own son, in *Une Vie*.

It is generally agreed that Guy de Maupassant modelled the heroine of this novel, Jeanne le Parthus des Vauds, on his mother, Laure Le Poittevin. Maupassant modelled all his characters on living persons, and as he is known to have felt for no one but his mother that sort of virginal tenderness with which the heroine of *Une Vie* is depicted, it may indeed be taken for granted that Jeanne's and Laure's fundamental emotions were one and the same. Their stories differed substantially, and so did their characters. Jeanne is described as blonde, innocent, utterly passive and aristocratic as a swan; Laure was dark, sophisticated, bitterly wilful, nervous, nostalgic, refined middle class. But the 'Veronese' touch of Jeanne's beauty did come from Laure; that sensual vibration of the skin which is hurt rather than satisfied by the fulfilment of desire. Laure's frustration, like Jeanne's, must have started, if not sooner, at her wedding night when she wondered: 'So is it *this* he meant when calling me his little wife?' Jeanne in the novel is the daughter of an aristocrat who still believed, as had his 'Enlightened' forefathers, in the wisdom of philosophers and the goodness of Nature; before handing his daughter over to her young husband, he took her out for a stroll and gave her an embarrassed lecture, in terms half Rousseau, half ecclesiastic, about the facts of life. (This, of course, could hardly have happened to Laure, who was the sister, and, in a way the disciple of the man whose 'Belial' asked, 'Is there such a thing as virginity at all?') But when faced with '*this*', preceded by the clinking of coins emptied out of the pocket before going to bed, and by the first sight of conjugal underpants, the delicacy of the female fibres proved to be more stubborn than the believers in sound instincts generally realize. Jeanne, alarmed in her new companionship, tossed all night the prey to inarticulate thoughts (and so, presumably did Laure, in spite of her wider knowledge of diabolist literature). The answer to her alarmed question came, in the small hours, in the sounds of a happy light snore from the lips of the handsome husband.

Jeanne's husband, Julian, found solace for his bride's nervousness in the arms of their servant, Rosalie. Gustave seems to have done the same. An additional reason for his impatience with Laure may have been that she was no longer young. She was actually her husband's age; they were twenty-six when they married – and that meant she was almost an old maid in nineteenth-century eyes. Her looks did not seem to have suffered from it; but that her gesture of virginal panic annoyed the bridegroom even more than if it had come from a budding girl can well be imagined.

They both were quite well-off at the time of their marriage – particularly on the Le Poittevin side – but their fortunes were dwindling. After the death of Paul Le Poittevin – Laure's father – his widow returned to her mother in rue Sous-le-Bois, Fécamp, which then became the centre of the Le Poittevin family, including the Maupassant couple. But Gustave was most inventive in finding excuses for journeys, either with or, preferably, without his wife. On return from their honeymoon in Italy, he was constantly on the move between Rouen, Fécamp, Etretat, La Nouville and Paris, which he preferred above all.

9 · 1848 and after

Early in 1848, the Parisians banqueted in protest against the Government, demanding 'La réforme!', which mainly meant the extension of the suffrage, up to then a privilege of the wealthy few. Banqueting was banned; demonstrations started in protest, and, to the surprise of their initiators, unleashed a revolutionary wave all over the Continent.

The French monarchy disappeared overnight. A Republic was proclaimed and universal suffrage enacted. All this was still in harmony with the traditions of the Great Revolution. But, in the meantime, the national *tricolore* of the Great Revolution was denounced as a symbol of capitalist exploitation, and the red banner of socialism was unfolded in the industrial suburbs. The first *soviet* of Europe was installed in the shape of the *Commission de Luxembourg*, presided over (like the first Russian *soviet*) by the *Menshevik* leader of those days, Louis Blanc, whereas the leading *Bolshevik* figure, Blanqui, forced his way into the Chamber and was only prevented by disagreement with his own lieutenants from grabbing the helm of the State. To provide workers with work and adequate pay was declared a Government responsibility, and National Workshops were set up with at least the pretence of discharging it. 'The battle up to now had been fought to do away with all privileges save property,' Tocqueville said, 'but now it was the privilege of property which was in jeopardy.' Indeed, in retrospect, the February of 1848 in France was no less a turning-point in European history than the July of 1789.

However, as a revolution, it came to a quicker end. Universal suffrage brought about the victory of its own opponents. The peasantry was conservative: the farmers because they were more *bourgeois* than the *bourgeois*, the farmhands because they held property in greater awe than did those who owned it. Royalism had ceased to seem a workable proposition, but the authority of the Church and the appeal of Imperial glory, both played down under the Protestant and Anglophile Guizot, were now given full play. By the end of the year, Napoleon Bonaparte was elected President of the Republic. The noblemen and the respectable *bourgeoisie*, whom he was about to save for his own use, received him with contempt but also with relief; the masses, whom he was about to disfranchise, received him with enthusiasm. Once the Paris riots had died down, only those very few who took ideas seriously kept up murmurings against him.

The freak Communism gave way to a freak Fascism. In four years' time, the 'National Socialist' authoritarianism of President Napoleon Bonaparte was finally consolidated into the Second Empire.

If the landlords were the real rulers of France under the restored Bourbons, and the bankers and industrialists under the Orleans, who, wondered Marx, were now the ruling class under this 'parody' of a Napoleon? It was *bourgeois*, no doubt; but certainly not in the orthodox sense. It was the 'artificial classes' which now took over, Marx concluded, that is the bureaucracy which was largely of Napoleon's own making, soldierly, clerical-ist and commercial. The broader basis of their power was the plot-holding peasantry, the near-proletarians of the land who tended to look backward. The consent, and even zeal, of the poor became the vehicle of new imperialist adventures and of the restoration of the former rule of the *épaulette*, the mitre and the purse.

It was in 1850, under the phoney Republic preparing for the phoney Empire, that Gustave de Maupassant and his wife moved to the château Miromesnil, just before, or just after, their first son, Guy, was born.

10 · *The child Guy*

Guy de Maupassant had no memories of Miromesnil; when thirty-two, he took a friend, Robert Pinchon, to show him as a matter of curiosity the window of the room in which he is sup-posed to have been born.[1] But he had very clear recollections of the less lordly château of Grainville-Ymanville, in the Goderville canton of Le Havre district, into which his parents had moved some four years after his birth. He described it, in *Une Vie*, as Jeanne's home, naming it 'Les Peuples' which (as he himself explains) would in the Norman use stand for 'Poplars' or the like. Though a very economical writer, he could dwell at great length on factual details (in this respect, Balzac's disciple even more than Flaubert's), for instance, when he felt the composi-

[1] Dumesnil, *Guy de Maupassant*, p. 77.

tion of a building more characteristic of the people living in it than their own thoughts. He says about *Les Peuples*: [1]

> It was one of those huge high Norman houses that are at once farm and château, built of grey stones that were originally white, and big enough to house a whole tribe.
>
> An immense vestibule divided the house itself, running from end to end opening its great doors on either side. A double staircase seemed to straddle this entrance hall, leaving the centre empty. On the first floor, its two flights were joined together by a kind of bridge.
>
> On the ground floor, to the right, was the enormous drawing room hung with tapestries on which birds disported themselves against a leafy background. All the furniture, upholstered in *petit-point*, illustrated La Fontaine's fables . . . On the same side as the drawing room was the library, full of old books . . . On the left were the dining room, with modern panelling and furniture, the linen room, the office, the kitchen and the little room containing the bath.
>
> The first floor was divided along its entire length by a corridor, along which were aligned the ten doors of its ten rooms . . .

As to the furniture, described in no less detail than the layout of the floors, 'there were pieces such as each generation leaves behind in a family and which turn an old house into a kind of jungled museum'. In front of the house, he goes on, there

> was a wide lawn, butter-yellow in . . . moonlight. Two huge trees reared up at opposite corners: a plane to the north and a lime to the south. Right at the end was a little wood which reached the end of the domain, sheltered from storms by five rows of ancient elms. The elms were twisted, gnarled and gnawed; the fierce perpetual wind from the sea had carved them in sloping tiers like a roof.
>
> The park – if one could call it such – was bounded right and left by two long avenues of poplars. These avenues shut off the landowner's house from the two adjoining farms . . .

[1] *A Woman's Life*, translated by Antonia White, Hamish Hamilton, 1949.

– and hence its name, *Les Peuples*. The sea was visible from its windows. There was the scent of jasmines in the air, mixed with the strong savour of salt in the breeze coming from the sea, and the 'damp, viscous smell of the seaweeds'.

Guy loved that. From early childhood, he felt a sensual affection for nature, for matter teeming with life; he was bemused with the majesty of old trees, with the perfume of fresh flowers, but even more with the 'damp, viscous' vegetation full of innumerable creatures, with the soil exhaling water, the water fertilizing the soil. His sensations in relation to animals were no less intimate though not always kind.

> I remember, [he wrote when thirty-five years of age] when I was a child, I already loved cats with the rough desire to strangle them in my tiny hands; and one day, at the end of the garden, where it led into the forest, I was suddenly struck by the sight of something grey rolling in the high grass. I went to see what it was; it was a cat, with its collar caught, suffocating, rattling in agony. It twisted and wrung itself, tore the soil with its claws, bounced and fell inert, and then started again, and its hoarse and rapid panting was like the noise of a pump, a horrid noise which I shall never forget.
>
> I could have found a spade to cut its collar off and set it free, I could also have looked for the maid or advised my father. – No, I did not move, and, my heart beating, I watched that creature dying, with tremulous and cruel joy; it was a cat! If it had been a dog, I would rather have cut that strip of leather with my own teeth than let it suffer for another second.
>
> And when the cat had died, when it was safely dead but still warm, I had to feel its body with my fingers and to pull its tail.[1]

In another section of this short story Maupassant reprinted Baudelaire's sonnet on the cats. He shared with that poet (and with his own uncle, Alfred Le Poittevin) the 'diabolist' pleasure of showing off with sentimentally tinged cruelty. He may also have been influenced by the Marquis de Sade in whose writings he showed a vivid interest. He was not at his best as a writer

[1] *Sur les chats.*

when he revealed these influences too obviously; his writing became shallow when he set out to exhibit directly the depths of his feelings. Yet these were liberating influences in his development as they helped him ultimately to face the cruelties of existence with a detachment that takes away the reader's breath, more than do his references to his own 'tremulous and cruel' enjoyments.

But as a glimpse of his childhood pastimes, this piece is revealing. Some called Guy de Maupassant a sadist, which he was not; others represented him as a good-hearted man, which he was not either; but he was rich in emotions and in the gift of recording them. Other children, too, would find pleasure in both the attractions and the sufferings of cats, not very differently from the way in which cats find their own pleasure in playing with mice. What distinguished the child Guy from most of the rest was the intensity of his identification with everything he saw creeping, flying or growing in and outside the garden, his drunken absorption with nature, the more remarkable that it did not prevent him from observing nature, as well as himself, with open eyes.

11 · Guy's parents

M. Lemoine, author of a deft *précis* of everything concerning Maupassant,[1] quotes Edouard Maynial, writer of the first comprehensive Maupassant biography,[2] as saying that Guy de Maupassant's 'history of life' was nothing but 'the history of his works'. One would be tempted, Lemoine suggests, to say that it was rather the other way round: 'the history of his *œuvre* was that of his life'. Indeed, both are right – and both for the same reason. Maupassant was a professional writer as instinctively as he was tender-hearted when he stroked a cat, or cruel when he pulled its tail; and to be a professional writer meant to him keeping his eyes open wherever he went, and recording everything he

[1] Fernand Lemoine, *Guy de Maupassant* (Classiques du XIXᵉ siècle), Editions Universitaires, Paris, 1957.
[2] *La vie et l'œuvre de Guy de Maupasssant.*

saw, first in his memory and later on paper. Yet he was not born with the idea that this was his job in life; he underwent, as Lemoine adds, 'many influences, especially those of the circles he frequented'. It was his epoch and entourage that enabled him to transform his passion for fact-recording into creative genius. But the passion – even obsession I would call it – was with him, from his early years of innocent illiteracy onwards; and it is due to this that his life appears as the frame of the fiction he wrote and that, at the same time, all his fiction writing could be reduced to what he saw, heard or experienced.

One can, of course, go wrong in identifying some splinters of his stories with the episodes of his life, but it seems safe to assume from his stories that, despite his thrill in adventures in the garden, the woodland and on the seashore, his childhood at Grainville was most unhappy and left deep marks on his character and outlook. The married life of his parents had become a hell. Its details can be traced, not only in *Une Vie* but in the short story, *Garçon, un bock!* [1] – by the way, a somewhat clumsy piece of writing, presumably on account of the author's great pains to hide the identity of his characters. He was haunted by the memory of a scene which he had somehow to get out of his system, but he had to rearrange the setting more radically than befitted the nature of his realistic imagination. 'I was thirteen,' his hero says as he tells his story, though the scene he is to describe betrays that the author must have been much younger when it actually happened:

It was a day of great wind. The whole row of trees bent under the squall, sighing, appearing to let out groans, the deep and hollow cries of forests in the tempest.

The leaves, torn asunder and already yellow, fluttered like birds, eddied, then landed and ran along the alley like swift beasts.

Evening came. It was dark in the thicket. Excited by the agitation of the wind and of the branches, I galloped round and howled in imitation of wolves.

[1] M. de Pradel de Lamuse, in *Mercure de France*, 1 September 1928, quoted by Dumesnil, *Guy de Maupassant*.

When I caught sight of my parents, I approached them stealthily under the branches in order to surprise them, as though I were a real rover.

But, overcome with fright, I stopped some distance from them. My father, overwhelmed by terrific anger, was shouting:

'Your mother is an idiot; and, anyway, it's not your mother's concern but mine. I need that money, I tell you, and expect you to sign.'

Mama answered firmly:

'I won't sign. That's Jean's fortune. I must keep it for him and I won't let you swallow it up, like that, with your tarts and your maids, as you did with your legacy.'

Then Father, trembling with fury, turned and grabbed at Mother's throat, and started striking her with all his strength with his other hand.

Mama's hat fell off, her hair came undone and fell over her shoulders; she tried to ward off the blows but she did not succeed. Father struck and struck again like a madman. She was rolling on the ground, hiding her face in her arms. He turned her over on her back and held her arms apart so as to cover her face with more blows.

. . . I started shouting madly, with my whole strength, without knowing why . . . My father turned round, got up and came towards me. I thought he would kill me and I fled like a wounded animal, far into the woods.

I kept on for perhaps one hour, or two, I don't know. Night came, I fell on the grass, bewildered, devoured by fear, gnawed by a chagrin capable of breaking a child's poor heart for good. I was cold, I was hungry perhaps. Day broke. I did not dare to get up . . . I might still be lying there, starved to death at the foot of a tree, had the forest guard not found me and taken me back by force.

I found my parents with their ordinary expressions. 'Naughty boy, what a fright you gave me,' Mama said . . .

The *visage ordinaire* after the gruesome scene, this is very strikingly his parents. They were both difficult characters, particularly with each other, but were really friends and could not easily part company for good. In spite of their disappointments, they could not help being impressed with each other. Intermittently they even slept together, and Laure wanted another child; she had a nightmarish fear of losing her beloved Guy and wished to make sure that, whatever happened to him, she would have someone upon whom to concentrate her affections and hopes. Gustave was reluctant; one claimant on the 'legacy' was more than sufficient for his tastes. Laure then pretended to be pregnant, which induced her husband to get her really with child, in the ninth year of their marriage. Hervé de Maupassant was born in what we know from his brother's novel as *Les Peuples* manor house in April 1856.

Whether the worst scenes between Gustave and Laure came before or after this event, is not known; but disharmony continued, and so did their mutual willingness to see, at any rate occasionally, each other's point of view. They agreed on 'friendly separation'; Gustave moved to Paris, and Laure with her two sons to Etretat. When Guy was thirteen, they agreed through a Justice of the Peace that M. de Maupassant was to support his wife and children with a yearly allowance of 1,600 francs (corresponding, roughly, to the purchasing value of £500 in the Britain of 1966).[1]

Guy remained on friendly terms with his father, wrote affectionate letters to him, often stayed with him in Paris or elsewhere, and his mother did not object. She found modified revenge in amusement at the little tricks played by Guy on his father, or at his cracks at Gustave's expense. Guy, when nine years old, wrote to his mother:[2] 'I was first in composition. As a reward, Mme de X . . . takes me to the circus with Papa. Apparently, she also rewards Papa, but I don't know what for.'

In another letter, he described how, when due with his brother, Hervé, at a children's matinée at Mlle Z—'s, he teased his father by fiddling about whilst dressing, and blackmailed him ultimately into fastening the children's shoes, because he knew that Papa was at least as keen to see Mlle Z— as were the children. These incidents, though years before the amicable separation, were typical of Guy's feelings for his father all

[1] Cf. Maupassant's list of monthly expenses on pp. 91-2.

[2] First recorded in *Souvenirs sur Maupassant*, ed. Lumbroso; and Maynial, *La vie et l'œuvre de Guy de Maupassant*.

through his adolescence. He did not take him quite seriously. As a true Frenchman, who will break any conventional tie more easily than that of filial attachment, he liked and even respected his father, though tongue-in-cheek, and with a faint touch of condescension. Surely it was not for him to bear a grudge against anybody for an interest in those 'tarts and maids', not even for 'eating up' some money in their company? Guy's filial resentment, like his filial respect, was tempered by a sympathetic smile of complicity. What he felt when remembering his father's brutality was not that his father was horrid, but that life was horrid, and married life unbearable.

12 · Etretat

The fishing village and seaside resort, Etretat, in the bay between Fécamp and Le Havre, where Guy de Maupassant spent most of his childhood, owes its character to the co-operation of God, the Norman race and Alphonse Karr. Its cliffs form two steep arches over the water, the 'Portes' as the inhabitants call them. Onésime Reclus described them as the 'most beautiful and proudest monuments of the architecture of the sea'; to Maupassant they appeared as the legs of a giant wading into the ocean, or an elephant plunging his trunk into it.[1] Where these eccentric cliffs end, fertile and well-cultivated farmlands begin and, at their meeting-point, is the village, 'a handful of houses planted at random turning their faces in all directions', as Maupassant saw them, 'affected, irregular and quaint as if they had been scattered from heaven by a sower and taken root where they fell'.[2] Most of its inhabitants toiled hard, either on the sea or in the fields, and lived on a lean diet; yet, they were prosperous enough to keep the shades of penury away.

The imaginativeness of Alphonse Karr had in 1833 added to the fanciful geological patterns of Etretat. Karr was an influential

[1] *Une Vie.*
[2] In his reportage on Etretat (about which see following pages).

writer throughout the greater part of the last century.[1] He was a Romantic, but a most practical one, who urged that nature should not only be admired but also enjoyed. As a protagonist of *villégiature*, he started a campaign to popularize this beauty spot amongst his fellow intellectuals and wealthy Parisians. 'If I had to show the sea to a friend for the first time,' he said, 'I would choose to do it from Etretat.' And a most efficient propagandist he proved to be.

By the time Laure de Maupassant with her two sons moved to Etretat, it had already been a fashionable place for some twenty years, and it remained so in their lifetime and, to some extent, ever after. Its *caloges*, the old barges transformed into huts and workshops, and scattered along the shingly beach, were dominated by the motley *Casino*, erected of wood, right in the centre of the scene. Newspapers, drinks, billiards and other civilized games were readily accessible to the lovers of nature, and so also was love, usually starting on the beach, under the canvas tents where the ladies sat, busy at their needlework, their eyes on their paddling children, and their ears tuned to whoever might call on them. Such was the *tableau* whilst the sun was shining: and when the moon and stars took over, the sound of the waves that broke on the cliffs was outmurmured by that of concerts, balls and gossip.

The Maupassants occupied an old house, *Verguies*, solid and quite spacious but not particularly decorous, with a vast garden and a local ghost story attached to it, as is the case with many Norman houses. Its name derived from the ancient form of *verger* (orchard), and its situation was rural rather than maritime. Altogether, it was an ideal home for one who liked to feel his roots without being attached to them, and keen as Guy always was on having access to people in all walks of life, indigenous folk and visitors, peasants, fishermen, craftsmen, postmen, squires, shopkeepers, artists, tramps, millionaires, *cocottes* alike. It was this mixture of unrestrained elementary forces, of tenacious husbandry and of easy-going worldliness that formed Guy de Maupassant; the unabashed surrender to the call of the

---

[1] Of his sentimental novels and satirical articles hardly anything has survived except his cruel witticism made in reply to the proposed abolition of capital punishment: 'que messieurs les assassins commencent'.

senses, of ready cash and of superficial artistry was always at the bottom of what he had to say, whether he himself said it in grand style or in light sketches.

He had already published, with Flaubert's affectionate and uneasy blessings, his volume of poetry and had just established himself, with the success of *Boule de Suif* in the 'Médan' collection, as a leading prose writer of his generation when, in August 1880, a piece of light reportage written by him about Etretat, and playfully signed 'The Devil's Cauldron', was published in *Le Gaulois*. As for its style, or outlook, it could have come from any moderately clever gossip columnist, but it was, on its own level, absolutely sincere. He revealed in it his fascination with the teeming society of the Etretat beach, Casino, hotels and villas; he found delight in its 'mixed territory where the artists and the bourgeois, these hereditary enemies, meet and join forces to keep out the invasion *de la basse gomme et du monde fractionné*' (the phoney smart society). He was most impressed with Offenbach's splendid villa and he enumerated many another villa owner, including fashionable painters, hardly remembered today; but he did not mention that Courbet and Monet, too, liked to visit Etretat, though he was not unaware of their importance.[1] In fact, many important people visited Etretat, politicians and bankers as well as scholars and artists. An encyclopaedia could be written of the visions and ideas it inspired. But, to judge by what is written of its intellectual life, nothing made a greater impact on this society of 'artists and bourgeois united' than did the pun created by the author, Marcel Schwob, at the expense of another author and important local villa owner, Prince Lubomirsky – *ni lu, ni beau, à peine mirsky!*

The idea that the boy, Guy, who grew up on the fringes of this society should be a man of letters came from his mother. She was determined that one at least of her two sons should become the man her brother, Alfred, would have been but for his early death. 'I have two children whom I love from the bottom of my heart,' she wrote to her old playmate, Gustave Flaubert, in March, 1866, 'and who will perhaps one day give me great joy . . . the elder is already a serious young man; the poor boy has seen and experienced much and is almost too mature for

[1] Cf. his article, mainly, on Claude Monet, 'La vie d'un paysagiste'.

his fifteen years. He will remind you of his Uncle Alfred, whom he resembles in many ways and I am sure you will love him.'

With Guy, Laure de Maupassant's passionate scheme worked perfectly. She was his first guide to Shakespeare and the beauties of nature, they read *Macbeth* and *Midsummer Night's Dream* together, they climbed the cliffs together, she sticking beside him in storm and hurricane and coming home with her hair tousled and her dress torn – on at least one occasion, she almost paid with her life for her alpinist ventures and was only saved, as she asserted, through Guy's presence of mind and bravery. *Verguies* was to become the successor to the billiard-room of the *Hôtel-Dieu*; she helped her son to organize theatrical performances there with his friends who formed a little gang of *farceurs* round him. It was not exactly like the days in Rouen, but it was under their spell. Alfred Le Poittevin had by then grown into a symbolic figure in the family shrine; and Flaubert into the acknowledged master of polished writing in France. The spirits of these great artists hovered over the gatherings, but the atmosphere was more that of an airy-fairy Offenbach-on-Sea.

Guy adored his mother with a devotion that was touching, chivalrous and almost obscene. She was the only person to whom he was unreservedly attached all his life and from whom he never dissociated himself, not even to the extent of a mischievous smile, except when giving away some of her weaknesses in the description of his female characters – a proceeding for which he might well have had her approval since it was an aid to artistic perfection and success. They were more than friends, they were accomplices. It was a link so strong bodily that proximity was not always needed to betoken it. Guy was a sturdy boy, broad-shouldered, muscular, and though companionable, a bit of a bully; a tough little guy he would have been dubbed some sixty years later. He was keen on exercise, on adventurous excursions with his pals and excelled in acquiring the fishermen's skill in navigation. In spite of his amorous attachment to his mother, he grew independent rapidly, and was early attracted by the female body. But she trusted him, even when he visited his father, although she might have felt that this was his greatest temptation to disloyalty. She knew that, wherever he moved, his success was her glory.

She herself taught him, with the assistance of a local *abbé*, until he was thirteen. Guy learned with ease, memorized well, especially poetry, and versified diligently, with a good sense for diction and cadence, and a premature lack of originality. He was not good at, nor even interested in, foreign languages; he learned Latin, which was essential for a youth preparing for an academic career in those days, but, though full of admiration for the poetry of other countries, antique and modern alike, he made no effort to get at their roots, or to study them in the original. On the other hand, he mastered the local *patois* as perfectly as any farm-hand from Tourville or Ymanville or Goderville who never spoke any other. He was fond of listening to people, and the way they told their stories stuck in his mind no less than did the stories themselves. He was good at picking up idiomatic phrases and accents, and at taking off women as well as men – he felt he was born for the stage.

He thus set out, simultaneously, on two separate tracks towards what he was to become as a writer. One was his – and his mother's – love for show, rhythm, poetic images, the whiffs of old Rouen, modern Paris, tourist-ridden Etretat; the other was his passion for rambling, his biological and social curiosity, his clinging to what he sensed, his instinctive belief that if life makes sense at all, it only does so because it can be recorded. With Etretat as his operational base, he discovered Normandy and, through Normandy, the human race.

13 · The discovery of Normandy

Normandy is a unique country; but, then, all countries or provinces, all cities, empires, tribes and hamlets are in some sense unique. There are some whose uniqueness is obvious, such as Venice or Tibet. One simple sentence suffices to drive home what their distinguishing features are. I do not think Normandy has such features. Edouard Herriot[1] described it as a 'unique landscape where the water mingles with the verdure', and this is certainly typical of its character, but typical of many another

[1] *La Porte Océane.*

part of the world as well. As to its mental climate, 'we are Norman', Flaubert said, 'in so far as we have some cider in our veins, drops of that tart and fermented drink which *fait quelquefois sauter la bonde*' – makes the heart leap, and crash the gates. But surely it was the romantic rather than the realist in him that made him say so.

The great *Flaubertien* and *Maupassantien*, René Dumesnil,[1] gave an admirable picture of Norman characteristics, convincing and challenging at the same time. The Normans, as he sees them, are a legalistic people, freedom-loving, insisting on time-honoured rights, and even more perhaps, on the rituals that symbolize them. He approvingly quotes d'Agnesseau's remark that, in that province, 'a change of religion would be easier to bring in than a change of jurisprudence'. This typifies even the commonest of its people in the commonest of their moments; when one of Maupassant's peasants, drunken and greedy, sells his wife 'by the cubic meter' to a mate, he says: 'It's a bargain. Shake on it.'[2] The handshake, Dumesnil suggests, is more Norman than is the transaction it confirms. Norman landscapes recall Sussex, and Norman traditions recall those of Great Britain; 'the Norman, great seeker of adventure and great wanderer in far-away regions', Dumesnil goes on, 'carries with him under all climates, like the Englishman, the confidence in his own country's superiority. He has the haughtiness of his race, the pride of his origins.'

But the Normans are not entirely like the English. Despite their Teutonic ramifications, they are in a way more Latin than any other racial mixture of the last four or five centuries; for instance, in their cult of food and drink – 'Normand, gourmand' – their cult of the lofty and of the bawdy, their rhetoric, their *gauloiseries* . . . The Protestant ideal of a distilled Christianity did not appeal to them; they would rather believe in Saints and miracles, or in nothing. They often believe in nothing *but* miracles, without the Saints, without even God; they tend to superstition as well as to scepticism. Their hearty laughter now and then gives way to reveries and melancholia; they meet cruel spectres in the tendrils of their gentle countryside. There is mist in the air, and brilliance in the mist; the fields, the orchards, the

[1] *Guy de Maupassant*, p. 40.   [2] *Une Vente*.

gardens burst with fertility. Whatever survived in the Norman of the Celtic, the Roman, the Viking, it is their compound which is unique, that utterly Western and European compound, rich in beauties, even richer in contradictions. It was a ravishing world as Maupassant saw it.

He also saw it as the very opposite of ravishing, as the province of drabness. Its vegetation exhaled the stench of aimlessness and decay, its homes that of sweaty underwear and stale food, and majestic Rouen was transformed by the rainy season into 'the chamber-pot of France'.[1] Its inhabitants were soulless toilers and money-grubbers, when not idle and sluggish gentry and tramps, and their boisterous fun petered out in boredom. Was this to hate it all? It was to love it, without illusions. If existence was dull, its details were not. Such details could be as colourful as they were ugly, and as amusing as they were tragic. The misfortune of the peasant farmer branded as a thief for picking up a piece of string had its setting in the market-place at a moment when the trivialities of rural and industrial life were on festive display. Maupassant was thirty-three years of age when he published this amusing story,[2] but its introductory paragraphs reflected the things he had observed, the things that had enthralled him ever since his childhood.

Along the roads around Goderville the peasants and their wives were making their way towards the town, for it was market day. The men were proceeding with unhurried steps, their bodies thrust forward with every movement of their long crooked legs, deformed as they were by hard work, by putting pressure on the plough which made them at the same time raise the left shoulder and twist the body, by cutting the corn which made them stand with knees apart to keep a firm stance, by all the slow and painful toil of the countryside. Their blue smocks, starched and shining as if varnished, with little white embroidered designs at the collar and cuffs, puffed out from their bony bodies like balloons ready to carry them away. From each of these balloons a head, two arms and two legs protruded.

[1] *Mademoiselle Fifi.*   [2] *La Ficelle* (The Piece of String).

Some led a cow or a calf by a rope, while their wives walking behind whipped the animals' haunches with leafy branches to hasten their progress. The women carried large baskets on their arms, from some of which emerged the heads of chickens, from others ducks. And they walked with shorter, quicker steps than their menfolk. Their spare, upright figures were wrapped in scanty shawls pinned across their flat bosoms, and their heads were tightly swathed in white linen topped by bonnets.

Then a wagon passed drawn by an old nag at a jerky trot, which rudely shook the two men seated side by side in it and the woman who sat in the bottom of it holding on to the sides to lessen the jolting.

In the main square of Goderville there was a great crowd, a mixed throng of human beings and animals. The horns of the cattle, the tall brushed silk hats of the rich peasants, and the head-dresses of the peasant women rose above the surface of the gathering. And the discordant voices, shrill and loud, created a continuous clamour, which was drowned now and then by a great shout of laughter from the robust lungs of some countryman or the long-drawn-out bellow of a cow tied to the wall of a house.

The whole scene smacked of the stable, the dairy and the dung heap, hay and sweat giving forth that sharp, unpleasant odour, both human and animal, peculiar to the people of the fields.

Maître Hauchecome of Bréauté had just arrived – and here the story proper starts. He picked up anything he thought worth a tiny fraction of a *sou* because he was 'economical like a true Norman'. For – *pace* Dumesnil – there was nothing more Norman, in Maupassant's experience, than the naked love of money. With the more passive species of the peasantry, it was simply stinginess; with the active, the prosperous and rising kind of peasants it was greed, obstinate, astute, murderous and comic. The 'Normand, gourmand', sitting at the table, eating and drinking and cracking coarse *gaulois* jokes, and eating again, from 2 p.m. to 8 p.m. or longer, especially at wedding feasts, was a familiar sight indeed;[1] but so, even more, was the labourer's

[1] *Farce normande.*

family round the soup tureen, a spoon in the right hand, a crust of bread in the left, for they hardly ever ate anything else. They were very poor, most of the peasants, but not all. There was 'mère' Magloire,[1] who owned a handsome little farm, but lived on that sort of diet because she was used to it, and who ultimately lost her life just because she deviated from it. Her neighbour, Maître Chicot, killed her with brandy in order to get hold of her farm – very Norman. The Norman farmer's son anxious to see his parents dead lest he should have more to pay for their care,[2] the Norman mother advising her pregnant daughter to hide her pregnancy from the coachman who would give her a free lift as long as he felt like using her body,[3] these were the typical characters Maupassant came across in his homeland, particularly in the villages, where life was hardest. A family tortured their blind son to death because, as Maupassant understandingly adds, 'in the fields to be useless is to be harmful, and the peasants would be quite glad to act like the chickens who kill the disabled in their midst'.[4] They were not thoroughly wicked, however; at the funeral of the blind fellow whom they had so badly maltreated, 'they even cried'. Maupassant did not judge them; he pitied them, almost as much as he pitied their blind victim, albeit without tears. Such was Normandy, he felt, and such was life.

He was, all the same, a Norman patriot, more indeed than a French one. He loved his Norman brethren not for being better than the rest of mankind but for being so very strikingly like them. He paid tribute to the flesh-and-blood Norman by stripping him of all myth: 'the Normans', he said, 'were not so much conquerors as they were *curieux*' – curious to see things for themselves. This was fundamentally a confession. It revealed Maupassant's pride in belonging to the Norman community. He certainly wished to see everything with his own eyes. What he saw most often was awkwardness, boredom, cruelty, but he found comfort in portraying them precisely.

---

[1] *Le Petit Fût* (The Little Cask).
[2] One of Maupassant's recurring subjects, e.g. in *Le Vieux*.
[3] *L'Aveu*. [4] *L'Aveugle*; see also *Le Gueux*.

14 · The discovery of sex

Guy as a child spent much of his time at his grandparents' home, in Fécamp, that old city of liqueur-manufacturing monks, fishmongers and well-to-do traders; and there, his memory is still alive. The derelict old houses on the quay smack of the gaiety and bleakness that he used to equate with middle-class family happiness and, round the old church, Saint-Etienne, the jovial *patrons* and *patronnes*, not at all touchy about the unflattering portraits of their ancestors in the Maupassant stories, indulge in guesses about the antecedents of this or that respectable inn today, which may have served as a model for the *Maison Tellier* some eighty years ago. Or is it true that the real model stood in Rouen, but that Maupassant 'had some reasons to transfer the story to Fécamp', as he himself told his faithful manservant, François Tassart?[1] This conjecture struck some of the Fécamp citizens with whom I talked as almost a slur on their city's character. The more they held of Maupassant, they felt, the better.

In Etretat, it is different. There, the Maupassant monuments are more clearly identifiable but more isolated, less penetrating the air. It may have been mere chance, but, as it happened, when I visited the towns and villages of Caux, in the autumn of 1962, I did not meet in Etretat anybody with affection for Guy de Maupassant. I talked to a well-bred and highly educated old lady who had some family recollections of the Maupassants. 'O *she*,' the old lady sighed, referring to Laure de Maupassant, 'she was a terror. A liar, a snob . . . simply unbearable. And *he* [Guy] was a good author but nothing more. He wrote some entertaining stories. He was a most repellent character. You know he was really a sadist,' and the story of the cat followed, a bit over-stressed as if it had been Guy's lifelong pastime to watch animals writhe and perish. 'His brother,' the old lady added, 'was much nicer.'

Poor Hervé, he would have been quite glad to hear that

[1] François Tassart, *Souvenirs sur Guy de Maupassant par François, son valet de chambre*, Plon, Paris, 1911. See also Chapter 35.

posthumous tribute near the garden of the house where his short and dismal career had started. He hated his brother, with the stubborn hatred of a lazy and stolid mind. Their relations were uneasy from the very beginning. Guy may or may not have bullied Hervé systematically, but he tortured him with his practical jokes, frightened him by dressing up as a ghost[1] and so on, and above all was so much superior to him in skill and wits, as well as in age. The difference between them was too great for the younger to compete. His defence was passive ill-will. His strategy was to make his mother feel guilty. Guy, when grown out of childhood, was too considerate a son to hate him back; his attitude towards his brother was that of irritated and patronizing tenderness. No wonder Hervé felt humiliated. Though physically tough and brave, psychologically he was crippled, as well as a nit-wit. But he has been vindicated, at least, by the Norman gentry who, for some mysterious reason, maintain that he rather than his brother deserved to be a success.

Guy was a frantic and hilarious hoaxer, with intermittent spasms of melancholia and spiritualist experience. He was remembered as 'the little blighter' in Croisset, Flaubert's house. Once left alone with his cousin, Louis Le Poittevin, in the study, he eagerly seized the chance to explore, with Norman curiosity, the objects within his reach and broke the master's favourite pipe. Flaubert, discovering the damage, immediately boxed Louis's ears, and learned from Guy's hearty chuckles that the wrong boy had been chastised.[2] Flaubert's niece, Caroline, had to play boats with Guy, he being the skipper and she the crew. She recalled later that Guy used to collect insects with passion, mainly huge spiders with a view to terrifying his grandmother. 'Meanwhile, every now and then,' she added, 'Guy would suddenly sink into unexplained sadness . . . and refuse even to eat.'[3]

---

[1] Described convincingly although, no doubt, with hostility towards Guy, by Hervé's childhood friend, the author, Jean Lorrain in 1897 (quoted in the Introduction to Lorrain's novel, *Villa Mauresque*, by their countryman, Georges Normandy; published by Editions du Livre Moderne, Paris, 1942).

[2] Descharmes. See footnote 1, p. 34.

[3] Quoted by Pierre Borel, in the Introduction to *Lettres inédites de Guy de Maupassant*, Editions des Portiques, Paris, 1929.

On the whole, however, he was polite and likeable, occasionally displaying moments of chivalry. In Etretat, many of his playmates were fishermen's sons and the like, and when on one occasion a lady friend of his mother's, casually handed over to one of them a basket to carry to the station, Guy took it and said, 'We shall carry it in turns, Madam, and it is for me to start.'

When preparing for his first communion, Guy underwent a religious crisis. But after that he became an agnostic and indifferent to religious matters – at any rate, in so far as flirting with belief in spectres, fights with demons and making fun of both religion and anti-religion could fit in with an agnostic and indifferent attitude. But he often relapsed, if not into the religious crisis, at any rate into the state of mind underlying it. He did not believe in God, but struggled with Him.

After entering the seminary of Yvetot as a boarder, in his thirteenth year, this struggle took the shape of a violent pagan protest. He found the discipline and the bigotry of the school intolerable, and reacted fiercely. If ever he was a revolutionary and anti-clerical – even anti-religious, as distinct from simply non-religious – it was in this period of his life. He wanted liberty. It was not the sort of liberty for which, by then, three revolutions had been fought in his country, but the liberty of his senses – to eat and drink, to ramble and go boating as he liked, and to read about love-making, and not merely to read about it. Though his ideas did not smack of Jacobin *vertu*, his defiance of the established order and traditions were reminiscent of the zeal with which his late uncle, Alfred Le Poittevin, had defended the Republican heritage. And one of his favourite books at that time was *La Nouvelle Héloise*. His sensual appetite was slightly coloured with sentimental and humanitarian dreams.

He several times ran away from the seminary and only returned at his mother's entreaty. But he would not behave himself. With some of his mates, he stole the *proviseur*'s bundle of keys, ransacked the cellar for brandy, held a party on the roof, 'revelling like hell till four in the morning', as he later boasted to his servant,[1] adding that he had accepted full responsibility for the venture when questioned by his masters. Then his teachers discovered a letter of his to a young lady, actually a

[1] Tassart, *Souvenirs sur Guy de Maupassant* . . .

cousin, containing a poem in the style of rather *risqué* gallantry, praising her carnal charms and cursing that prison of 'girdles' and 'surplices' where he suffocated whilst longing for her.[1] Now it was the Reverend Fathers' turn to ask Mme de Maupassant to remove her son from the seminary. Laure received her Guy in tears, and with the devotion due to a martyr of the Enlightenment, for which she showed enthusiasm on some occasions, although usually respectful of the clergy. Albeit shaken by events and worried about Guy's future, she was delighted to have him back for a while.

About Maupassant's early sex life our most dependable source is his own obscene poetry, composed in his later years, with slightly boastful yearning for his adolescence. I call these poems obscene because he did so, for instance, when he asked his friend, Robert Pinchon, to help him in recovering one of the pieces which had gone astray; the little I have seen of them (since most are still unpublished or have been lost for good) do not reveal particular imaginativeness in that genre but are valuable as background material to his stories. In their atmosphere, there is, again, something of Alfred Le Poittevin's sentimental and diabolist self-praise for assiduous love-making, with quasi-sexual attachment to the shores and fields of Caux, the theatre of their first live dramas. One day, when thirteen, he tells us in a poem, he fell asleep in a barn and as he woke up he caught sight of their servant and the maid.

> Ils étaient enlacés je ne sais trop comment,
> Et leurs derrières nus s'agitaient vivement.

He, Guy, guessed that what they were doing was 'une chose très bonne'. One would be tempted to surmise that his knowledge of such details must have dated from much earlier, but, in any case, it seemed to him a convenient experience with which to introduce the Register he drew up of his own amorous adventures, as befitted an admirer of *Don Juan*.

His first partner had been fourteen-year-old Jeanne with whom he 'tried to imitate the grown-ups'. She must have been an emotional little country girl; Guy would always remember the

---

[1] Dubosc, *Trois Normands*.

forceful pressure of her arms in his loins, and the 'fire of happiness' that 'ate itself into our bones', and the way she fell back
crying 'enough, enough!' with her eyes closed. And, since then
. . . a somewhat boastful and dreamy enumeration follows of the
types of women he has entertained in his bed, the fair combined
with moonlight and the dark figuring in lascivious gymnastics;
there was a soft giantess and there was a hairy lady attractively
smelling of goat, there was the *jeune fille* and there was the
adulteress, etc., etc., but, in spite of all, the poet concludes, he
has always been tied to Jeanne in his souvenirs, and he sees her
again and again as she was, 'dinky, fresh and blonde – as she
walks away showing her round buttocks'.[1]

As an emotional rapid scale passage, this is rather common-
place, but its visual emphasis deserves some attention; that
roundness was for Maupassant the essence of delight.

15 · Meeting Swinburne

Guy was fourteen when one morning on the beach at Etretat
he heard shouts of 'help!' Somebody, he learned, had been
carried away by the eddies and was now struggling for his life
under the Petite Porte. Guy dived to rescue him, but by the time
he got there the stranger had already been dragged to safety on
board a fishing-boat. All the same his valiant gesture was
appreciated, and he was invited to lunch on the following day by
the stranger, who was, he discovered, the English poet, Algernon
Charles Swinburne.

Swinburne was staying in Etretat in a remote little chalet,
named 'Chaumière Dulmance', with a young admirer – 'another
Englishman', in Maupassant's words,[2] or a 'Welsh squire', as
noted by a most punctilious Maupassant commentator[3] – any-

---

[1] French text in Appendix 1.

[2] *Notes sur Algernon Charles Swinburne*: Maupassant's Preface to
Swinburne's *Poèmes et Ballades*, translated into French by Gabriel
Mourey, Savine, Paris, 1891. The outlines of this Preface could already be
found in Maupassant's sketch, *L'Anglais d'Etretat*, published in *Le Gaulois*,
November 1882.

[3] Albert-Marie Schmidt, *Maupassant par lui-même*, Seuil, Paris, 1963.

way, apparently, a most intimate friend, called G. E. J. Powell. A third member of the strange *ménage* was a monkey, Nip by name, who hopped around all the time and, in contrast to the kind and cordial human hosts, exhibited his xenophobia in shockingly uncivilized forms. Whilst Swinburne and Powell were 'talking art, literature and the humanities' to their young Norman guest, Nip hit him on the head. Ultimately, as Guy was later to learn, Nip came to a bad end at the hands of a young valet, and they buried him in the neighbouring lawn and marked the place with a huge granite tombstone and the laconic inscription: NIP.

Rumour had it that the two Englishmen used to get hold of fresh adolescent valets from England every few months and instruct them in the theories of the Marquis de Sade, honoured by Swinburne as a great benefactor of mankind.[1] Maupassant, in his *Notes*, does not tell us whether Nip's executioner belonged to that category of servants, nor whether his masters were willing to condone his blood-thirstiness; in the spirit of orthodox Sadism, they ought to have been most indignant, remembering that the Marquis, whilst sympathetic to the lust for torturing, was adamant in opposing capital punishment.

Guy was bedevilled by this encounter. The contents of his hosts' utterances seem largely to have escaped him, except that Swinburne raved about Victor Hugo; but the atmosphere reminded him of Edgar Alan Poe, who since Baudelaire had been regarded by the *literati* in France and other countries as the *non plus ultra* of Anglo-Saxon sophistication,[2] the embodiment of all that is loftiest in morbidness, of phantasmagoria truer than facts, of a logic so refined as to evaporate in poetic dreams. And Swinburne struck the adolescent Guy as 'a sort of idealist and sensual Edgar Poe'. The unusual junk in the chalet, including

[1] Referred to in Goncourt's *Journal*, which quotes young Maupassant's account of this adventure; according to this, Maupassant said he had called three times at Swinburne's chalet and seen pornographic photographs mainly of the male body.

[2] This predilection for Poe, especially with reference to *The Raven*, has ever since then prevailed amongst English readers in non-English-speaking countries, as pointed out with some astonishment by Aldous Huxley in his essay, *Vulgarity in Literature*. In Hungary the translations of *The Raven* hitherto printed amount to quite a large volume.

fantastic photographs and various bones, *ossements*, scattered about the table, enhanced the favourable impression made by his highly educated hosts. He was delighted to accept another invitation to lunch. This time, monkey-on-the-spit was served, with a stench that made Guy feel that this was over-sophistication. His second lunch was the last he had in the *Chaumière Dulmance*.

But he faithfully kept two souvenirs of these meetings. One was a shrivelled hand, one of the *ossements*, given to him as a present by Swinburne, which was to crop up in various corners of his varying residences. He loved to think it must have been a parricide's hand. He was haunted by that ugly relic, which became inevitably a subject both of his Grand Guignol phantasmagoria and of his practical jokes. It also inspired him to write an early ghost story (rather dull in itself), *La Main d'écorché*.

More interesting, but less clearly identifiable, is the mark that this encounter left on Maupassant's outlook and character. Schmidt[1] tends to think that Maupassant's numerous excursions, literary and practical, into that shrill mixture of sadism, amorous reveries and schoolboy scatology, which was certainly characteristic of him, must have dated from that encounter. I think this is rather far-fetched; Guy had that in him, so to speak, from the cradle. The artistic part of it can be traced back to his ancestral ties with all the 'Don Juans', 'Valmonts', as well as the 'Gargantuas', and mainly to the sensual inquisitiveness of his late uncle, Alfred, whereas the coarseness of Guy's ribaldries was clearly his own contribution. Yet, there was some shade of wistful poetry added to it under Swinburne's influence. He could not read Swinburne's poems in the original, but his friend Turgenev's off-hand translations, in the course of informal talks, made the greatest impression on him (though, by the way, Turgenev was not uncritical of Swinburne). On the grounds of these and other translations, and of what he had learnt about Swinburne's career and difficulties 'in that immoral and prudish England, the queen of hypocrisy', he wrote: 'The poet [Swinburne] is often obscure and often magnificent; he breathes antiquity, that of Greece, but is, at the same time, inextricably complicated, in that entirely modern way of MM. Verlaine and

[1] *Maupassant par lui-même.*

Mallarmé . . .' And he recalled their meetings in the chalet, Swinburne's extraordinary appearance and his 'almost supernatural personality, as he constantly trembled from nervous shocks'. Both Swinburne and Powell seemed to him 'sick visionaries, drunken with perverse and magic poetry'.[1]

Maupassant was attracted to the penumbra of magic, to the poetry of perverted angels, and often dabbled in their unearthly activities. But when he did so, he almost always failed. For one thing, he was hopelessly earthy and limpid; like Ovid, who was unable to write in prose 'for whatever I tried to put in words put itself into verse', Maupassant was unable to prevent his words from grouping themselves into easily intelligible images. His accounts of the supernatural – or even of the transcendental – sound like spiritualist penny-paper reportage; even if empirically truthful, they ring like cheap coin.

He rings like gold when he speaks about cheap coin. His safest realm is sex and greed, sex when trivial, greed when petty; the daily complications produced by love and money dryly and factually reported. But his sense of the weird and magical helped him in doing so. It is that which permeates his dryness with pity, his factualness with vision, his sentences with rhythm, and which reveals the living soul within the flesh, and even in the dry bones of a business deal.

16 · Coached by Bouilhet and Flaubert

In 1867,[2] Maupassant entered the Lyceé of Rouen as a boarder and, in July 1869, he matriculated, as a *bachelier ès lettres*. This time, things went quite smoothly. His rebelliousness had gone and, already in his inter-school period, his mother had found him 'quite aggravatingly mature for his age'.[3] The Rouen school, too, seemed more liberal than that at Yvetot; but the main improvement was due to the fact that he could now join,

[1] Preface to Swinburne's *Poèmes et Ballades*.
[2] In 1867, according to some biographical notes; in May 1868, according to others.
[3] See her letter to Flaubert in 1866, quoted in Chapter 12.

as a poet apprentice, the middle-aged rump of the erstwhile *Hôtel-Dieu* children's gang.

Flaubert's two oldest friends had deserted him: Alfred Le Poittevin, as will be remembered, by capitulating to the temptations of barristership, marriage and death; and Ernest Chevalier, by sinking into 'philistinism', that is, by becoming an impeccable magistrate. Their vacant places had for years been filled by two agitated and prolific men of letters, Maxime Du Camp and Louis Bouilhet. The two seem, in retrospect, most contrasting characters: Du Camp, the efficient literary organizer and publicist, historian of his century, editor of periodicals, enormously ambitious and clever in everything except in hiding his ambitions; Bouilhet, poet, playwright, librarian, tender in feelings, polished in style, *parnassien par excellence*, licentious in fantasies, but shy in life. Yet their role in Flaubert's life will mainly be remembered for an episode in which they acted in perfect unanimity. In 1849 Flaubert read out to them, with sonorous diction, his *Tentation de Saint-Antoine*, in which his tortured soul projected itself in Christian and blasphemous visions, written in inspired and overwrought sentences. It took four days and eight hours each day to read it, and the two friends listened to the reading, as previously agreed, without comment until the end. Then, they advised him to throw it into the fire. He had better, they suggested, try something on an entirely different line, as for instance, a piece of trivial news from a newspaper, and elaborate on that, so as to get nearer to reality. Cruel as the advice was, it proved fruitful. Flaubert picked on a news item and, by 1856, *Madame Bovary* was ready for publication.

Du Camp, then joint editor of a literary magazine, was moderately happy about the result. He accepted, and passed on to Flaubert, his colleague's opinion that there were good things in it, no doubt, but that the whole was boring as it stood, and it should be cut by half – 'leave it to us'. Flaubert did not give way this time, anyway not easily. 'Gigantesque!' he remarked on the friendly editorial advice. And when at last a Rouen magazine and Du Camp's *Revue de Paris* started publishing his novel, publication was interrupted by a prosecution for obscenity. The prosecutor, Pinard by name, was a stern and carefully dressed gentleman, dignified looking and known to be a writer of bawdy poetry. Flaubert was acquitted in court, but not cleared of all accusations in respectable society. For years to come, *Madame Bovary* was 'one of those books you simply can't have in an honest home'.[1] One reviewer, Cassagnac, called it a 'dung-heap'; another, Ambineau, in a leading paper of the Right, *L'Univers*, described it as 'full of filth' (*ordure*); whereas Mazade, in *Revue*, mainly deplored that it lacked originality.

To be shocked by such judgments would today be as preposterous as it would be to endorse them. They were the reflection of a great and superstitious epoch, adventurous, imaginative, creative, but too easily ready to equate *vertu* with ignoring the facts of life. In France, this epoch started with the collapse of the monarchy, in the 1780s, and ended with the collapse of the restored monarchy, in the 1870s: in some other countries it had come into being earlier, but faded out much later. It may seem puzzling that an age which had made such headway in biology and embryology should have been so prudish about the facts of life, but it happened like that. Previously, under the *ancien régime*, the body of a prince was revered openly because it was created princely by God's grace; under the subsequent rule of qualified egalitarianism, the industrial princes and their families did not claim such privileges but expected to be regarded in public as exemplary citizens whose bodies did not exist below the waist. Majesty had given way to Decency.

This particular brand of decency and hypocrisy, was fighting its most aggressive rearguard action under Napoleon III. The battle was still undecided. Inspired by the findings of Darwin and Strauss, science asserted its claim to enquire into the origins of man and his God; Renan, a conservative liberal – more conservative by nature than even Flaubert – was the living proof that it was impossible for a scholar to put up with the limits set under the ruling moral code. Simultaneously, for writers and artists, the right to see people as they were, even inside their clothes, was gradually being recognized as one of the Rights of Man. But bigotry and prudishness were still able to strike mortal blows. Renan and Flaubert only got what they had asked for, but they did not have long to wait for recognition. As to

[1] La Varende, *Flaubert par lui-même*, Seuil, Paris, 1958.

Flaubert, he earned high tributes from the best critics and poets, from Sainte-Beuve to Baudelaire, and if the Académie Française was reluctant to include him in their invitations, Princess Mathilde was not. *Madame Bovary*, as well as *The Life of Jesus*, became best-sellers, although some present-day readers may be inclined to feel that, however petty and envious Maxime Du Camp was, there is something to be said for his opinion that that perfect novel could have been made even more perfect by judicious deleting . . .

As time marched on, Flaubert became estranged from Du Camp, not because he was too critical of *Madame Bovary* but because he was too anxious for fame and honours. But Bouilhet, his 'spiritual brother', his 'conscience', remained with him. Bouilhet was not an important writer himself, but had an important part to play in literary history. Until Flaubert's new circle of friends developed – a circle consisting broadly of his followers and admirers in *belles-lettres* and their opposite numbers in scholarship – the friendship between these two men stood for a hidden Academy. They were at one in that religious belief in unreligious truthfulness and uncompromising craftsmanship which can be seen, in retrospect, as the Romantic impulse of the artist towards a social and anatomical reality which was anything but romantic.

That workshop of verbal perfection was to become the laboratory of Guy de Maupassant's genius. His mother had wished it, and he was delighted to comply with her wishes. It was fun to talk sex and poetry with these two middle-aged men who were as kindly as they were misanthropic, and artists to their fingertips. They were both exceptionally well-read, erudite, highminded and, at the same time, completely devoid of pomposity and reassuringly responsive to jokes. They received young Guy with confidence and affection. Flaubert loved him. Guy reminded him of Alfred. He was moved by their resemblance which on occasions struck him as alarming; 'now and then I am really startled by it', he wrote to Laure de Maupassant, 'especially when he bows his head as he recites verses'.[1]

How far did that resemblance go? Alfred Le Poittevin, of whom no portrait remained, would appear from literary recol-

[1] Cf. Introduction by Borel to *Lettres inédites de Guy de Maupassant.*

lections as a frail, dark-shaded figure, tingling with nervousness and death-ridden. Young Guy was thick-set, broad-shouldered, imposingly muscular, but inelegant in his proportions, looking like a giant whilst rowing, and then shrinking to a stocky lad as he stood up on his short legs. With his bristly chestnut hair, his thick neck, his regular, handsome, rather conventional features, he would seem to suggest a character very different from his uncle's. He had, however, a slight nervous tick from his childhood; and his eyes, 'pale and cryptic' according to some, 'glowing topaz' according to others, contradicted the robust and healthy vulgarity of his features and figure. Taine compared him to a 'sad bull'; Goncourt saw in him the 'type of a young Norman horse-trader'; and Georges de Porto-Riche noted: 'At close quarters he appears to me to resemble one of his peasants. Like them, he is a misanthrope and a farce-maker, patient and sly, a dreamer *malgré lui* and a libertine.'[1] Although these observations were made some twenty years later, they help to give an idea of young Maupassant's appearance.

What really attracted Flaubert towards sixteen-year-old Guy, under the spell of the dead Alfred Le Poittevin, was youth in its heavy effervescence, youth in the full blossom of its grace, resilience and *gaucherie*, the roughness of instincts longing for the sublime yet facetious about it, the abundance of muscles combined with some melancholia and morbid quivering. It was also a projection of Gustave Flaubert's own youth, his childhood's reminiscences carried on from one generation to another, from the corpses watched in the *Hôtel-Dieu* to the fresh and gossipy breeze of the Fécamp quay and the Etretat beach conveyed to him by a lyrically inspired adolescent. It was not, by any means, Guy de Maupassant's talent; of that, neither of them had or could have had any idea at that time. Guy actually hesitated whether to devote himself ultimately to lyrical poetry or to stage-craft; and his voluntary but systematic tutor was actually Bouilhet, in whose home he spent most of his Sundays and who went through his verses with him, patiently pruning and polishing them, always mindful of the rules and finesse of prosody. Occasionally Flaubert also warned Maupassant against accepting

[1] Schmidt, *Maupassant par lui-même*; Paul Morand, *Vie de Guy de Maupassant*, Flammarion, Paris, 1942.

hackneyed formulas, against letting himself be carried away by ideas and images that were not genuinely his own. He must learn to see things with his own eyes, this was the essence of their advice. But no one had a notion of what those eyes could see, only of how movingly they could be lowered during poetry-reading.

Bouilhet died in July 1869 – the very month when Guy obtained his *baccalauréat*. His literary coaching was now taken over directly by Flaubert. 'Had Bouilhet lived longer,' Laure de Maupassant later said, 'he would have made a poet of my son. It was Flaubert who wanted him to become a novelist.'[1] It was true. That giant genius was made by others who loved it without having an inkling of its own nature.

17 · A vision of cosmic boredom

There was one moment in Maupassant's youth when he rose above mediocrity, during his poetic apprenticeship at Louis Bouilhet's side. When, after Maupassant's death, his unpublished manuscripts and documents were unearthed, the Lycée of Rouen produced a poem by him on *Le Dieu Créateur*, written in 1868 but hidden up to then in the Honour Book of its *classe de philosophie*. It was not included in his volume of poetry published some twelve years later, *Des Vers*, nor apparently, did any of his friends think it worth publishing; and, in a way, they were right. It is, on the whole, a loquacious and rather immature piece, slipping into the theistic rhetoricism of pious unbelievers. But René Dumesnil is justified in saying that 'in spite of its *gaucheries*, it makes one think at places of Vigny';[2] and, in its visions of the manned and man-less phases of the universe, it reveals a metaphysical curiosity, probably enhanced by his reading of Schopenhauer, which was to remain an undercurrent

[1] Maynial, *La vie et l'œuvre de Guy de Maupassant*.

[2] In 'Notice' to the volume *Poésies – Théâtre*, in *Œuvres complètes illustrées de Guy de Maupassant*, Librairie de France, Paris, 1938 (where the whole text of the poem can be found); and also in his own *Guy de Maupassant*.

of his sensual and realistic story-telling all through his life, although it never found such articulate and elegant expression as in the best verses of this clumsy poem. Its beginning is fascinating;[1] it visualizes an Almighty as the prisoner of his own omnipotence that is bound to stretch the present moment into eternity, and bored to death and beyond it, for if it were death that threatened him he would not be Almighty. 'The Great God who can do everything cannot not be!'

This is indubitably Maupassant, no less than his bawdy verses. The essence of life is the smile of round female buttocks, under the shadow of cosmic boredom.

18 · *Practical jokes, women, tragedies*

After the scenes he had witnessed between his parents, the selfishness and coarseness he had observed (and quite often liked) in others, and the lessons in disillusion he had received from Flaubert and Bouilhet and, indirectly, from Alfred Le Poittevin, he may have seemed the most disillusioned of men by the time he reached his seventeenth year. In a way he was; but no disillusionment can be complete. It certainly had not been with Le Poittevin, visionary of a cosmic progress, nor with Flaubert and Bouilhet, believers in Art. Maupassant inherited their disbeliefs; but only sparks of their beliefs. Spiritual disciplines and a sancrosanct *métier* were not the things to absorb him at that time; his abundance of physiological energy – sexual as well as muscular – and his desire to 'drink colours with his eyes' kept him on the move all the time. He liked to feel his strength and planned to sign up as a seaman on board a big sailing-boat which was to cross the ocean.[2]

His days, when he could afford it, were packed with exercise on land and sea and river, with drinking parties, farcical stage performances and practical jokes. He enjoyed dressing up as a girl. One day, in Etretat, after catching sight of an English lady tourist whom he suspected of belonging to the most respectable, shy and shockable category of middle-aged women, he put on

[1] See Appendix 2.   [2] *Cahier d'Amour*. See Appendix 8.

a dress of his mother's, pasted lots of powder on his face and introduced himself to the good soul as 'Mademoiselle Renée de Valmont', an innocent young girl who had just arrived after a long journey. The lady at once extended to the young stranger her protective sympathy:

'Oh Mademoiselle, to make such a journey alone!'

'That's all right, Madam, I've got my two maids with me,' he answered.

'Even with maids, to be so far away, for a *jeune fille*!'

'No, I have no reason to be afraid. I have also a dragoon and a cuirassier waiting on me.'[1]

The joke came off, the lady was flabbergasted, and her expression of bewilderment and despair made her the laughing-stock of the village, especially its younger members of both sexes. Guy, who laughed loudest, never forgot the poor lady's expression. It was that, supposedly, which, some fifteen years later, made him write his heart-rending *Miss Harriet*, the story of the bird-loving and bashful old spinster who threw herself into a well after the shock of seeing the young painter, with whom she had unsuspectingly fallen in love, kiss Céleste, the buxom peasant maid. Then, the story goes on, it was the painter who held vigil over her body in the lonely room of a small farm-house, and pressed a long kiss on her cold lips, 'the first perhaps they had ever received'.

The 'broad fat face' of Céleste was one attraction, and the pallidness of tall slim Harriet was another. Maupassant saw one woman as betrothed to death by her aloofness, sensitiveness and awkwardness; another as attractive through her gay and coarse ebullience; another as ravishing with her mischievous smile when she admitted to having lied and cheated; yet another as fascinating through the falseness and emptiness of her worldly splendour. Would it be right to say that he was disillusioned over them? It would be, had he not derived more thrill out of the dissipation of illusions than he could possibly have had from fulfilment.

[1] 'Guy's Childhood.' Anecdotes told by Mme Laure de Maupassant to Mlle Ray and Dr Balestre, quoted in *Souvenirs sur Maupassant*, ed. Lumbroso.

But, again, this was not completely true; under the crust of disbelief and disenchantment of any being who still clings to life, some more layers of illusion can be unearthed, even quite banal illusions at that. Seventeen-year-old Guy had learnt from Flaubert that for a man of letters to marry was 'apostasy'; from what he had seen at home and elsewhere, he had learnt that to marry was misery; and, besides, marriage or no marriage, he liked to see women as subjects of poetry, not as partners in it. Yet, there was in Etretat a girl, Fanny Le Cl—, who he hoped would be a companion soul, in his rhymed reveries. He left a batch of his poems with her, and expected to receive a word from her as she had promised. As he had waited in vain, he went to call on her; and happened to overhear her, through the door, reading out his poems facetiously to her pals, and making fun of the poetically minded *amoroso*.[1] Maupassant, apparently, could never forget this.

19 · In Paris and on the battlefield

In October 1869 Guy de Maupassant joined his father in Paris, to read Law at the University, but, in 1870, his academic career was interrupted by the Franco-Prussian war, in which he served as a soldier.

From the Rouen district he retreated to Paris as the Prussians advanced. He wrote to his mother in Etretat:

> I managed to save myself with our routed army . . . the Prussians almost caught me. I passed from the vanguard to the rearguard to hand over an order from the Intendant to the General. I made *15 leagues* [about 38 miles] *on foot*. After marching and running all the previous night with the orders, I slept on a stone in an icy cave; if it hadn't been for my good legs, I'd be a prisoner now. *I'm fine.*

And somewhat later, already settled in besieged Paris:

> The Prussians approach by forced marches. As to the outcome of the war, that can no longer be in doubt; the Prussians

[1] *Cahier d'Amour.* See Appendix 8.

have had it. They themselves feel this and their sole hope is to conquer Paris by one stroke, but we are prepared to receive them here.[1]

Then he would write to his mother about his petty arguments with his father, and about having enjoyed *Muette* at the Opera to which he had been given a free ticket . . . But when his optimism in strategics started to prove unfounded, he exclaimed, 'Anything rather than the Prussians in Paris! Anything, even the Republic!'[2] In fact, he got both the Prussians in Paris and the Republic. As to the latter, he did not mind it; though he never was profoundly Republican, he was even less a Monarchist. But his hatred of the Prussian military survived. And so, even more, did his nausea and loathing for war.

20 · *Condoning murder, hating war*

Indeed, if he had any political passion at all, it was his rejection of war. Whether lasting peace could ever be achieved was none of his concern; nor was he particularly horrified by massacres and cruelties, however sympathetic he might feel towards the victims. The fact that man killed man did not shock him; but that the industry of war by which man killed man should be glorified was more than he could stomach.

In the course of his life, his revulsion against war, and even more against the myth surrounding it, took various forms. For almost ten years, he contented himself with occasional curses on the war-lords and politicians who had landed the country in such a mess. As time passed, his recollection of what French society at the crucial moment had been like grew clearer: it had been an undramatic nightmare. *Boule de Suif* starts with the description of Rouen just before and during the Prussian occupation, up to the moment when 'it became the duty of the defeated to show themselves accommodating to the victors'. And then:

[1] Cf. volume *Études, Chroniques, Correspondance* in *Œuvres complètes illustrées de Guy de Maupassant*.

[2] Morand, *Vie de Guy de Maupassant*.

After a short time, when the first panic had subsided, a new calm descended on the town. In many houses the Prussian officer ate at the family table. He was not infrequently a gentleman, and out of politeness expressed sympathy with France, saying how much he disliked having to take part in the war. People were grateful to him for this sentiment; moreover, one day they might need his protection. If they were nice to him, they might perhaps have fewer men to feed. And why make things unpleasant for him, when they were entirely at his mercy? This would be rashness rather than bravery. And rashness is no longer the fault of the Rouen shopkeeper, as it had been in the days of heroic defence, which had on so many occasions in the past shed glory on the city. They put forward traditional French good manners as their final justification; they reflected that politeness inside their own houses was quite permissible, provided they did not fraternize in public with enemy soldiers. In the streets they cut each other, but at home they chatted freely, and every evening the German stayed later, warming himself at the fire with the family.[1]

War, as Maupassant saw it at that time, was not so much cruel as dull and hypocritical. It was not fought for patriotism; the more heroic hoped for promotion; the others fought because they were too cowardly to resist the orders to fight; military honours were awarded for deeds of heroism never performed.[2] There was but one variety of heroism that Maupassant believed in: that of the unsophisticated civilian who killed intruding soldiers out of revenge and disgust, as in the story of the old Norman peasant who butchered sixteen Prussians on successive nights and spat in the face of the Colonel on whom his life depended,[3] or of the Jewish prostitute who at the end of her Grand Guignol story married a 'patriot with no prejudice' and became 'a lady as worthy of respect as many another'.[4] The right answer to jackbooted arrogance was active hatred on the part of the individual.

[1] *Boule de Suif* . . ., translated by H. N. P. Sloman, Penguin Books.
[2] *L'Aventure de Walter Schnaffs.*
[3] *Le Père Milon.*   [4] *Mademoiselle Fifi.*

In this hatred, he backed his own countrymen against the Prussians; but he later sided with the natives of Algeria and Tunisia against his own countrymen. In 1881, when he visited Algeria, and during the subsequent three or four years of French expansion in North Africa, he indulged in a violent campaign against the colonizers and the financial interests backing their ventures – an attitude noticeable not only in his newspaper articles but also in his novel, *Bel-Ami*, published in 1885, and in his short stories later on. In his rhetorical outbursts against these conquests, in the expression of his horror at the inhumanities committed by the conquerors, he now and then sounded almost like a believer in humanitarian ideas. 'We have remained brutal conquerors,' he complains in the tone of an anti-colonialist gospel-reader, 'clumsy and infatuated with our own entirely artificial ideas. All that we do seems nonsensical, a challenge to this country [Algeria], not so much to her first inhabitants as to the land itself.'[1] And when international armed conflict threatened on account of imperialist rivalries, he got into a rage: 'Whenever I hear the word *war*, I feel bewildered as though people talked about sorcery or the Inquisition, about far-away things, abominable, monstrous, contrary to nature and deeply buried in the past . . .' Why should there still be wars? 'Well, there is National Honour, that very strange honour which drives us to take what does not belong to us; National Honour feeds on theft . . .'[2] Sudden echo of Proudhon's formula, 'Property is theft', in this utterly property-ridden mind; and not by accident only, it seems, for he carries on: 'I talked the other day to an ex-member of the Commune whose acute mind pleases me, I confess.' This man had said, 'Let them fight if they like over such stupidities. I shall keep myself ready for the civil war.' Maupassant was amused.

But it would be wrong to seek any coherent idea, either pacifist or other, behind these utterances. Their emphasis and reasoning shifted all the time, according to the story to be told or the daily event to be commented on. The one feeling consistently voiced in them was impatience with the high-falutin' pretences of the warmongers. There was no greater insult to human in-

[1] *Au Soleil*, a travel diary.
[2] *La Guerre*, in *Gil Blas*, November 1883. Also in *Sur l'Eau*.

telligence, he felt, than for Field Marshal von Moltke to call the reluctance to fight 'materialism'. So to kill one man was murder, but to kill *en masse* was idealism? He had no more use for his own country's Moltkes either. And in the same way as it pleased him to think of *le père* Milon and *la fille* Rachel who had excelled in killing Prussians, he was sympathetic towards the revengeful Arabs, liking them as they were, 'unknown, mysterious, mendacious, sly, subdued, smiling, impenetrable'.[1] 'Unknown', he meant, to the European colonizers, notably in Algeria, and he predicted that their rule would be submerged in horror.

Like his first important work, *Boule de Suif,* his last novel, *Angélus,* of which only some two chapters were written, had for its background the Prussian invasion of France. The intruders, particularly their officers, were, as he saw them, always the same: repellent in their brutality and conceit, and even more irritating perhaps, when trying to be polite, in their heel-clicking smartness. The tragedies he saw developing around them changed from that expressed in the hot tears of a kind-hearted *cocotte* in the first story, to the crippled baby of a brutalized châtelaine in the last. It had been ghastly and unforgivable,[2] but the idea of France paying back in kind did not appeal to him. Revenge, yes; *revanche,* no. He was against war, except at one moment, in the early days of 1892 when he urged his servant: 'François, are you ready? We have to leave at once, war has been declared,' and he was anxious to hurry to the German frontier.[3] Within a week he was interned in the asylum of Dr Blanche in Passy. (See Chapters 46 and 47.)

21 · Birth of the Third Republic

The outcome of the Franco-Prussian war in 1870–1 brought about what went down in history as the first Commune, the Second Reich (in Germany) and the Third Republic (in France).

The Commune of Paris seems in retrospect to be more, but was in fact less, of a landmark than had been the Commission

---

[1] *Allouma.* [2] Cf. *Deux Amis.*
[3] Tassart, *Souvenirs sur Guy de Maupassant* . . .

of Luxembourg of 1848. Compared to the workers who in the short spell of the Second Republic had first unfolded the red banner of proletarian internationalism in the Paris suburb, most of the 1871 *communards* were but frustrated patriots, fed on Jacobin reminiscences and lower middle class in background.

The initial feeling of the Parisians of 1871 was bitterness against the intruding Prussian military and, even more, against the French Establishment held responsible for the national disgrace; once they had decided to take a revolutionary course, they could not stop short of subverting the whole social order, but the measures adopted to that end took them by surprise as they did everybody else. One day the column in the Place Vendôme was pulled down because citizen Courbet, the painter, thought it incompatible both with his aesthetic principles and his dislike of the Bonaparte dynasty; another day, bakers were forbidden to start baking in the small hours because citizen Frankel, the Hungarian goldsmith, found this practice unbearable for the workers concerned. The enthusiastic Parisians did not really know what to think about all this, for, socialism or no socialism, they liked a majestic column in an elegant public square and were unanimous in loving fresh *brioches* with their breakfast coffee – so long as *brioches* and coffee were available at all (for towards the end of the Commune, rat-meat even became a delicacy). Other measures were less puzzling. Rents were abolished for the three past or coming quarters, which came as a relief to many, but as an outrage to others. Flaubert found it an outrage to common sense and complained in a letter written from his country place, that if these *communards* thought what belonged to you should belong to someone else, they must have very confused ideas . . . which, in fact, was true. They had a vague vision of Proudhonian socialism, with political techniques inspired but not controlled by old Blanqui (who was held in captivity by the Government of Versailles). Responsible socialist leaders (such as Louis Blanc) had stepped aside and the *communards* had the half-hearted support of the Workers' International, whose aims they had not really endorsed. In fact, all they really wanted was to vent their heroic disgust on those who had dragged them into the war, then let them down, and now proposed to rule hand in glove with the arrogant conqueror.

Their disgust was justified; but was it sufficient basis for a viable policy? Marx doubted it; he had warned the French workers against any foolish revolutionary adventure in September 1870 and looked upon the declaration of the Commune in March 1871 with misgivings. Only when it was over, and the bloodthirstiness of Versailles had turned it into a lugubrious and glorious leaf in French revolutionary chronicles, did he adopt it as an inspiring chapter of the international labour movement and as a memorable attempt to achieve the 'democratic dictatorship of the proletariat'.[1] The victors of Versailles had every reason to represent the Commune as an international socialist plot; they needed to justify their own cruelty in crushing the people of Paris and their appeasement of the Prussian conquerors. Right and Left played into each other's hands in spreading an image of the Commune which has overlaid its true character – the hysterical idealism of despair.

The defeat of the Paris Commune by Versailles, and the proclamation of the Prussian-ruled German Empire in Versailles, was followed by the consolidation of the French Republic, a republic no less phoney in its first decade than that under the presidency of Napoleon Bonaparte some twenty years earlier. It owed its existence to the inability of the monarchists – Legitimists, Orleanists, Bonapartists – to agree amongst themselves about the succession to the throne, and to the cautious pressure brought to bear upon them by Chancellor Bismarck who, a full-blooded authoritarian, thought, typically, a Republican France would necessarily be weaker and more manageable as a neighbour than a monarchy. He did not reckon with Clemenceau.

The State was headed for two years by old Thiers, astute and level-headed spokesman of Big Business, who, unlike most of his associates, could claim credit for having opposed the adventurous war on Prussia from the outset. After Thiers' resignation, the Duke of Magenta, Marshal MacMahon was elected President almost unanimously; like many a war-lord, he was rewarded for battles lost to the enemy, and for toughness in butchering his own rebellious countrymen, with the highest honours of civic virtue. Under his personal rule the administration of France became not less but more authoritarian than it

[1] See Appendix 3.

had been in the last, liberalized decade of the Second Empire. The Duke–Marshal–President acted as the trustee of all those who despised the Republic sufficiently to accept it as a convenience. The liberal intelligentsia hated him. Flaubert and Maupassant saw in him the embodiment of what was lowest, most bigoted, most impudent in France. Maupassant, apparently, could have forgiven him for not knowing the difference between constitutional and unconstitutional proceedings; but that he did not know Renan from Littré and still dared to control the lives of Frenchmen, that was worse than patricide.[1]

After the downfall of the Second Empire, as Maupassant later put it,[2] the directors of Government offices became Republican *par instinct de conservation*, by which he meant the instinct of self-preservation as much as that of conservatism. In a way, this applied at that moment to the whole population which, shaken and decimated by war and civil strife, wanted only to survive, and to convert the *corvée* of rehabilitation into a business boom. On the whole they succeeded. France, whilst licking her wounds and mourning for Alsace and Lorraine, was still able to pay war compensation to Germany ahead of schedule, and her commerce and industry were forging ahead. The Republic, for all its authoritarianism, was eclectic and hybrid enough not to hinder the prosperous from becoming more prosperous. The *bien-pensant* middle-class man had become the backbone of the nation, whilst the erstwhile revolutionary tricolour now stood for Law and Order, for Church, Army and Property.

Measured in years, they were about halfway between the Great Revolution and the Astronauts. Looking at the recent explosive changes in speed, in science, technology and social engineering, one might think that our world had undergone a more thorough change during the ninety years since the establishment of the French Third Republic than during those preceding it. But this is not so in all respects. Take, for instance, the dress of the educated man. If, in the London Athenaeum Club or in a comparable Paris restaurant, a gentleman were to come for lunch today dressed like those directors of Government

[1] Cf. his letter to his mother, 11 September 1878.
[2] *Les Dimanches d'un bourgeois de Paris.*

offices in the 1870s, he would strike people as whimsically old-fashioned, no doubt, but not nearly so absurd as he would have appeared in the 1870s dressed in the white wig and the velvet *culottes* of the Rococo. The average white-collared townsman as we know him today is really the product of the development which, in France, had proceeded from the collapse of Louis XVI's throne to the erection of MacMahon's presidency. His basic characteristics still prevail, in Moscow as well as in New York, London and Paris itself.

After the Franco-Prussian war, Guy de Maupassant settled in Paris to make a living as a Government employee and, as he then thought, to finish his university studies. There were no motor-cars or electric lights as yet, but the railway was already ousting the stage-coach, and gas was replacing the candle and the oil lamp. The types Maupassant discovered can be rediscovered, with slight modifications, in any metropolis today.

22 · *Amongst clerks*

Poor middle-class young man in a rich capital, with a dreary office to work in, with sordid digs to live in, with the daily struggle to fill his stomach and to appear in presentable clothes, with an aristocratic *particule* which in the circumstances became its own parody, with family fortunes dwindling and family feuds buzzing round what had remained of them – this was Guy de Maupassant's existence in the 1870s after he had been demobilized.

Flaubert dissuaded him from taking up writing as a profession; partly because he was not convinced of his talent, but even more perhaps because he thought a writer worthy of the name should sacrifice his life for writing rather than make money out of it. Maupassant accepted this advice for reasons of his own; as a true Norman he wanted some solid financial ground, however modest, under his stocky feet. He applied for admission to the Ministry of the Marine and was at first refused but later accepted; in 1872 he joined the staff of the Ministry as an unsalaried library clerk. In February 1873 he was promoted to an office in the Directorship of Colonies under the same Ministry with a salary of 125 francs per month, plus an annual bonus of 150 francs. In December 1878, with Flaubert's help, he succeeded in obtaining a somewhat less drab job in the Ministry of Education, a post which in retrospect appears as his passage to the literary profession. These were the milestones in his eight years of Civil Service.

Once his fame as an author had been established, stories started circulating about his shortcomings as a civil servant, particularly as far as his ability to write was concerned. Rumour had it that his chiefs had found him unable to compose a 'memo' correctly; and it depended on the story-teller's mood whether the story came off as a dig at the wooden-headed bureaucrats who could not recognize good writing, or at the fashionable writer whose unsophisticated appearance and obvious fear of theoretical discussion offered a provoking target for the facetious erudites. The rumours were followed by counter rumours suggesting that he had been a brilliant composer of memoranda, recognized even by his superiors . . . In fact, he had been neither bad nor outstanding; he was just 'upper middle'. He was quite punctual, quite conscientious as an official, though always anxious to steal as much office time as possible without inviting reprimands for his favourite pastimes – boating, rambling, love-making, Flaubert and composing prose and verses. He read in his spare time quite a lot, though less, apparently, than he used to during his adolescence. His eyes quickly became tired of reading – an early symptom of his fatal illness.

Guy's grandfather, Jules Maupassant, the one well-known for his marriage romance and his hospitable country house, had in the meantime lost all his fortune. He sold his properties and moved to Rouen, where he worked first as a tobacco warehouse-keeper and later had to rely entirely on the support and hospitality of his daughter, Louise, widow of Alfred Le Poittevin, who later married Charles Cord'homme, a respectable wine merchant and zealous republican and democrat who was to figure quite prominently in Maupassant's works. Guy's father, Gustave de Maupassant, carried on a prosperous but muddled existence in Paris, living partly on the dowry of his separated wife, partly on an inheritance from his grandmother and partly on money made on the stock exchange. Guy had to depend on his allowance, especially whilst he had no income from the Ministry, but there were incessant quarrels between father and son as to the amount due to him. Guy, who had looked upon his father with humorous tolerance at the time of the melodramatic parental conflicts, completely lost his detachment now when arguing about petty problems of cash; in a letter to his mother (in November 1872)[1] he reported at length an argument with his father, going on and on about it:

> I showed him my accounts for the month and pointed out that there was more to pay for light and heating ... I said quite gently that it was simply a matter of heating ... and there were microscopic slices of meat in my modest diet. He answered in a rage that dinner in his home consisted only of one plate of meat and a piece of cheese ... He got absolutely furious and said it was not his fault that his father took 50,000 frs. from him; I answered it was not my fault that all businessmen agreed that he could have saved at least 40,000 frs. if he had tried ...

And so forth. And then came detailed figures of his own living expenses:

Received for subsistence per month 110 *f.*

Paid:

rent	10
mending	3.50
coal	4
firewood	1.90
matches	0.50
hairdresser . . .	0.60
2 *sulphuric* baths . . .	2
sugar	0.40
ground coffee . . .	0.60
fuel for lamp . . .	5.50
laundry	7
postage	0.40

[1] *Correspondance inédite de Guy de Maupassant*, edited by A. Artinian and E. Maynial, Dominique Wapler, Paris, 1951.

30 lunch	.	.	.	34
rolls during day		.	.	3
dinner 1.60		.	.	48
tobacco	.	.	.	5
soap .	.	.	.	0.50

126.90

He paid me 8 dinners, that is   12.80

114.10

He also paid the tobacconist .   5

109.10

Well, he counted 5*f* for my miscellaneous entertainment, but the sole entertainment I can afford is to smoke my pipe. So I spent 4*f* on tobacco, sad as a luxury and very modest . . .

Again, the true Norman. In another similar calculation he proved that his father had at least 1,474 francs per annum to spare, even with living in comfort, and could thus easily increase his son's allowance.

Jules Maupassant died in 1875. His suffering, his death, his funeral and all the arrangements connected therewith, gave a new impetus to these quarrels, not only between Gustave and Guy but with practically all members of the family, and Guy's letters to his mother in Etretat, often bearing the dignified heading 'Ministère de la Marine et des Colonies', poured out detailed accounts of and curses on the meanness and pettiness of one or another of his relatives. He did not have to go far, in his later years, to find a model for middle-class families who start litigation round a coffin not yet nailed.[1]

To this background should be added the drudgery of his office work and the company of his colleagues whose adolescent jocularity struck him as more depressing even than their priggishness.[2] He loathed them and their way of life,[3] but not without feeling deep sympathy for them, precisely on account of

---

[1] *En Famille.*
[2] *Les Dimanches* . . . and *L'Héritage.*
[3] *L'Héritage* and the beginning of *Bel-Ami.*

the way of life to which they were condemned. Remembering them later as a journalist, in an article on *les employés*,[1] he took up their case with passion, arguing that to toil in *redingote*, stooped over a writing desk, was more killing than even the most exhaustive manual labour.

23 · On the Seine

Yet these eight drab years were the happiest period in Maupassant's life. His adolescent torments had abated, his fatal illness was not yet overpowering his nerves, and he knew how to squeeze pleasure even out of drabness. His main defence against it was to observe it without illusions. His scathing observation of the ways in which Civil Servants got promoted amused rather than depressed him, and his poor opinion of the sense of humour of his colleagues did not prevent him from sharing in it, and even less from recording its expressions with gusto. It was at that time that he discovered the 'little men' of Paris and their 'great miseries'.[2]

He also discovered the Seine. The name of that river stood for everything he cared for – fresh air, exercise, love-making, practical jokes, gay and bawdy company. He had a sentimental attachment for everything alive in nature, the fish and the weeds, as well as human flesh. In his later years of splendour, of literary and financial success, in 1890, he would recall those sensations with nostalgia; and it was not simply the longing for his lost youth. It was the longing for the time when the lack of illusions was endurable because there were compensations in sensual pleasures, curiosity and farce.

> What a lot of funny things, and funny girls, I used to see in the days gone by when I went boating . . . I was an office worker without a penny; I am, today, an *arrivé* who can afford to throw away large sums for the caprice of a moment. Then I nursed a thousand modest and unrealizable desires which gilded existence with all sorts of imaginary expectations.

[1] Cf. *Le Gooulois*, January 1882.

[2] *Grandes Misères des petites gens;* he was planning to write a series of stories under this title, as he told his mother in a letter in 1875.

Today, I really don't know what fantasy would be needed to make me leave the easy-chair in which I am dozing.

This, I feel, has been a bit touched up so as to fit an average middle-aged man; in fact, in his twenties, he had never given any sign of having unrealizable expectations and, after achieving success, he was less able quietly to drop off in an easy-chair than he had been in his youth. But otherwise it is factually and emotionally correct:

How simple it was, how good, and how difficult, thus to live between the office in Paris and the river at Argenteuil. My great, my only, my absorbing passion for ten years was the Seine. O, that beautiful, calm, varied and stinking river, full of mirage and rubbish! I loved it, it seems to me, because it gave me the taste of life. O, those strolls along the steep banks covered with flowers, and my friends, the frogs, who used to dream with their bellies turned to the breeze, on nenuphar leaves, and the coquettish and fragile water-lilies amidst the long and slender reeds which, beyond a willow, suddenly threw open for me the leaves of a Japanese album as the kingfisher fled from me like a blue flame! I loved all this with the instinctive love of my eyes that spread through my whole body a natural and profound delight.

As others have memories of tender nights, so have I of the sunrise in morning mist, in floating, drifting vapours, white like a cadaver before dawn and then, with the first rays sliding across the meadow, turned into a brilliant pink that tore at one's heart; and memories, also, of the moon that silvered the trembling current in a splendour which made all dreams blossom.

This was the symbol of eternal illusion, and I found it on the putrid water that carried the refuse of Paris to the sea.

Then follows the story which, though a bit tearful in mood, certainly lacks the sentimental pantheism of its invocation: it is about a happy-go-lucky girl nick-named 'Fly', who was shared by five boating companions, and about the complications involved by her pregnancy . . .[1] The ambivalent approach in this

___
[1] *Mouche.*

particular story may strike one as crude, but the compound of
sentiment and flippancy was genuine in Maupassant's writings
as well as in his personality. His love was for the colours and
the scents of the Seine; but it could not become real without
love-making, that is, without the excitement of passing women
and of sympathetic pals.

24 · 'Young bull at large'

Guy de Maupassant was a sexomaniac in more than one respect.
His appetite for copulation was enormous; his ebullient strength
and his morbid sensitiveness equally accounted for that. Had he
died before he was thirty he might have been remembered by
his friends as a sturdy young fellow bouncing with health, like
'a young bull at large', about whose 'heroic amorous exploits'
plenty of stories had been 'whispered round'.[1] Later, with some
hindsight, however, it was not difficult to discover the stimulus
of bacteria on his unquiet nerves. He was utterly promiscuous;
he quickly tired of any woman and, even if he did not, he was
attracted by all types, for one reason or another, and ready to
change his partners all the time. He could hardly see a woman
without contrasting her with others; they were superimposed
one on another in his sensations. Though keen to pick them up
for a ride in his boat, and apparently clever in handling them,
opportunities did not always offer themselves, and just as his
Bel-Ami who ended as the Prince *gigolo* of France, he found
himself now and then so forsaken that the partnership of the
plainest and dreariest female would have come as a solace . . .
As to prostitutes, in whom he was always interested, he usually
could not afford them – as can be guessed from his monthly
accounts, detailed in his letter to his mother.

His mind was as sex-ridden as his body. Irrespective of whether
he was sexually starved or glutted, he was obsessed with sex as
a subject; the hypothesis that aphrodisiacs are only required by
men who lack physical powers certainly did not apply to him.

[1] Pol Neveux, Preface to Maupassant's *Œuvres complètes*, Vol. I (*Boule
de Suif*), Conard, Paris, 1908.

'Dirty stories' were an essential part of his life, including, as they have done from time immemorial, excretion as well as proliferation. He liked them not only told but also acted dramatically, in company of course.

His comrades-in-bawd were, in the first place, his boating partners with whom he had developed a sort of adolescent gang ritual, each of them holding a ceremonial nick-name, such as Petit-Bleu; Tomahawk; La Toque (conspicuous for his flat cap); N'a Qu'un Œil (who wore a monocle); and finally, Joseph Prunier, which was – besides Guy de Valmont – one of Maupassant's early pen-names as well as his pal's name. Some writers and painters and colleagues from the Ministry would also sometimes join them.

It was pornography embodied in modest, middle-class social gatherings, and most literary pornography at that. Above the bodies and bodily symbols fluttered the spirits of Aristophanes and Rabelais, of the Abbé Prévost, of Laclos, of Sade; and, from amongst the living, of Flaubert and Baudelaire. *The Temptation of St. Anthony* had a role to play which Flaubert, though by no means prudish, would hardly have imagined when he was toiling at it; it was through that heavy jewel of visionary writing that Maupassant discovered Crepitus, who had been in ancient Rome the god of wind from the bowels. Maupassant organized a society of *Crépitiens* whose standard joke was defined by its denomination. This joined forces with the sexier *Société des Maquereaux* which had quite an echo in the literary circles of the day.[1]

Dumesnil warns against making 'teratology'[2] out of Maupassant's life story, and I should like to pay heed to his wise and noble words, but, at this point, it is not easy to do so. Maupassant's impetuous drolleries and debaucheries were the deliberate preparatory school of his art, no less than were his simultaneous exercises in literary composition. He loved farce, both by temperament and by philosophy – or even as an act of hilarious protest against philosophy. The show should be 'as farcical as possible', he urged 'La Toque', Robert Pinchon, when pre-

---

[1] Schmidt, *Maupassant par lui-même*, p. 48.

[2] '*teratology*, dealing in the marvellous (Biol.) study of animal or vegetable monstrosities' (The Concise Oxford Dictionary).

paring with him an amateur stage performance in Etretat,[1] and later, as an *arrivé* author, he wrote stories in praise of 'the real farce, the good farce, the happy and simple and healthy farce of our fathers'.[2] No joke could be too simple for him to enjoy, and the dirtier it was, the better.

Another shade of implied protest in his pleasure was his passion for shocking *les bourgeois* – the Le Poittevin–Flaubert heritage, coloured now by Baudelairian 'Satanism'. He would talk about the taste of human flesh, and when asked by a staggered listener at a dinner whether, for Heaven's sake, he had ever eaten man, answered, 'O no, never man; only woman', and added a gastronomic description of the meal. Hoaxes, of course – but too frequent, and too much a part of his gradually developing obsessions, to be dismissed as hoaxes only. The liturgies of the Crépitiens–Maquereaux brotherhood included wilful sacrilege, of a facetious and self-torturing rather than anti-clerical character – O Baudelaire! – and the initiation included tests of sexual strength, of fortitude to face putrefaction and horror, and to endure physical pain, somewhat reminiscent of what young Guy had learned in Swinburne's entourage. An office colleague of Maupassant's is supposed to have paid with an early death for these tests, and Maupassant almost boasted that he was unrepentant about it.[3] This assertion, too, may have been made in jest, but the participants in these liturgies liked to believe themselves to be serious; the atmosphere was really 'teratogenic'.

Yet beneath all this we find the simple pleasure of a young civil servant, who liked to indulge his sensual and slightly *larmoyant* lyricism. He got up in the small hours to drag his boat to the river; he smoked a pipeful of tobacco; he had a short swim; and then started rowing and, as he said of his favourite painters, 'ate with his eyes' the changing scene, absorbed in bliss and melancholia. He constantly needed company, both male and female, yet he only truly found himself when alone with Nature.

[1] 8 September 1877.   [2] *La Farce* (1883).
[3] In a letter from the Ministry of Education, presumably in 1879, to an unknown lady jokingly addressed as 'Charmante Princesse'. *Correspondance inédite*, edited by A. Artinian and E. Maynial.

25 · Alfred reincarnated

It was really Flaubert who ruined Maupassant. Maupassant, when still quite young, went to see him in Rouen – or maybe it happened when Flaubert visited Paris – and he, Flaubert, took him to a brothel with his friends, telling them he would show them a prodigy: Maupassant *tirant six coups de suite*. Indeed, Maupassant possessed quite amazing sexual potency, and he ended by taking some pride in it, becoming almost an exhibitionist. One day, the syphilis came . . .

This part of a longer narrative, coming from a reliable source,[1] is rather naïve; surely Maupassant did not need Flaubert's assistance? Yet it was typical. A similar, or maybe the same, venture of young Maupassant, has been recalled by Edmond de Goncourt[2] as a memorable event in French literary life: a tart acclaimed Flaubert as 'Béranger!', and the tears rolled down Flaubert's face from laughter. He liked to refer to that light and popular poet as the symbol of the lyrical philistine. It was the epoch of brothel-crawling as it was of middle-class respectability; and of boisterous ribaldry chequered with romantic musing.

Flaubert now had his beloved Alfred reincarnated in a robust youth; he was attached to twenty-three-year-old Guy whom, as he told his mother,[3] he saw as 'a good child, charming, intelligent, full of good sense and wit'. There was a gentlemanly and provincial *gaucherie* in young Guy which appealed to the older writer, tired of the loquacious over-cleverness and bohemian forwardness of most of the young men who turned up as his admirers. Guy talked little, particularly about theories; he did not try to impose his views on others and, in fact, did not hold many views. He was kind and attentive to his elders. His indecencies were restricted to dirty stories and practical jokes, and stopped short of tactlessness in discussions on values and ideas.

[1] Paul Léautaud, 'Journal littéraire', vol. VIII, pp. 270–1, *Mercure de France*, 1960, quoting Claude Berton, whose father was a personal friend of Maupassant and a particularly close friend of Maupassant's doctor.
[2] See Appendix 4.   [3] In a letter of February 1873.

He was not of the type one would expect to become an important writer; but he belonged to the 'gang', and Flaubert agreed with Laure de Maupassant that he should try his hand at writing.

Maupassant went to see Flaubert in Croisset, Rouen, as often as he could, finances, job and women permitting, and they also met in Paris, especially after Flaubert had established a *pied-à-terre* there at rue Murillo.[1] Besides, they kept up a long correspondence, all these years, on all kinds of subjects, and as literary in spirit as it was informal otherwise. These letters were not devised for posterity. In fact, they were carelessly written, especially by Flaubert, who did not bother even about spelling mistakes when writing to his intimates. Indeed, he ordered his letters to be burnt after his death, but his ambitious niece Caroline, Mme Commanville, published them after removing as much as she could of what she considered offensive. Regrettable though this pruning was, the dutiful execution of the Master's will would have been even more regrettable.

Maupassant submitted to his *cher Maître* his literary sketches and designs – theatre, poetry, epic prose and also literary criticism – and Flaubert went through them with devoted patience, meticulousness, and a degree of rigour and outspokenness tempered only by the affection it betrayed. 'I don't know whether you are gifted for writing,' was the refrain of his paternal criticism; but you must try, and try again, sacrificing all wordly pleasures, flouting money and success, despising the opinion of journalists, not caring for anything but the artistic perfection of the work. Talent was, in Buffon's words, 'nothing but long patience'; and, as demonstrated by Flaubert, patience mainly in self-torture. Why should anybody wish to acquire talent at that price? That was the one question Flaubert never tried to answer. Ostentatious about his disillusionment and his refusal to share in any metaphysical belief, he failed to admit – or even to recognize – that he was serving a mystical ideal, which he called 'Art', and expected his beloved ones, as well as himself, to burn themselves up with zeal for it. It was all right for Guy to indulge his faunal desires so long as he knew that, in the final analysis, life should only be regarded as subject-matter for writing. But, later, 'think of the serious things, young man.'

[1] He later moved to his niece's apartment in faubourg St Honoré.

Flaubert thus never stopped prodding Maupassant. His complaint against him from the outset was, as he told Laure de Maupassant (in the above quoted letter) that 'our young man is somewhat of a *flâneur* [vagabond]', and he urged him to try his skill on larger compositions – not, apparently, because size had any value in itself, but simply because that would be more likely to keep him glued to his writing-desk and make him concentrate on the subject he had chosen. About the plans submitted to him by Maupassant, Flaubert was most appreciative; but the manuscripts themselves were blackened with his corrections and often were buried ultimately in the waste-paper basket.

'Young man,' Flaubert kept on repeating, 'you must work ...' And even as late as August 1878: 'You complain that women's buttocks are *monotonous*' (which, by the way, meant in Maupassant's philosophy that the essence of life was monotonous). 'Well, there is a fairly simple remedy: do not avail yourself of them.' He found Guy guilty of: 'Too many whores; too much boating; too much exercise!'

He was always worried about Guy – his prospects as a writer, his prospects in practical life, his finances, his health. He got quite excited over Guy's eye troubles, and discussed at length the medical details. And, when the *flâneur* had disappeared for a while – presumably with a girl in his boat – he wrote to a friend: 'Give me news of Guy, his last letter was pathetic. I have since written to him but got no reply. He may, I fear, be ill ... If, however, the above-mentioned young man turns out to be in good health, you are authorized on my behalf to *foutre* a kick in his arse.'[1]

26 · *'Absolutely lubricious'*

The above-mentioned young man, in the meantime, was growing into a middle-aged, pleasant and, seemingly, most pedestrian shadow of his adored master. He assisted Flaubert, his office duties permitting, both in research for his work and in

[1] July 1878. Morand, *Vie de Guy de Maupassant*.

receiving his friends. *Bouvard et Pécuchet*, the last great work started by Flaubert, required an enormous amount of reading in practically all branches of science in which the two dunderheads were supposed to dabble. But the *flâneur*, Guy, preferred to leave the reading to his master and do the fieldwork instead; in his letter of 3 November 1877 he described in great detail the scenery in and round Etretat where Flaubert was planning to set his characters. 'You cannot,' he wrote, 'make your *bonhommes* start from Bruneval in order to go to Etretat because . . .' – there were natural obstacles on that particular route, obstacles he knew from his own experience and in which Flaubert was interested, though not sufficiently to go and see for himself. Was such research necessary at all? Could a bush or precipice not be pushed aside in order to fit in with the geography required for the story? Certainly it could, and was when called for. Yet interest in the minute facts was most characteristic of both Flaubert and Maupassant – as it was, for all differences in character, of Goncourt and of Zola – because they were all writers moved by an almost mystic passion for factual authenticity.

Flaubert's *pied-à-terre* in Paris was a simple little apartment – for he loved bright colours and rich ornaments everywhere save in his own home – where he received his friends on Sunday afternoons, in his wide, tobacco-coloured gown, usually showing them in himself as the servant was having his day off. They stayed until the evening, then Flaubert would doze for an hour on his broad divan, slip into his tail-coat and go off to the *salon* of Princess Mathilde there to meet some of his guests again – the established *élite* as it were which throve side by side with, but was clearly distinguishable from, high officialdom and the Académie.

The regular callers on those Sunday afternoons included the Russian novelist, Turgenev – he often arrived first and was received by Flaubert with 'brotherly embraces' as Maupassant later described. Then there were many of the leading French intellectuals of the day, scholars, novelists, poets, critics, men such as Taine, Renan, Goncourt, Zola, Daudet, Heredia, Catulle Mendès, Huysmans, Paul Alexis . . . To most of them, Maupassant was known as a likeable and unimportant youngster, a good mixer though not a great talker, and a bawdy and innocent farce-maker. 'What a pity,' Turgenev sighed after reading one of his essays, 'that he will never have any talent.'

In this period, ending with the seventies of the century, there was really only one work with which Maupassant made any impact on the literary world, the play *A la feuille de rose, Maison turque*, written and acted by him in co-operation with his boating partners – some of them men of letters themselves – and with other young men, such as Octave Mirbeau, Maurice Leloir, Georges Becker. This treats of the adventures in a brothel that specializes in amorous gymnastics symbolized by 'rose leaves', and in dressing its girls in 'Turkish' style. The details are more typical of the *crépitien* Maupassant than of the erotomaniac – as far as the two can be contrasted. The tone is set by a scavenger whose job was to clean the cesspool discussing his findings with a valet of the establishment (who washes contraceptives). Barely hidden homosexuality also came into the performance; only men played the parts, with huge symbols of the female sex when required, and the climax of the play was a pornographic ballet danced by these 'women'.

There is also a plot with the perennial comic triangle of the cuckold, the adulteress and the sly seducer in it. A *bourgeois* couple, a provincial mayor and his wife, take a room in the *Maison*, mistaking it for an ordinary hotel; they have been tricked into this by a friend who is in league with the *maquereau* to seduce the wife. The members of the 'harem' are shown to strangers as a special favour, for high fees. The husband catches his wife *in flagrante* with the seducer, but by then he has himself committed adultery with one of the 'ladies' of the harem – namely, Maupassant – and is blackmailed into silence by the *maquereau* who threatens him with the sword of the Sultan. The *maquereau* gets money from everybody: that's the happy ending. Other familiar characters are the bragging *Marseillais*, who fails at the moment of action, and the sight-seeing Englishman to whom the harlots are presented as wax figures and who is enraptured with their verisimilitude.

Two performances of *Maison turque* are on record, both in Paris: the first, in Leloir's attic, transformed into a temporary theatre, on the Quai Voltaire, in April 1875; and the second for those who had missed it, in Becker's studio, rue de Fleurs, in

May 1877. A prosecution followed – by authorities who refused to regard the performance as 'strictly private', but this was stopped, so Léon Daudet reports,[1] on Alphonse Daudet's intervention. It had not, however, been printed till 1945, and then only in a sumptuous edition, for *gourmets*.

Unlike other works by Maupassant before 1880, this was, at least, discussed. Invitations had been sent to 'men past twenty years of age and women previously deflowered', and the selected audiences which turned up, especially for the second performance, included the French literary *élite* with its Russian honorary member, Turgenev, and some five or six women, notorious vamps of the day, such as the fascinating blonde, Voltesse de la Bigne, a live model of Zola's Nana, and the actress Suzanne Lagier, known for her Rabelaisian sense of humour. Princess Mathilde, having heard of it, had also thought of attending in a mask, but Flaubert managed to dissuade her in time. Flaubert himself was seen to arrive fully dressed. Panting heavily he climbed the stairs, ridding himself of one article of clothing after another on each landing until he joined the audience in his shirt-sleeves, with his wardrobe over his arms. But he was amply rewarded; he burst into laughter again and again in his boisterous way at the sight of those sexy phantasmagoria, with his Guy in the role of a strumpet. 'How refreshing!' he exclaimed. There was loud applause and some faint censure. Edmond de Goncourt took great pains to 'disguise his disgust', as he noted, for he felt it would be awkward for an author like him to appear to be prudish. He also reported that Voltesse de la Bigne seemed rather bored behind her courteous smile, whereas Madame Lagier left in protest before the end. What shocked Goncourt most was to see the author's father, Gustave de Maupassant, so amused by his son's obscene production.[2] He might have been even more shocked to learn that Maupassant when preparing for the first performance in March 1875, boasted to his mother that it was to be 'absolument lubrique' (absolutely lubricious).

[1] *Quand vivait mon père*, Grasset, Paris, 1940, pp. 38–9.
[2] Goncourt's *Journal*, May 1877.

Beside all these 'refreshing' ventures, Flaubert taught his disciple to concentrate on the 'serious things' of Art: originality
and style. By originality he did not, however, mean the Romantic 'intuition', but rather its opposite, a faculty which could be
developed by mental effort and self-restraint. To look at a
corner of life hard enough was to discover its hidden characteristics, to get rid of the *idée reçue*, and so see a trivial thing as
though it had never been seen before.

> There is something inexplored in everything, because we
> are used to using our eyes only with the memories of what
> others thought of the thing we are contemplating. The most
> minute thing contains something unknown. Let us find it.
> In order to describe the flames of a fire or a tree in the plain,
> we should stand gazing at that fire or tree until we find them
> unlike any other tree and any other fire. It is in this way that
> one becomes original.

Or else:

> If you pass a grocer sitting in his doorway, or a *concierge*
> smoking his pipe, or a rank of hackney carriages, show me
> that grocer and that *concierge*, their posture, their whole
> physical appearance . . . their whole moral nature, in such a
> way that I shall not confuse them with any other grocer or
> any other *concierge*, and make me see by one single word what
> distinguishes a certain hackney horse from fifty others . . .[1]

M. Paul Morand comments that: 'These gymnastics in
originality make one smile. Had Balzac had to proceed like this,
there would have been no Balzac at all.'[2] There might, perhaps,
have been a better Balzac – at any rate, according to Flaubert
who admired Balzac as a giant rather than as an artist. Maupassant, too, was most critical of the author of the *Comédie
humaine*, who, he said, was a genius, but 'having a hundred

[1] Quoted by Maupassant in his Preface to *Pierre et Jean* (which is
discussed below).

[2] Morand, *Vie de Guy de Maupassant*, p. 49.

times more material than is necessary for building a house, uses everything because he is unable to choose'. Subsequently, Maupassant complained about some minor editorial changes carried out in an article of his which would make him appear to be a greater admirer of Balzac than he really was. What would Flaubert think? 'For,' he carries on, 'I know that he [Flaubert] judges him [Balzac] absolutely as I do, and that whilst admitting his indisputable genius, he considers him not as an imperfect writer but as no writer at all.'[1]

Flaubert and his disciple may or may not have been right in a number of things; but what M. Morand does not seem to appreciate is that Flaubert, through his discipline of discarding everything that could not stand the test of personal perception, did provide the psychological key to a prose-writing unequalled in accuracy and articulateness. Not every horse he described was unlike every other horse; but his effort to grasp what was unique in the particular horse enabled him to grasp what was typical of horses in general. In my opinion there was nothing wrong with the Flaubertian advice, except perhaps the somewhat ambiguous use of the term 'originality', which might be taken to mean an effort to say strikingly new things in a strikingly new form. What Flaubert had in mind was rather *genuineness*; he wished to get at the naked facts, including the facts of daydreams and visions, by ridding himself of every image that had been accepted instinctively, merely for the sake of convenience. He had no faith in the originality of mental innocence.

Flaubert, like Balzac – or Stendhal, for that matter – was drawn by a vision of truthful story-telling; but, unlike them, he held that the proof of the writing was whether it rang true. Or, maybe, their ideas of ringing true differed; Stendhal seeking it in adequacy, Balzac in riches, and Flaubert in rhythm. For Flaubert, as Maupassant saw him, was 'an artist before all' and owed to certain old masters – Apuleius, Rabelais, La Bruyère, Cervantes – and, amongst his contemporaries, to the poet,

[1] Cf. Maupassant's articles (both signed 'Guy de Valmont') 'Gustave Flaubert' in *La République des Lettres* 23 October 1876, and 'Balzac d'après ses lettres' in *La Nation*, 22 November 1876; and his letters to Henri Roujon, dated 'This Monday morning' (in October 1876) and to Flaubert, 8 January 1877.

Théophile Gautier, more than he did to earlier novelists. Indeed, in Flaubert's view, prose-writing required even more sense of rhythm than did poetry, precisely because the rhythm of prose, though no less essential, was less definable by rules. He did not aim at verse-like prose, but rather a crystal-like prose condensed from the stream of freely spoken words. He tested everything he had written through his ears as well as his eyes, reading it aloud and not satisfied until he found it flawless. Maupassant relates in his *Gustave Flaubert*:[1]

> When he read to his friends his story *Un Cœur simple*, some found fault with that passage of ten lines in which the old girl ended by confusing her parrot with the Holy Ghost. The idea appeared to be too subtle for a peasant woman's mind. Flaubert listened to them, pondered, admitted that the objection was legitimate. 'You are right,' he said, 'but then . . . the *phrase*, the sentence, would have to be changed.'

> That very evening, he set to work; he spent the whole night trying to alter the words, blackened and erased twenty sheets of paper, and ended by not altering a word, unable to find another sentence with a harmony that could have satisfied him.

> At the beginning of the same story, the last word of a paragraph, which introduced the subject of the one that followed, seemed somewhat ambiguous. His friends drew his attention to this; he conceded their point and tried to modify the sense of the words, but since he did not succeed in reestablishing the sonority he had in mind, he gave up and exclaimed, 'So much the worse for the sense; rhythm before all!'

This, then, was Maupassant's schooling in literature. How much did he accept of it? Everything, on the surface. This is how Henry Roujon, assistant editor of the literary magazine *La République des Lettres*, describes Maupassant's *début*. One day Catulle Mendès passed on to him a manuscript, the poem *Au bord de l'eau*, by Guy de Valmont.

'Who is he?' – 'A *protégé* of Flaubert. Flaubert has sent it himself asking me to publish it . . . Guy de Valmont is a

---

[1] First published as the Preface to the *Correspondance of Flaubert and George Sand*, Charpentier, Paris, 1884: not to be confused with the above-quoted article by 'Guy de Valmont' in 1876.

pen-name. Flaubert says his young friend is employed at the Ministry of Marine, working under a man who dislikes poetry. The real name of the poet is Maupassant; but he is going to come and see us himself.'

He did come. There was nothing romantic in his appearance. The plump, suffused features of a land-lubber, with frank and simple manners. 'My name is *Mauvais-passant*' [punning on his name], he repeated with a *bonhomie* that gave the lie to the threat. His conversation was restricted to the recollections of the lessons in literary theology inculcated in him by Flaubert; he expressed his admiration, with more liveliness than profoundness, for what he was expected to admire in that artistic religion; in addition he had an inexhaustible supply of bawdy anecdotes, and poured out violent invective against the personnel of the Ministry of Marine. On that subject he could never stop. In fact, he did not say much, he did not give himself away, he did not say anything about his future plans. He continued to write verse . . . He was liked for his easy-going manners and the equanimity of his temperament.[1]

This seems a very trustworthy account, not in spite of, but rather because of the contradictions it contains. Maupassant was an 'inexhaustible' talker on some matters though on the whole, he talked very little; and he was noted for not looking romantic, though he belonged to a world where a romantic appearance, especially for a young poet, was a rule rather than an eccentricity. In his ideas, one would think, he was more of a Flaubertian than was Flaubert himself; as can be seen in his dictum in the Preface to *Pierre et Jean*, written in 1888: 'Whatever we may wish to say, there is but one word to express it, one verb to enliven it, one adjective to qualify it. One must search until one discovers that word, that verb, that adjective.'

This was, indeed, Flaubertianism over-simplified; but he wrote it in a somewhat aggressive mood, challenging, amongst others, Goncourt, who with his *écriture artiste*, though no less keen on the 'right word', sought it in a very different direction.[2]

[1] Dumesnil, *Guy de Maupassant*.   [2] See Chapter 39.

Maupassant was aware of his enormous debt to Flaubert, and paid tribute to him in most generous praises and in touching personal recollections. But while the author we know as Guy de Maupassant was really of Flaubert's making – he substantially differed from his maker. They had mainly three things in common. First there was their humility towards facts. This, to some extent, was the common religion of the whole *élite* of those days, of practically all the scholars, artists and men of letters who met in Flaubert's little apartment on Sunday afternoons, and was at the bottom of so many *isms* of their century: positivism, scientism, realism, naturalism, even impressionism as a method of recording the reflections of minute physical details on the mind, after ridding it of any preconceived idea of what the whole must be like. Not that it was an epoch of documentary rather than imaginative literature. Epic *belles-lettres* in France and in the whole western world – including, not least, Russia – flourished during the middle and the late nineteenth century more than ever before or since. It was taken for granted that the facts observed must be grouped or selected or coloured or modified so as to fit into an artistic composition; the facts of the Norman or the African coast could be set aside if it was found necessary, but, in the 'theology' of Croisset, they *must not be ignored*.

A more personal, more intimate link between Flaubert and Maupassant was that created by the superimposition on one another of poetic visions and ostentatious disillusionments, which stemmed from those children's stage performances in the *Hôtel-Dieu*. It was a philosophy more clearly manifest in emotional experiences than in ideas; the tender memories of Alfred Le Poittevin, the dear and sophisticated friend, and of Laure, the devoted mother, clearly came into it, as did the partnership in brothel excursions and in ventures such as the *Maison turque*. Flaubert, biologically undersexed, and Maupassant, oversexed, were both equally haunted by those shapes and colours in nature that suggested the desire for copulation, and the melancholia that followed both its fulfilment and non-fulfilment. The sensual vision of Flaubert, unlike that of his predecessors, was ascetic and self-denying. It was the positivism, realism and sensualism of the Romantic turned anti-Romantic through self-torture; it was an act of faith of one who treasured the gloom of his faithlessness as a source of inspiration.

Maupassant joined him with his own deeper disbelief, more genuine lack of illusions, and more superficial intellect. He was a positivist, a realist, a sensualist by instinct; in so far as he felt nothing was genuine unless borne out by sensations. These sensations, according to Flaubert, were only justified in so far as they enabled an artist to create a work in which the artist himself was invisible: 'L'homme n'est rien, l'œuvre est tout.' And this was the point at which Maupassant, though without contradicting him in so many words, was really an unfaithful disciple. 'I write for money'; 'as a matter of fact, I prefer a pretty woman to all the arts';[1] statements like these, from his private correspondence, or his recorded dialogues, though certainly over-simplified and intended mainly to shock some high-falutin' fellow-writers, expressed, at any rate, the negative facet of the truth. He considered art and letters merely as a part of life; and if life as a whole was senseless, why should there be more sense in a part of it? 'Maupassant, c'est Flaubert moins la foi en l'art' – Maupassant is Flaubert without his faith in Art – says one of our contemporary *Maupassantiens*,[2] and he is almost right.

Almost – because it still leaves open the question why Maupassant wrote, and why he did so frantically and with a self-devouring passion. He loved women and money, and women who could be bought for money, no doubt; but he was willing and, indeed, anxious to forget them all for the sake of recording his impressions and experiences, and to 'learn his *métier*', much before he had the slightest assurance of making any money out of it. He was unable to live without trying his hand at literary work of a higher or lower order – plays, verses, sketches, notes, stories. However strong his sensual appetites, he needed the constant stimulus of self-expression to feel that they were real. An urge to re-create what he sensed in order to sense it convincingly,

[1] In his correspondence with Marie Bashkirtseff (about which more later).

[2] Lemoine, *Guy de Maupassant*.

seems to have been the most important driving power in his art; life if properly expressed was sad, but if not put into words it was worse than sad, it was hollow. His adherence, though tongue-in-cheek, to Flaubert's 'literary theology' provided him with the rituals to escape that hollowness.

The first thing in which the two met was thus their love for what Maupassant called 'l'humble vérité';[1] the second, their love for sensual imagery, in a mood of frustration and melancholia; and the third, their love for clear expression, for that beauty in style without which not even the ugliness of existence could be brought to life – the rhythm in prose.

We shall have to dwell on the intricacies of Maupassant's apparently simple style in some later chapters; it should suffice to say here that it could hardly have developed without Flaubert's example and assistance. It was Flaubert's virtuosity to draw out the lyricism of a sentimental dreamer, in long waves of prosaic melody, in sentences which contained *impassible* descriptions of sceneries and events; and then to interrupt them, whenever a breath was required, with the clap of short sentences, and now and then a metaphor or a factual statement that hinted at an aphorism untold. Maupassant developed his own gift for this technique both through his listening to Flaubert and by looking through the pages 'blackened and erased' by the master in his search for the perfect cadence. The rules of that perfection could hardly be defined; Flaubert's horror of alliteration, or his aversion to repetition of words, was certainly but a fraction, and not even the most important, of what he was aiming at. They were not, and could not be, hard and fast rules; they were not passed on to Maupassant as a textbook but through emotional and professional intimacy.

Flaubert's style, like his philosophy, was watered down by his disciple. Lemaître called Maupassant's style *Flaubert détendu* – Flaubert less tense. It was cheaper stuff than the master's, no doubt. But its very deterioration reflected an advance both in readability and in practical wisdom. Maupassant's style compared to Flaubert's was as applied science compared to pure science; Flaubert's was the abstract equation, but Maupassant's was the machine that worked.

[1] In the motto of *Une Vie*.

Maupassant knew that; and he acknowledged his debt to Flaubert with a mixture of tender irony and remorse for his own irony. He adored his master; but there was inevitably a touch of patronizing respect in his adoration. Anyway, he could not have written sincerely about Flaubert without stressing those characteristics in which he differed from him.

> Ever since his [Gustave Flaubert's] early childhood, the two distinctive features of his character were a great *naïveté* and a horror of physical action. Throughout all his life he remained naïve and sedentary ... This penetrating and subtle observer appeared only to see life with lucidity from a distance. The moment he touched it, or when it concerned his close neighbours, one would have said he kept his eyes under a veil. His extreme straightforwardness by nature, his unshakable good faith, the generosity of his emotions, and of all the impulses of his soul, these were undoubtedly the causes of that stubborn *naïveté*.
>
> He lived off life, and not in it. Well placed to observe, he did not have the clear sensation of contacts.

This is an admirable analysis of Flaubert's approach – one wonders why the very man who wrote it, and who followed in Flaubert's footsteps, only found empty platitudes to say when, in the same essay,[1] he tried to analyze some of Flaubert's works. Maupassant saw Flaubert perfectly; and to see a man perfectly means to see also his imperfections. Without that faint shade of contempt, Maupassant's respect would not have been real. He made a great effort to pretend blindness about Flaubert's weaknesses; but when once Dumas-*fils* remarked, 'O Flaubert! he cuts down a forest to build a barge,' the devoted *Flaubertien* was unable to suppress a mischievous and affirmative smile.[2]

Maupassant was anything but naïve; he lived *in* life, as intensely as any writer could, and was second to none in conveying 'the clear sensation of contacts'. His notion of perfect beauty was as hazy and indirect as was Flaubert's experience of sexual ecstasy; his knowledge of world literature as fragmentary as was Flaubert's of the shrubs on the Norman sea coast. He was as

[1] *Gustave Flaubert*, 1884.
[2] A. Vial, *Maupassant et l'Art du Roman*, Nizet, Paris, 1954.

industrious in rambling, sailing, love-making and money-making as was Flaubert in reading. His contemporary, Henry James, saw him mainly as a *roving* writer,[1] or reporter. Especially after discovering his real talent for story-telling, as distinct from poetry and drama, he was constantly hunting for 'subjects'; already as a young civil servant, he urged his mother to collect them for him! He knew he lacked imagination. He also knew, as a good Flaubertian, that his originality did not come from God; it had to be acquired. According to the 'literary theology' of his master, there were no free gifts from Nature to an artist or to a thinker; talent had to be sharpened by constant hard thought and observation, and looking at written and printed texts even more than at natural phenomena. If Maupassant read less than his master – and far less after his decisive success in 1880 – this was not for contempt of what could be learned from reading. It was simply on account of his physiological and nervous disposition. His eye troubles, his impatience, his physical appetites, his curiosity to observe landscapes and people, his ambitions to become a popular writer, all these drew him away from literary studies. Flaubert's *naïveté* consisted in his absolute devotion to Art, and not in mistaking its nature. About the latter Maupassant saw eye-to-eye with his master and quoted approvingly what he had repeatedly heard from him, that 'talent is nothing but long patience'. But with a slip typical of the differences between them, he attributed the aphorism to Chateaubriand instead of Buffon . . .[2] Surely nobody is safe against such slips of memory,[3] yet there is something ironical in praising accuracy inaccurately, or in paying tribute to long patience in a noticeable hurry. Not that Maupassant despised learning, but Buffon meant very little to him; his own long patience was that of the expert

---

[1] In the Preface to the first English edition of Maupassant's short stories, *The Odd Number*, Harper & Brothers, New York and London, 1889.

[2] He did so in his essay on *Roman*, first published in *Figaro Littéraire*. In the course of a subsequent press controversy, he apologized for having 'made Flaubert say this stupidity' and, when the essay was republished as a Preface to *Pierre et Jean* (1888), he set it right.

[3] Not even Flaubert. The eyes of Emma Bovary change colour several times, and though this is convincingly explained by the varying light effects, it could be argued that it was originally due to the author's forgetfulness (see La Varende, *Flaubert par lui-même*, pp. 101–2).

motorist impatient to keep his vehicle moving, or of a reporter racing with time. And speed is an enemy of perfection.

The strange thing is that the final result, at any rate in the best pieces he was to mass-produce, was all the more perfect for these imperfections. Natural inspiration could not work literary miracles, but schooling through sensual and intellectual intimacy could; Guy de Maupassant came out of the mental laboratory of Croisset and rue Murillo fully equipped to observe life 'originally' and to record his findings in the 'rhythm' aimed at, in a language as limpid and easily readable as it was concise and, when required, poetic. His reporter's hunch and superficiality, his haste and worldliness, his anxiety to sense everything for himself, to record what he had sensed and to see in print what he had recorded, all his earthly passions and weaknesses enabled him to add to the Flaubertian art that 'clear sensation of contacts' which Flaubert himself lacked. The magnificence of Flaubert's style may outshine his characters, and 'cela empêche l'atmosphère', as his devoted friend, Turgenev, complained.[1] Indeed, the very impeccability of those masterpieces makes them tiresome now and then, even that *Cœur simple* in which he was understandably unable to alter a word . . . It would be easier to alter a word here and there in *Boule de Suif*, or *Le Petit Fût*, or *Miss Harriet*, or *Le Mal d'André*, or *L'Héritage*; but why should one? There is beauty in them, no doubt, for the style is Flaubert diluted, and Flaubert even when diluted is beautiful. But there is not too much beauty to distract the reader from the characters, to disturb the atmosphere. There is just that spark of vulgarity in them which would be needed in any Heaven to make it appeal to human beings more than any sordid earth. 'The little blighter surpassed us,' Flaubert triumphed after reading *Boule de Suif*, and he was right; what he did not, perhaps, realize was that his disciple owed his superiority to his apostasy in ritual as much as to his faithfulness in theology to his master. Maupassant's masterpieces were achieved by concessions to the common reader made at the expense of Flaubertian ideals by one who was sufficiently akin to both. This could not have been brought about without his shortcomings; nor, of course, without Flaubert.

[1] Quoted by Paul Bourget, *Nouvelles pages de critique et de doctrine*.

29 · The turning-point: 1879–80

The years of 1879–80 marked the turning-point in Maupassant's career. It was then that he introduced himself to a wider public first on the stage, then with a volume of poetry and, most important of all, with the publication of *Boule de Suif.*

His plays are only of interest because they indicate his longing for colourful and worldly performances, and his sense of the dramatic, without which he could not have become the storyteller he was. Today, one may surmise, he would have found in television his proper medium for representing life in action; but the stage in his time was less suitable for condensing dramatic effects than was the printed word, and he did not think of trying to break through its barriers. He went on struggling throughout his life to become a successful playwright, but he was not gifted in that direction. In his letters to his friend, Robert Pinchon ('La Toque') he complained early in 1878: 'I have wasted almost my whole winter on rewriting my play and I am not happy about it,' and then he vowed, 'I swear I shall never touch the stage again!' However, he broke this pledge and tried, again and again.

On 19 February 1879 his play *Histoire du Vieux Temps* was performed on a stage so modest as to make it only a symbolic *début.* Flaubert, as enthusiastic in popularizing Guy's writings once they were released, as he was severe in pruning them so long as they were in manuscript, planned to have it performed in Princess Mathilde's *salon*; this private view would have meant more to the young author than a public performance. Flaubert had had similar plans for a previous play by his disciple, *Une Répétition*, which the Vaudeville theatre had found *trop fine* for staging. Nothing came of these plans, but Maupassant himself was introduced to the *salon* of the Princess and thus socially joined the *élite* before doing so as a writer.

Maupassant's poetry appears today as nothing but a preparatory exercise in polished prose. His poems were mostly versified short stories, fairly banal both in form and in content; but it was in them that he first expressed that 'deep sensuality', sometimes elegiac, now and then flashing up in mischievous bawdiness, which pervaded his view not only of human beings but also of rivers, marshes, fields. His prosody, despite the careful coaching by Bouilhet and Flaubert, was not impeccable; Lemaître, though certainly not a pedant, reprimanded him for some unnecessary *enjambements*; but it had a smooth and vigorous beat which was to continue later, freed from superfluous padding, in the descriptive paragraphs of his novels and short stories. His second-rate poetry, like his third-rate stage-craft, provided the bricks and mortar for his first-rate narrative prose.

His sole volume of poetry, *Des Vers*, published in May 1880, was of importance in his career only because it was his first work published as a separate volume;[1] and because of the 'immorality' scandal with the authorities that preceded its publication. The scandal was a rather trivial affair, more fussed about by Maupassant and his friends than by the authorities and their crusading prudes; it had some echoes of the prosecutions, many years before, against the authors of *Madame Bovary* and *Les Fleurs du Mal*. But it was typical enough to be told in some detail.

The story dates back to the middle seventies when the young poet and literary chronicler under the *nom-de-plume* of 'Guy de Valmont', or occasionally 'Joseph Prunier' or 'Maufrigneuse', toured the editorial offices of newspapers and literary magazines in the hope of placing some of his writings or of obtaining a commission for more or less regular journalistic work.

He was socially welcome everywhere, but the willingness to print his works was less unanimous. The lady editor, Mme Adam, was happy to entertain him in her home and explained to him most eloquently why she could not print his work in her

---

[1] Discounting plays in serial publications.

Nouvelle Revue, despite Flaubert ... The *Revue des Deux Mondes* also rejected his poem which left, for long years, an aching scar on his soul. He found, however, some space for his articles in *La Nation* and *Le Gaulois*, and so earned a few francs to add to his slender salary at the Ministry. Flaubert, normally contemptuous and scornful of journalism, which he considered as the very opposite of true literature, did not mind his Guy's dabbling in it; in fact, he gave him advice how to make his articles 'sensational'. His paternal anxiety about Guy's future overruled even his belief in Art for Art's sake. Besides, he may instinctively have felt, despite all his pedagogic harangues to his erring disciple, that the same rules of conduct could not be applied to both of them, and that without some journalese excursions, Maupassant would not be Maupassant. In fact, in the development of that great fiction writer, journalism played a role even more essential than poetry and stage-craft.

At the office of the important literary magazine, *La République des Lettres*, Catulle Mendès and Henri Roujon received 'Guy de Valmont' in a mixed mood of sympathy and hesitation; the recommendation of Flaubert was *too* enthusiastic to be trusted. They read and re-read the long poem submitted to them by Guy, *Au bord de l'eau* and then decided to publish it. They no doubt did the right thing. That poem, though overrated by Flaubert, is quite a pleasant but chattering piece of pastoral eroticism, the recollections, in lulling Alexandrines, of a young man on how he made love with a peasant laundress by the river, and then made love again, and then again.

Years had passed when in 1879 Maupassant decided to drop his pen-name and published his volume of poetry. The publisher, Charpentier, was not keen on the venture, but Flaubert besieged him, and even his wife, with so many letters entreating, imploring, almost threatening them – 'I am asking this as a *personal favour* ... I insist ... I love him [Guy] as my son,' and 'If your husband doesn't give way I shall be unable to forgive him' – that they did give way and the publication of *Des Vers* was at last agreed upon. The selection of the pieces was discussed between the disciple and the master, though it was noted later that some were included without submission to Flaubert; Maupassant feared, apparently, that they would be found too facile. On this ground, Flaubert tried to persuade Maupassant to leave out *Désirs* as 'unworthy' of so serious a poet, but Maupassant defied the advice, though he carried out a great number of corrections in order to meet Flaubert's objections.

Whilst these preparations were going on, Maupassant got in touch with a provincial *avant-garde* periodical, *Revue Moderne et Naturaliste*, published by Auguste Allien, a literary-minded and generous master printer, of Etampes, and edited by Harry Alis (whose real name was Hippolyte Percher). This Harry Alis, then twenty-three or twenty-four, was an 'angry young man' of his time, a dynamic and versatile novelist and polemist, and founder and/or editor of various periodicals, a Republican in politics and spokesman for the dissenting spirits in art, a crusader against hypocrisy, bigotry, Jesuitism, Bonapartism and everything he found reactionary in the Third Republic. He passionately fought prudishness, irrespective of whether its background was Christian authoritarianism or Republican *vertu*. As to the *Parnassiens*, he advised them, in the introductory manifesto of his *Revue*, 'to look for readers amongst the old mummies of Keops, the only ones able to understand and to appreciate them'. In a word, he fought everybody. He was killed in a duel at the age of thirty-seven.[1]

Maupassant had nothing to do with Alis's crusades or, for that matter, with any crusade; he simply showed some of his poems to Alis, who was so impressed by *Au bord de l'eau* that he reprinted it in his *Revue*, under the new title *Une Fille*. Strangely enough, though he was only too anxious to provoke the prudish authorities, he thought it wise to cut some of the lines deemed to be too *risqué*. Maupassant later said that all this had happened without his knowledge, but he seemed to approve it, as he did not complain about it and, furthermore, submitted to Alis another – unpublished – poem, *Le Mur*. This was printed in the *Revue*, also with some cuts for the sake of propriety, but with an editorial note calculated to anger the authorities: 'At the moment of going to press we learn that we are getting more

---

[1] Ironically, he died a champion of French imperialism, and received warmest obituaries from the enemies of French democracy, the witty *aventurier ès lettres*, Maurice Barrès, and the spiteful bore, Charles Maurras.

and more immoral,' it read. 'A trial is threatening us . . .' As to Maupassant's *Le Mur*, it was a poem somewhat paler than, but rather similar in character to, *Au bord de l'eau*; it described, also in erotic and lulling Alexandrines, the play on a white wall of two black shadows which then merged into one.

The authorities of Etampes would not normally have paid much attention to such poetry, and they were even less interested in the fate of the *Parnassiens*, but there were other issues at stake all over France. It was in the years following MacMahon's fall, with the genuine Republicans trying to seize power from the network of crypto-Monarchists who had up to then ruled the Republic. Politically, it was a most delicate moment. And Harry Alis belonged to that set of people whose activities can in such circumstances be most embarrassing to what is called today the Establishment. He had just taken over, simultaneously with his literary *Revue*, the editorship of the periodical *Abeille*, up to then a rather drab little sheet used mainly for local judicial advertisements, and transformed it into an instrument of political warfare. The authorities felt they had to do something against him; and they decided that the most convenient way of discrediting him was to prosecute – not his *Abeille* but his *Revue Moderne et Naturaliste*, and not on political but on moral grounds.

This was the reason why the magistrates of Etampes suddenly discovered an interest in modern and naturalist *belles-lettres*. They dug up copies of the *Revue*, sent one piece after another to the Attorney of the Republic to rouse his moral indignation until at last some were found shocking enough to start a prosecution. Amongst these pieces was Maupassant's poem, the one already published years before. Investigations and hearings started. Maupassant, too, was interrogated. He pointed out that his poem had already been published years earlier in a national literary magazine without causing any trouble. The magistrate listened to him sceptically, but while he was hesitating, the more recent issue of the *Revue* (that of 1 February 1880) containing *Le Mur* came into his hands. So the charge of 'outrage on public morality' on account of *Au bord de l'eau* was dropped, but sustained on account of *Le Mur*.

Maupassant became scared and excited, and Flaubert even more so. The legal punishment, or fine, that threatened the author was negligible, but his post in the Ministry of Education was in danger. Besides, it would be unpleasant and, indeed, an insult to literature to have to omit the incriminated poems from the forthcoming volume. So they ran from pillar to post in their attempts to get the prosecution withdrawn. Flaubert sent Maupassant a long list of influential persons to be approached on the matter. Both the honour of the Muse and the salary of Guy had to be saved.

Then they had second thoughts about it. Would it not be a pity to waste the publicity that a 'public morality' scandal would bring? Maupassant was never reluctant to consider such points; nor was Flaubert when the question concerned not himself but Guy. He recalled that he owed 'three-quarters' of *Madame Bovary*'s success to the prosecution against it. So why not let *Des Vers* also profit by such a *réclame gigantesque*!

It would, however, be wrong to think that they plotted in cold-blooded frivolity. At the critical moment, they were really in despair. 'I shall defend my poem at whatever cost and shall never agree to withhold it from publication,' Maupassant wrote to Flaubert. And then he outlined his great request:

I should need a letter from you, a long comforting, paternal and philosophical letter, with high ideas about the moral values of literary trials ... It should include your opinion on my piece *Au bord de l'eau* from the literary point of view, as well as from the moral point of view (artistic morality is nothing but Beauty), and expressions of affection. My lawyer – a friend – gave me this advice which I think is excellent ... This letter would be published in *Le Gaulois*, in an article on my trial ... Your exceptional, your unique position as a genius prosecuted for a masterpiece, acquitted with difficulty and then honoured, and definitely classed as an incomparable master, recognized as such by all schools, would secure me such support, my lawyer thinks, that the whole affair would be quashed after the publication of such a letter ... Now, should this for any reason be distasteful to you, we will not discuss it further ... Forgive me, my dearest *maître*, for this heavy *corvée*. But what am I to say? I have to defend myself alone, my livelihood is threatened, I am without support from my family or my relatives, and unable to afford the fees of a great lawyer [And in postscript:] If it would be a nuisance for you to write for a newspaper, don't send me anything . . .

Nuisance or no, it was for Guy's sake, so it had to be done. Flaubert, despite his sturdy appearance, had always been a sick man, liable to epileptic fits and heart attacks since his early twenties. Since the middle 'seventies he also suffered from financial difficulties through his reckless generosity towards his niece Caroline and her husband, Commanville, and he had had to apply for a State pension which was granted to him in 1879. Maupassant had pulled the strings to hasten the decision, and these worries were now over; but his nerves were in a bad state. He was working feverishly to finish *Bouvard et Pécuchet* and his other work, for he felt he had not much longer to live. And now he had to push all this aside and write for a newspaper! It must have been a *corvée* indeed; though perhaps, after all, he enjoyed this excursion into public polemics. In any case, he was prompt in replying. In a long letter, he eloquently called up all the classics of world literature in defence of *Au bord de l'eau* and attacked the philistine magistrates with exasperation and sarcasm. He must have toiled a great deal at it. He even agreed to a revised version being published at the head of a new issue of *Des Vers*. Twenty-five variants have been identified of these two authorized texts – quite typical of the way Flaubert's mind worked, struggling towards sonority but chary of grandiloquence. First he said about the prosecutors: 'Are they paid to devaluate [*démonetiser*] the Republic, by showering contempt and ridicule on it?' In the second version this read: 'Do they wish to devaluate the Republic? I should think so.' And in the course of such alterations the share of the scandal in the success of *Madame Bovary* shrank from 'three-quarters' to 'two-thirds'.

Flaubert concentrated his fulminant *plaidoyer* exclusively on *Au bord de l'eau* and completely ignored *Le Mur*, the poem for which Maupassant was actually prosecuted. The reason may have been that he preferred the former to the latter and that it seemed more effective to deal only with the piece which had already been printed, without causing any stir, several years before.

Maupassant's various biographers have done an immense amount of research on the many conflicting documents relating to this case, but all that really matters is that on 27 February 1880, not quite a week after the publication of Flaubert's letter in *Le Gaulois*, the prosecution was withdrawn. At the moment of its publication, as a matter of fact, it had already been decided, under the pressure of influential friends mobilized by Flaubert, to withdraw the action; but once having gone so far Maupassant was determined to make capital out of the publicity, and he had his master's full support in this. Certainly it was a rewarding little scandal. Though his Minister, in spite of being Flaubert's personal friend, showed 'some coolness' towards him, he could in the final event only congratulate himself on the results of that cowardly and hypocritical attempt to save 'public morality' from 'naturalism'.

Within a few weeks Flaubert had in his hands the first printed copy of *Des Vers*, with its most humble and affectionate dedication to himself, and read it, as he admitted, with tears in his eyes. After his death, only a short time later, his by then famous letter in defence of *Au bord de l'eau* was republished in the third edition of that volume.[1]

Was it necessarily hypocritical, the reader may wonder, to accuse Maupassant of immorality? Not if sex is considered sinful. Under both the traditional Christian and the puritanical Republican conception of *vertu*, sex indulgence *was* a sin. Maupassant, without any doubt, did indulge in it, both in fact and in his writings. To pretend that sex in a work of art is sublimated and that the audience or the reader enjoys it without responding to the sensual desires it depicts – the conventional line of defence of erotic art against prudishness – is in fact no less hypocritical than to condemn eroticism in public and to enjoy it in private. So long as sex as a subject was taboo, there was reason in objecting to erotic art.

[1] This account has been based mainly on Chapter IV, Part II, of *La Vie et l'Œuvre de Guy de Maupassant* by Edouard Maynial, and Chapter IV, sub-chapters 1 and 3, of *Guy de Maupassant* by René Dumesnil, the latter dealing thoroughly with the research on the Etampes prosecution by René Descharmes, Alexandre Zevaes, etc.

Maupassant had really asked for trouble with the upholders of *vertu* through the publication of his poems, and the fact that he got away with it so easily only showed that the concept of virtue was on the decline. The case was hypocritical on other grounds; namely, that those responsible for the prosecution were not in the least interested in morality, and that it was only a cover for action against that intransigent Republican, Harry Alis. Too cowardly to go into battle on the political issues, they tried to strangle Alis as a pornographer. If they had had it their own way, Maupassant would have fallen victim to their political manipulations, although the one thing of which he was certainly innocent was political conviction.

In the event, however, outraged morality was found ineffective as a weapon. Prudishness in art had disappeared amongst the relics of old-fashioned philistinism; the new philistine paraded as a bohemian himself, and the liberal *haute-bourgeoisie* was as ostentatious in its flippancy as had been the *marquis* and *marquises* a hundred years before. This was not the case in all comparable countries; certainly not in Victorian Britain. But in France, ever since 1880, art had been free of the shackles of sex morality, and artists only got into trouble with the authorities on that count when they had tried to obtain that notoriety very hard indeed. Maupassant, to some extent, was their precursor.

31 · Zola's young men

Simultaneously with *Des Vers*, appeared *Boule de Suif* and, with it, the manifestation of the perfect craftsmanship of which Guy de Maupassant was capable.

Its antecedents, again, show Maupassant as the disciple and *protégé* of Flaubert, admitted to the intimate circle of qualified literary men before he had displayed any quality to be amongst them, except for being a companionable fellow.

About the atmosphere of the literary gatherings that led to it, there was a paragraph in the gossip columns of *La République des Lettres* of 13 April 1877: 'In the restaurant Trapp, destined to become famous, near Gare Saint-Lazare, six young and enthusiastic Naturalists, who were also to become famous, MM. Paul Alexis, Henry Céard, Léon Hennique, J.-K. Huysmans, Octave Mirbeau, and Guy de Valmont, entertained their masters: Gustave Flaubert, Edmond de Goncourt, Emile Zola. One of the guests let us have the menu: soup, *purée Bovary* . . .' and so forth, in honour of the *trois maîtres*; and the paragraph concluded with the innocent witticism that Flaubert deplored the absence of pigeons *à la Salammbô*. The dinners *chez Trapp* have since become an important chapter in the history of literature. Those young men met regularly, once a week at least, either there or elsewhere, now and then in the company of other artists and writers whose names are still famous, such as the novelist, Alphonse Daudet; the poet, François Coppée; the painter, Paul Cézanne, Zola's childhood pal and schoolmate who quarrelled with him more often than not . . .

They also met as Zola's guests at 21 rue Saint-Georges, today rue des Appenins. Later he bought a *bicoque* (shanty), in Médan, which was to become their favourite meeting-place. Zola, attended by his dark, stout, responsive wife, was an excellent and most dynamic host, especially for vigorous and intelligent young men. In his home, crammed with artistic junk, he ate and entertained them to enormous meals, took them walking, shooting, boating, and showered on them what Maupassant called his 'anti-patriotic sermons'. Barbey d'Aurevilly labelled him a 'cerebral belly'. Cerebral he was but certainly not heartless, perhaps even overflowing with heart. He combined the taste of a glutton with the zeal of an apostle. In art, he was Manet's prophet; in literature, mainly his own. He was not egocentric, it was the world that interested him – both as subject-matter and for its responses – but that very interest was so constantly at boiling point and so creative as to overpower other voices, other personalities. He loved his work as a novelist and was uninhibited in wishing to make it a success, financially as well as morally. Besides, he knew he had a calling in this world and was adamant about it. Along with his remarkable appetite for money, honours and good dishes, there worked in him a fearless and relentless urge – often, seemingly, quite Quixotic – to tell the truth, the whole truth and mainly what was most embarrassing in the truth. Some twenty years later, it was this urge which drove him into challenging the Government, the Church, the Army, the Courts and, not least, public opinion in defence of an unjustly convicted captain with whom he had no connection. It was the same urge that had made him stand up for Impressionist art in defiance of contempt and ridicule. As an author he concentrated his apostolic attention on dung-heaps and chamber-pots, on illicit trade in goods, securities and women, on the hunger for food and sex, on the tyranny of the body over the soul and of putrefaction over the body; on things about which it was *not done* to talk. He was not the first to talk about them; but it was he who made a faith of doing so. That faith he called Naturalism. He may be compared with Flaubert as Luther with Erasmus. Whereas the free contemplation of senses for Flaubert, like free Bible-reading for Erasmus, was a means to humanist self-perfection; for Zola, or Luther, they were the cornerstones of a creed. Flaubert pursued truth for the sake of Art, Goncourt for the sake of Curiosity, but Zola pursued truth for the sake of Truth.

Neither the truth about the dung-heap and the rest, nor the intelligence of its believers must be underrated. There was no question of denying that everything beautiful revealed an aspect of the truth, whether through the gods of Homer, or the kings of Shakespeare, or even the divine and royal slum-dwellers of Victor Hugo. Zola, in particular, was far from insensitive to the meanings of such imaginative writings. But he rightly felt that the time called for writers to add the facts to the symbols, however drab and shocking they might be. In collecting factual details, though certainly not in brooding over them, he outstripped even Flaubert. With a notebook in his hand and epic visions in his heart, he set out to depict life more frankly than ever before, especially life under the Second Empire, that bugbear of the intelligentsia to which he belonged. Altogether, he succeeded admirably. The touch of strict factuality may have escaped him, but the Muse of narration did not. Thanks to his theories, or in spite of them, he was a great artist.

Maupassant owed very much to Zola. Many have denied this, mainly on the ground that Maupassant did not profess the Naturalist creed. This is true in so far as he did not profess any creed at all. When Catulle Mendès, in 1876, invited him to join the Freemasons, Maupassant first casually agreed and then in a letter which, for him, was an unusual confession of faith, withdrew his consent and declared:

> Through egoism, wickedness, or eclecticism, I do not wish ever to be linked with any political party, any religion, any sect, any school . . . I wish to be entitled to attack all good gods . . . I am scared of the smallest bond, whether it comes from an idea or a woman.

There was some narcissism in this declaration, as in confessions in general, but it was sincere. According to Maupassant, wrote Henry Roujon, 'to hold a political opinion was a painful weakness';[1] and, in the course of discussions about Naturalism, he made it clear that his attitude towards trends in literature was similar. His argument in favour of Naturalism, and of matter-of-fact writing in general, was that it was an inevitable 'reaction' to Romanticism,[2] and whether it was a good trend or not, it appealed to him.

For if Zola held the faith that to mirror the facts of life was the main contribution that he and his generation could make to literature, Maupassant had the ability to do so; but, lacking faith, his mind required Zola as a guide to embark on it. Over-responsive to sensual impulses, obsessed with the desire to record his sensations, and detached about practically everything else, he was born to be a 'naturalist', but he needed the encouragement of Zola's example and philosophy, as well as Flaubert's coaching in craftsmanship and 'originality', to do what he was born for. It was Zola who opened his eyes to the importance, in literature, of biological details. To dwell upon them was not only a reaction against Romanticism, and also against solemn Classicism, but a return, in a way, to some earlier masters, mainly Rabelais, whom Maupassant considered, as he explained in an essay on old French poetry,[3] the very greatest *poet* France had ever had. But that traditional, and more or less officially admitted, version of literary bawdiness atoned for its crudeness by its setting in fantasies and jokes; to deal with them in factual

[1] *Souvenirs sur Maupassant*, ed. Lumbroso, pp. 316–17.
[2] Cf., *i.a.*, his answer to Albert Wolff in *Le Gaulois*, 28 August 1882.
[3] 'Les Poètes français du XVIe siècle', *Nation*, 1877.

detail, in the colloquial style of a novelist, was an offence against taste even more than against the norms of moral behaviour. Zola defied this taboo. His inscription in his novel, *L'Assommoir*, to Flaubert read: 'A mon grand ami Gustave Flaubert, en haine du goût.' Flaubert liked this idea, but with some qualification; Maupassant was all for it. In his letter to his mother, on 3 April 1878, he wrote: 'As to that literature which steps on coquettish heels, I know it and will have none of it; and my only wish is not to have any taste, because all great men lack it and invent a new one.'

Maupassant thus joined Zola in his search for distasteful truth. Zola did so because he believed in it; and Maupassant, because he discovered that he was no good at anything else. He never denied his debt to Zola, though. In his essay on him[1] he dared to prophesy that Zola would certainly be in the public eye as an advocate of new noble causes. This forecast, amply borne out in the decades to come, was made with his tongue in his cheek, but, all the same, in sincere admiration.

As the young poet, 'Guy de Valmont', Maupassant made himself useful in Zola's entourage and in the Naturalist circle of young men, in his own un-literary way. In Médan, his finest hour came when Zola decided to attach a barge to his property. Maupassant, well versed in matters like these from his early days in Etretat and Fécamp, assisted him in buying, equipping and launching the barge, and also in setting her in the right literary perspective. When the question arose what the barge should be called he suggested 'Nana'; because, he added, 'tout le monde grimpera dessus'.[2] This argument, even more than the wish to do justice to Zola's novel, decided in favour of his suggestion.

In Paris, Maupassant was most active in organizing the fraternal meals at Trapp's and other restaurants, cafés and bistros, the reason for frequent changes being more often than not dissatisfaction with the cooking. The parsimonious and the *gourmand* Norman struggled in Maupassant all the time; he could not easily be reconciled to the fact that for the two francs he was prepared to pay he was unable to get a good and opulent din-

[1] In *La Revue bleue*, 1883.
[2] Armand Lanoux, *Bonjour, Monsieur Zola*, Hachette, Paris, 1962, p. 158.

ner.[1] All the same, he was hospitable, and often entertained his friends in his own modest home. Throughout most of his years in Government service, he lived in a most dismal room, 2 rue de Moncey, on the ground floor, with only one window; but at the end of 1878, as his finances had slightly improved, he moved into a more comfortable apartment at 19 rue Clauzel, consisting of two rooms and a kitchen, with a separate entrance. There he could invite his friends. Of his old boating partners, two were to crop up again and again in the years of his literary career: 'La Toque' and 'Petit-Bleu'. The former, Robert Pinchon, was a childhood friend from Etretat, and his co-playwright; the latter, Léon Fontaine, an intimate friend who was to publish interesting recollections of him. His new friends were mostly novelists: J.-K. Huysmans, Henry Céard, Léon Hennique, Marius Roux and that most enthusiastic of Naturalists, 'Zola's shadow', Paul Alexis. Maupassant also quite early made friends with young Paul Bourget, a contributor to the *Revue Moderne et Naturaliste* and one of Zola's admirers, but who never really belonged to the circle and was later to become famous as a key figure in the reaction against their tendencies.

All this time Maupassant was writing poems, and also articles, and even some short stories, but none of them of any significance, and he did not attempt to pose as a prose-writer. He sent some drafts of novels and stories to Flaubert – the faint outline of *Une Vie* is detectable in one of them – but he was already approaching his thirtieth year without really trying to join Zola's circle in activities other than social. If asked about his intentions, he answered: 'Why hurry, I am learning my *métier*.' When asked about his aims in writing, he insisted that he wanted to earn money – which he certainly did, but if that was what really interested him he would hardly have rejected out of hand 'that literature which steps on coquettish heels', which offered quite good returns in cash.

[1] Cf. Stanley Jackson, *Guy de Maupassant*, Duckworth, London, 1938.

The most significant outcome of these informal gatherings was an anthology of contemporary short stories, *Les Soirées de Médan*. Several participants later described how it had been planned, and Maupassant was the first to do so, in an article for *Le Gaulois*, acting, so to speak, as the voluntary publicity agent of the enterprise, but his over-dramatized report can hardly be trusted in its details; in fiction, he liked to keep to authentic facts, but in journalism, he was carried away by his taste for mystification. The gist of these accounts is, however, concordant and evidently correct. Zola and his young men talked war, by which they meant the war with Prussia almost ten years ago, near enough to be sensed, and far away enough for an open-eyed writer not to be blinded by its passions. War stories followed, and the question 'Why not publish such a volume?' It was the obvious idea that Zola's own piece should head the anthology, to be followed by young Naturalists, actually five of them. 'In preparing this book, we had no anti-patriotic intentions, indeed no intention whatsoever,' Maupassant wrote in a letter to Flaubert, on 5 January 1880:

> we only tried to record the war in the right tone [*donner . . . une note juste sur la guerre*], to strip our stories of the chauvinism *à la* Déroulède, of that false enthusiasm that has up to now been thought necessary . . . Our good faith in appraising military facts makes the whole volume appear as shockingly strange [*drôle de gueule*], and our wilful detachment about these matters, into which everybody brings his own passions unconsciously, will exasperate the bourgeois more than would a frontal attack. It will not be anti-patriotic but simply true.

Then referring to his own descriptions of war-time France, quoted in an earlier chapter:[1] 'What I said about the people of Rouen is still short of what was true.'

In a word, there *was* an intention, and even a political one;

[1] Cf. pp. 82–3.

in one way or another, all contributions were anti-war. Accordingly, the idea was to name the whole volume *Invasion comique*,[1] but this was dismissed as too provocative. It was decided to proceed tactfully.

One of the young authors, Céard, suggested the volume should be named *Soirées de Médan*, and the rest agreed, 'in honour of Madame Zola', as some explained. Flaubert found it a 'stupid title', but his role was no more than that of a patron saint, informed by Guy about some but not all details until the book was out.

Second in order of the short stories published in the volume was Maupassant's *Boule de Suif* (The Dumpling). That longish story of the kind-hearted and patriotic *cocotte*, exploited and then snubbed and humiliated for her sacrifice by a batch of respectable gentlefolk, has gone down as the *non plus ultra* of what a piece of Naturalist fiction-writing could be, truthful, economic, elegant, witty and emotionally effective in more than one way without either sentimentality or rhetoricism. Its reputation is well-earned; in the textbook merits of that genre, that story has never been surpassed even by Maupassant.

About its background in actual life, much has been written and there are conflicting accounts, but so much seems clear that Maupassant invented practically nothing. The stage-coach taking off from Rouen towards Le Havre could have been followed inch by inch by his contemporaries; the inn in Tôtes, that *Hôtel du Commerce* in the story, was *Hôtel du Cygne* in reality, but there was many another *Hôtel du Commerce* in Normandy. The plot woven round the gallant blackmail by a Prussian officer is likely to have been related to Maupassant by his uncle, Charles Cord'homme, wine merchant and passionate Republican, who is identifiable as the passenger called Cornudet in the story. And 'Boule de Suif' herself, the plump little brunette, with puffy fingers and deep black eyes, was without any doubt modelled on a Mademoiselle Adrienne Legay, a courtesan who was exceedingly helpful to many of her countrymen under the Prussian occupation.

Adrienne Legay was born in 1848 in the village of Eletot, not far from Fécamp, and came as a young girl to Rouen where,

[1] Dumesnil, *Guy de Maupassant*, p. 162.

when twenty, she was known to be the mistress of a cavalry officer. A year or so later, a cotton trader was her main patron, who then enlisted for military service in the war and was stationed in Le Havre, whilst Adrienne remained in Prussian-occupied Rouen. She several times went to see her lover, and obliged his comrades and their relatives by taking messages to and fro. It was on such an occasion that something on the lines of the *Boule de Suif* adventure is supposed to have happened to her, though she herself denied this and added a most feminine comment: 'It's a fake! Well, it's the revenge of Monsieur Guy, for I wouldn't give in to him. He was not my type but then, how could I have guessed that he would become a famous man?'[1]

It seems strange that she should call it 'revenge', this glorification of self-sacrifice, but Adrienne, apparently, found it an insult because, whatever the setting and the motivation, it represented her as one who *did* sleep with an enemy. Uncle Cord'homme, too, was incensed; not only because of the skit upon his Republicanism but also because, by the time *Boule de Suif* was published, he was actually having an affair with Adrienne, who in the story refused his advances. A lengthy family feud followed this literary success.

The other passengers of the stage-coach, too, were all recognizable as living persons by contemporaries. One of them was supposed to be the Senator, one-time Minister, Pouyer-Quertier, known as a tremendous eater, drinker, smoker and talker, who was said to have had an egg-eating race with Bismarck in the course of diplomatic talks and to have won by it a strip of territory for France.[2] Guesses and gossip about the other characters in the story went on right into the thirties of this century.

The reception of the *Médan* volume, and its aftermath, followed a pattern typical of literary policy; the reviews expressed opinions that could have been foretold before reading the stories. Literary chroniclers have always been star-watchers and scapegoat-hunters rather than aesthetes; their first concern about a new piece of writing is to classify it under an *ism*, their second

---

[1] *Souvenirs sur Maupassant*, ed. Lumbroso, p. 353.
[2] I was told this by M. A. Dubuc, President of *Amis de Gustave Flaubert*, Rouen.

to estimate the reactions that may be expected from others, and then at last they may be induced to sound their own reactions.

No doubt, however, those Naturalists knew this and faced its consequences with gusto. The *Médan* volume, released to the public on 15 April 1880, carried this preface in which one can detect Zola's apostolic self-righteousness combined with Maupassant's frolicsome liking for publicity:

> We expect to be attacked and to be received with that bad faith and ignorance which have been displayed towards us by current literary criticism. Our sole concern has been publicly to affirm our genuine friendship and, at the same time, our literary tendencies.

The first public response thus simply showed that some liked and others disliked these 'literary tendencies'. One of the quickest responses was that in *Evénement* from Léon Chaperon who thought it was high time for people to give up the habit of 'always finding excuses for murderers, nymphomaniacs, gamblers and – mainly – Naturalists'.

As a work of art, and also from the sales point of view, however, Maupassant's piece was best of all. This was recognized by his companions – Zola himself and Hennique, Huysmans, Alexis, Céard – when they decided that it should occupy the place second only to Zola in the volume. This opinion of the selected – or self-selected – few became the general opinion in no time. It would be an exaggeration to say that Maupassant's genius was ignored by his fellow-writers and the critics; once they discovered *Boule de Suif*, practically all recognized his gifts (Turgenev among the first, in hasty atonement for his previous disparagement), but the decisive verdict in his favour came from the masses of middle-brow readers, from the *salons* of the liberal plutocracy and from the middle class which followed in their footsteps.

On 19 April 1880 Albert Wolff wrote in *Figaro*: 'This little gang of conceited young men, in a preface of extraordinary impudence, flings the gauntlet to the critics ... *Les Soirées de Médan* is not really worth one single line of criticism. Except for Zola's story it is mediocrity of the basest order.' Yet barely two years later, on 21 July 1882, the same critic in the same newspaper wrote: 'Among the new novelists, there is no one whom I like as much as I do M. Guy de Maupassant; and none of them irritates me so much . . . Believe me, Monsieur de Maupassant, it is not necessary always to drag one's pen in low haunts for the sake of being a man of talent.' Albert Wolff's ideas of respectability, good literature and vulgarity had not changed in the course of those two years; he had simply discovered that, in the firmament of literary policy, the starlet Maupassant had to be allotted a place.

If, at the moment when the *Médan* volume was published, critics tended to dismiss its young contributors, including Maupassant, as boastful would-be Zolas, later they tended to belittle the links between Zola and these followers of his, especially Maupassant. Both these over-simplifications were prompted by politics. In 1880, Zola, though a controversial figure, held the undisputed reputation of a vigorous innovator; for the conformists who disliked him, it was convenient at that time to accept him as a strange and unique phenomenon whilst showing contempt for the young men in his following. In some years' time, as the appeal of Zola as an innovator was fading and that of Maupassant's charm increasing, it was more convenient to deplore that such a nice and entertaining young man should ever have mixed in that sordid company. And after the Dreyfus case, when Zola's name had become a symbol of political radicalism, he was made responsible for all the evils and excesses of Naturalism by all schools of thought who were shocked by his outspokenness; the high priests of the Ivory Tower and of Roman Catholicism made common front against his memory, and they were joined by nationalists and militarists, including the defeatist militarists of Vichy and, not least, by many a communist critic, particularly the orthodox followers of Zhdanov, who found his interest in the facts of life detestable. Towards Maupassant, they were more lenient; because, as cleverly set forth by Paul Morand, himself the embodiment of Vichy France, Zola's anti-militarism smacked of the 'Français de fraîche date', a Frenchman with Italian ancestry, whereas Maupassant was 'a Norman exiled in Paris' and had worn the uniform of the Army he denigrated. Incidentally, the believers in Norman racial purity never forgot to find fault with Maupassant for his Lorraine ancestry; but the application of the 'blood and soil' principle to literature has always been most elastic.

In 'anti-patriotism', there was no difference between Zola and Maupassant; for all their differences in character, style and approach, they were agreed that the only thing they could do about national idols was to tell the truth. They had to do it crudely to do it well; this was what Maupassant learned from Zola. That he did it more smoothly, with more elegance and cynicism, was due to his personal gifts; and also to what survived in him of Flaubert.

33 · Flaubert's triumph and death

There was gossip, even more absurd than that which turned Maupassant into Flaubert's illegitimate son – that *Boule de Suif* had really been written by Flaubert. It only deserves mention to show how silly gossip-mongers can be. For one thing, Flaubert could never have done it; he was far too noble to be so perfect a story-teller. Furthermore, it seems that Maupassant purposely hid the manuscript of *Boule de Suif* from his master until the eve of its publication, and was rather reluctant to inform him of the doings of the Médan group in general. It was meant to be a tribute to Flaubert, but not in his spirit; it was, vis-à-vis the master, a venture in humble heresy.

Flaubert looked upon the *Médanites*, on the whole, as likeable *enfants terribles*. He admired Zola, but disapproved of his school: they forgot about Beauty ... 'I am most anxious,' he wrote to Maupassant on 2 January 1880, 'to see the patriotic lucubration' [obviously a hint at – or slip for – 'anti-patriotic lucubration', Maupassant's term for Zola's table-sermons]. 'It must be very strong to shock me.' And then, he kept enquiring: 'You refer to *our* proofs. Who are "we"?' Maupassant answered apologetically, on the 5th: 'My very dear Master, – I see you have forgotten what I told you when I last saw you in Croisset about our forthcoming volume of short stories, and am anxious to explain the thing now.' Then, he did explain, apparently with some stage-fright; and by February, Flaubert had read *Boule de Suif*.

Once he had read it, there was no doubt. On 1 February he

wrote to his niece: '*The story by my disciple, which I read in proof this morning, is a masterpiece*: I insist on the word, a masterpiece of composition, of comedy, and of observation, and ... [for it was typical of Flaubert to be shocked at the fact that others could be shocked at a libertine work of art] ... and I wonder why Mme Branine [who had seen the story and disapproved of it] is shocked? It makes me dizzy. Is she a fool?' Three days later he repeated the word, 'masterpiece', in his letter to Guy himself. 'Yes, young man, neither more nor less, this came from a master ... That little story *will live* [*restera*], be assured.' This letter deserves to 'live' no less. The passionate aesthete mingles with the enthusiastic, paternal friend in it. '... The poor wench weeping whilst the other is singing the "Marseillaise" is sublime. I'd like to hug you for a quarter of an hour!' Then, two suggestions for minute alterations, on passages that 'are not bad at all but could make the idiots shout' – *imbéciles*, standing for prudes.

Flaubert was in a mood of ecstatic triumph. It seems to be the sole moment of his life when he forgot his pessimism. It was barely three months later, on 8 May, that he died of apoplexy. His funeral was fixed for the 11th. Maupassant arrived in Croisset on the eve of the day; he kept vigil, he assisted in closing the shutters, he received the callers. Came the Commanvilles, Flaubert's niece and her husband; they buttonholed Maupassant and persuaded him to keep out of the procession an old friend of Flaubert's with whom they had been entangled in a financial squabble. Came Zola, Daudet, Heredia, Goncourt, the Médan young men and many others. In Flaubert's study were his handkerchief, his pipe, a volume of Corneille opened some days before. The coffin was carried through gentle countryside to the cemetery by the old church. Goncourt was unusually moved, but watchful as usual; thinking of his *Journal* and posterity. He observed that people were talking of brill *à la normande*, and of duckling with orange sauce, and commenting on the absence of Hugo, Taine, Renan, Dumas and, most of all, Flaubert's old intimate, Du Camp. And once the holy water had been sprinkled on the coffin, he noted, the whole thirsty crowd hurried down towards the town with faces betraying their keenness to have a good time.[1]

[1] André Billy, *Les Frères Goncourt*, Flammarion, Paris, 1954, p. 354.

PART TWO

THE MADNESS OF LACKING
ILLUSIONS

34 · The turning-point passed

'Guy de Maupassant ceased to be a happy man at the moment when he had completely become a man of letters,' a childhood friend of his says in his recollections.[1] He is right though somewhat mistaken in dating and explaining that turning-point, as he goes on: 'We are in 1875. Guy de Maupassant is introduced by his master in the literary circles. Emile Zola, Alphonse Daudet receive him . . . He takes to prose . . . By abandoning the muse [of poetry] he bids farewell to his youth. Glory takes its usual toll of disquietudes from him.' Yes, but five years elapsed after 1875 before that glory came. And then it was not the entanglements of his career that killed his flashes of happiness. It was the aggravation of his illness; and, at the same time, his inability to find satisfaction in anything but his writing which, paradoxically, he did not really enjoy. Once he had mastered his *métier*, he became its slave.

An additional reason for his unhappiness was that, with the disappearance of his 'spiritual father', he had irrevocably *grown up*. This may sound ironical; for in a way he had been grown-up ever since the time of overhearing the rows between his parents, in early childhood; and if to be an adult means to take nastiness for granted, to dispense with daydreams and to compromise with facts, then he was certainly more so than that eternal child, the incurably good, sympathetic and irascible Gustave Flaubert. But a child-like father is still a father, especially if chosen for his spiritual magnitude; he might be side-tracked as he had been with the Médan anthology but as a stimulus, as an ideal or pacemaker, his position was unshaken. Without him, after the success of *Boule de Suif*, it was no longer difficult for Maupassant

[1] Adolphe Brisson, in *Souvenirs sur Maupassant*, ed. Lumbroso, p. 147.

to achieve fame and glory, but it was impossible to grope his way towards a new pattern of sensing and expressing things. His intellectual receptivity dried up. His mind worked brilliantly but between stone barriers, and when he tried to break through them he went mad.

The decade starting with his emotional coming-of-age in the summer of 1880 and ending with the first unmistakable symptoms of his lunacy was thus the most adventurous, glamorous, creative and yet on the whole, the dullest period of Maupassant's life. He was a famous and highly prosperous writer, a notorious and somewhat braggart dandy, a 'lion of the *salons*', a 'Don Juan' and a most enterprising traveller in all kinds of vehicles, including his own yacht, *Bel-Ami*, and an early airship named after his morbid story, *Le Horla*. He also was an extraordinarily prolific author, and whilst a great part of his output was average in quality, at his best he was at the peak of contemporary writing. His career was, however incongruous the expression when applied to a pessimist, a constant march of triumph through life and literature. Yet there was something dreary in the way it was performed. All the time he was only drawing on the mental resources which he already had at his disposal by 1880. He neither became stale nor monotonous; the scenes of his stories changed a great deal as he moved in different countries, different surroundings and listened to people coming from different walks of life, but his approach to people and events and his method of visualizing them remained unaltered. His cautious excursion, largely under Bourget's influence, into 'psychology' provided the only exception to this rule, and this was a most unspectacular exception. Though he never tired of observing people and collecting subjects, and though many of his writings were prompted by daily events, most of what was best in them could be traced back to recollections of his earlier years; he was up to date with colonial war crises, with the intricacies of the book trade, with the daily gossip about boudoirs and gambling clubs, but in their description he only rose above the mediocre when he reapplied to them what he had experienced long before. That tense and eventful third decade of his life may therefore be regarded, psychologically, as the explosive culmination of the preceding two; and also as an introduction to the final years of decay.

As success had come with the *Médan* volume, Maupassant set himself to building up his position as an independent and prosperous author with an ecstasy and a caution that were typical of him. He still was not sure whether he could earn his living as a free-lance writer; he thought it safer first to apply for one year's leave without pay from the Ministry. This granted, he undertook a journey to North Africa, notebook in hand, and whilst carrying on with his newspaper articles, he worked on the subjects kept in store for coming short stories.

The year that followed, 1881, was marked by the publication of the short stories *La Maison Tellier* and *Mademoiselle Fifi* which, together with *Boule de Suif*, made Maupassant appear as the expert writer on prostitution, notably on the kindliness and patriotism of whores. *Mademoiselle Fifi* which takes the reader back to the Prussian occupation of Normandy is altogether a second-rate story. It contains a splendid description of the conquerors billeted in a castle near Rouen, frustrated and racked by boredom, isolation and rain. Apart from this, it develops melodramatically the conflict between the arrogant conqueror and the patriotic harlot; the *fille* kills the Prussian officer, and in the end becomes respectable as a *mater-familias*. The author showed himself, if no less of a whore-worshipper, at least more of a patriot than he had done in *Boule de Suif*.

Maison Tellier, on the other hand, was a peace-time idyll, dealing with religion in the way its two sister stories had dealt with patriotism and military virtues. Maupassant had braced himself to perform this feat in the spirit of a bet. His inspiration was sparked off by one of his many chats about sex and tarts, in the course of which a friend mentioned to him that the brothel in rue des Cordeliers, Rouen, had been shut for several days, whilst a hand-written notice, in clumsy, uneven letters, explained on the door:

Closed because of First Communion

According to Edmond de Goncourt, the person from whom

Maupassant heard this was Hector Malot, the most Victorian of the French novelists; René Dumesnil thinks it more likely that it was Charles Lapierre,[1] editor of *Nouvelliste de Rouen*; but testimonies agree to the effect that Maupassant's mind caught fire at once and that the more his friends seemed doubtful about whether this *could* be the subject of a story, the keener he became on carrying it out. The idea was to depict first the bewilderment of the customers at the locked door with so surprising a reason given, and then the festival and temporary respectability of the brothel inmates in honour of the budding girl, *Madame*'s niece, whose First Communion was taking place. The story once conceived, there was no doubt as to what the main effects would be. Maupassant, when meeting Jules Lemaître that year in Algiers, told him he was writing a story 'with its first part in a bawdy-house, and with the second part in a church',[2] whereupon Lemaître thought that that dedicated practical joker was just pulling his leg. Lemaître was not entirely wrong; an itch for leg-pulling was in Maupassant's mind all the time during its preparation, as was the wish to squeeze as much publicity and money out of the subject as possible.

It seems most likely that all the characters in the story and all the episodes, indeed even the stones in it were modelled after life, though Maupassant shifted the scene; instead of the Rouen brothel, he described one at Fécamp, near the Church of St Etienne, and instead of the church of Boisguillaume, where the First Communion had actually taken place, he chose one in a village in the district of Eure. Maupassant himself mentioned this change of scenery to his valet, François, but did not explain his reasons; his friend, Robert Pinchon, thought he may have felt a smaller town more suitable for the evocation of that homely spirit amongst the prostitutes that he had in mind. Anyway, he knew the whole terrain perfectly. There was but one minor detail which required some research: to find out what his English sailors should sing in answer to their French colleagues' 'Marseillaise'. On this, as on questions of English language and literature in general, he consulted his paternal friend, Turgenev,

[1] *Guy de Maupassant*, p. 186.
[2] Maynial, *La vie et l'œuvre de Guy de Maupassant*.

and it was on the Russian novelist's advice that he made them sing 'Rule Britannia'.

The eagerness to shock the shockable, to enrapture those finding pleasure in flippancy, and to cash in on the victorious vogue of unreligious and sexual licentiousness is unmistakable in *Maison Tellier* and is even more conspicuous in what we know of its pre-history. It is all the more astonishing then that it is a masterpiece, profound, amusing, authentic in all its observations and, above all, devoid of that cruelty or emotional crudity which often makes Maupassant's brilliance as embarrassing as it is fascinating. The 'pessimist' does not completely deny himself in *Maison Tellier*; the miseries in the background of all these gay and voluptuous and piously lachrymose characters, money-grubbers, harlots, paupers, traders, peasants, children, can be glimpsed in the few words said about each of them; but what is actually seen is only their healthy appetite for food, drink, colour, fanciful clothes, entertainment, sex and godliness. *Impassibilité* this time is so perfect as to hide even itself; and sarcasm so clever as to take the shape of fable-loving joviality. Really, it does not hurt anybody.

The respectable middle-class husbands and fathers who regularly patronize that seaport *lupanar* turn its 'salon de Jupiter', reserved for white-collared customers, into a second home, smooth and cosy and adapted to sound routine. Should this read as an indictment of their duplicity? It may just as well be taken as a proof of their single-mindedness. When free to indulge their licentious desires, they carry on basically in the same way that they do during office hours and family meals. Their secret selves turn out to be very much like their public attitudes; in the bawdy house, it is not they who reveal themselves as crypto-lechers, it is their entertainers who reveal themselves as crypto-housewives. Family life, in Maupassant's stories,[1] is usually sordid; but when mirrored in the nostalgias of prostitutes and the habits of their customers, it becomes embellished. Similarly, religion discloses an uncommon appeal when the prostitutes join in the holy ceremony; it is made fun of, no doubt, but it is also vindicated as a spiritual power that shakes the hearts even of professional sinners. When Rosa la

---

[1] *Une Famille* is perhaps most typical from this point of view.

Rosse, the little 'ball of flesh', known to her Fécamp customers as an inexhaustible spring of songs and laughters, now in the village church, remembering her own First Communion, feels a few teardrops on her eyelids and then bursts into a torrent of sobs – not only her colleagues and their *Madame* but the chuckling reader, too, feels tempted to cry with them. It is but a short and discreet temptation. In this story nothing is overdone, not even the sympathy for the ridiculous. And it is told in no more words, and no more onerous ones, than are fitting for a dinner-table anecdote. A masterpiece, yes; mainly of economy, and of tenderness.

In comparison with *Boule de Suif*, *La Maison Tellier* is milder not only in exposing the bourgeoisie and its ideals to contempt and ridicule but also, despite its more *risqué* subject, in its references to sex. There is in the former, for instance, that episode when one of the bourgeois passengers, Loiseau, wine merchant and champion *farceur*, finds out that his zealous Republican fellow-passenger, Cornudet, is making passes at the *cocotte*, 'Boule de Suif'. It happens like this.

At night in his hotel room, with his spouse already asleep, Loiseau is peeping out through the key-hole into the passage. He sees the young woman, in blue cashmere dressing-gown, candle in hand, go to the lavatory and, on her return, at her own door, argue with Cornudet who, standing there in his braces, is apparently trying to enter her room. Of their conversation, Loiseau just manages to catch a few words such as: *He*: 'Really you are a fool, after all what does it matter to you?' *She*: 'No, my dear, there are moments when things like that are not done. Well, here it would be a disgrace.' And then again, after some noticeable argument, she goes on: 'Why? You ask me why? When Prussians are about, in the neighbouring room maybe?' Whereupon Loiseau wakes up his unlovely wife to make love with her.

Surely this in itself is a fine piece of sex psychology. But the reason why it is perfectly in its place in *Boule de Suif* is that it gives a clue to the envy and feeling of frustration which is working in that happy-go-lucky fellow, Loiseau, when his facetiousness turns into malignity at the expense of the woman he covets, and of the man he envies for at least daring to try.

Loiseau takes his revenge by telling his respectable fellow-passengers in the inn all about 'the mysteries of the corridor' and making them roar with laughter.

No such depths of dirt are dug up in *Maison Tellier*; there is pinching of thighs in the railway compartment instead, and when the village joiner, whose daughter is partaking of the First Communion, has been caught trying to make his unholy best of Rosa la Rosse's presence, his wife brushes the thing off with good humour. The story has a happy ending, happy for everybody, including the bourgeois regular customers of the *Maison* who are granted free treats, and served with champagne at cut price, because, as *Madame* explains, 'Not every day is a holiday.' By the way, Hector Malot, so Goncourt tells us, thought that by this festival note Maupassant spoiled the story which in his (Malot's) original version ended up with *Madame* tartly ordering her girls, 'Tonight, then, *dodo toutes seules*!' – in bed alone! Malot's ending was perhaps more Maupassant-like than Maupassant's; but there is nothing wrong with Maupassant's either.

Is, then, *Maison Tellier* lighter stuff than *Boule de Suif* or is it more graceful? It is both. In its approach to the female body and male desires, it has less of Zola; in its manner more of La Fontaine, Laclos, the Abbé Prévost; and as to its moral, it has none. This time-honoured and harmless bawdiness made it go down more smoothly with his conventionally minded readers than Maupassant would have expected; indeed, the only thing he did not achieve as intended was to *shock*. His sales rose at high speed, and his talent was now unanimously acclaimed.

Turgenev, to whom *Maison Tellier* was dedicated, now acted as a substitute Flaubert in relation to Maupassant, praising and publicizing him wherever he could, mainly amongst his fellow Russians. He hastened to show the story to Tolstoy amongst others; we shall later see with what results. And when Maupassant's contemporary, Pierre Loti, a charming writer of romantic taste and exotic curiosities, called that short novel the most perfect literary work ever written in French, he showed the sound judgment, though possibly with over-enthusiasm, of those who know good style from bad, whatever the School it represents.

Maupassant's School was, without any doubt, that called

Naturalism; not because he happened to belong to the Médan group but because he was, more perhaps than any of his companions, destined for it by his gifts and temperament.[1] Zola, as the head of the School, was jubilant about Maupassant's success and wrote an enthusiastic review of *Maison Tellier*; but the battle between prudes and anti-prudes was still raging, and *Figaro*, for which it was meant, refused to publish not only this review but also any advertisement of the 'shocking' story. And Maupassant was reproached by critics with conservative leanings, not so much for this specific piece as for his fondness for the subject-matter in general. Besides Albert Wolff of *Figaro*, it was the famous dramatic critic of *Le Temps*, 'Uncle' Francisque Sarcey, looked upon as the oracle of the sound upper middle class, who, in *Le XIXᵉ Siècle*, under the heading 'The Law on Pornographic Writings', in the course of a review of *Mademoiselle Fifi*, made the most conspicuous attack on the author. 'Is it not high time for M. Guy de Maupassant,' he asked, 'to direct his taste for observation and his talent for style to different subjects? He had better be careful! The public is beginning to get tired of these ugly pictures.' The verdict of the readers, Sarcey argued, would ultimately be more shattering than that of the authorities.

In his reply to Sarcey,[2] Maupassant said:

> Literature today is tending towards precise information; and, in fact, woman has two functions in life, love and motherhood. Novelists, wrongly perhaps, have always rated the former function more interesting to their readers than the latter, and have primarily observed woman in the professional performance of the thing for which she seemed to be born.
>
> Of all subjects, it is love that touches the public most. It is the *femme d'amour* with whom people are most concerned.
>
> Besides, amongst men, there are profound differences of intelligence, owing to education, to environment, etc.; it is different with woman, her human role is restricted; her

---

[1] M. Pellissier, in 1901, made the point that Maupassant was the only real naturalist story-teller, precisely because 'he had no philosophy, or rather his philosophy was not to be concerned with what could not be sensed' (*Souvenirs sur Maupassant*, ed. Lumbroso, p. 169).

[2] 'Réponse à M. Francisque Sarcey,' *Le Gaulois*, 20 July 1882.

faculties have remained limited; from the top to the bottom of the social scale, they are the same. The *filles* once married become in no time admirable *femmes du monde*. . . .

There are no classes amongst women. They only count in society through the men who have married or patronized them. As to the men who take them as consorts, under law or not, are they always so scrupulous about their *provenance?* Must one be more so when choosing them as literary subjects?

Surely this is a smug, and even poorly written, watering down of what Maupassant learned from his ancestors, the gay erotic chroniclers of the French eighteenth century, affected by Schopenhauer's morose grumblings against women; but two at least of his points are genuine: his interest in the public's interest; and his fascination with the love-making female body.

Furthermore, he had a definite sympathy for the women who make love for money, especially if they do so in good humour, combining venality with attachment, preferably with a wise and cheery mother in the background like his Rondoli sisters;[1] this was just the natural thing for a woman to do, however phoney the social setting which developed that inclination in her.[2] Although, in his later writings, he did not concentrate on prostitutes and the *demi-monde* to the same extent, the idea remained with him all the time and was manifest, at the peak of his career, in his introduction to a new edition of *Manon Lescaut*.[3] 'In this character full of allurement and instinctive perfidy,' he wrote, 'the author seems to have embodied all that is most gentle, most captivating and most infamous in a female.' And he quotes with admiration what the Abbé Prévost, or his hero, says about the heroine:

Never had a girl been less attached to money than she was, but she was unable to be quiet for a moment with the worry of lacking it. She would never have wished to obtain a penny when she could amuse herself free of charge. She did not even inform herself of the origins of our riches . . . but it was so much of a necessity for her to be thus occupied with pleasure that, without it, you could not rely at all on her honour and on her attachment.

[1] *Les Sœurs Rondoli.*   [2] *Yvette.*   [3] 1885.

Mercenary-mindedness, combined with companionable good-will in bed and at board, was, in the testimony of Maupassant's writings, the best a man could expect from a woman; or, at any rate, it was the most steadily enjoyable. He was not unaware of passions higher or deeper than that, and his point was not that they were less genuine, but that they were less bearable. He has a story about a man who married the woman he loved and then cut a sad figure though he did not really cease to be enchanted with her, nor she with him. It was the tension of happiness which made them, or at any rate him, unhappy. The narrator describes his sickish looks in the suffocating climate of mutual affection. Then, one night, the narrator finds him relaxed, cured as it were, and another man steps in: obviously the lover, the lightning-conductor, the relief. The husband excuses himself from them so as to have a little stroll with his old friend and, when in the street, he whispers, 'And now how about a call on the *filles?*'[1] Venal love, in Maupassant's universe, is not a substitute for true love; men require both, each according to his own taste, and he himself seems to have been more attached to the ideal of a piece of pretty flesh rewarded for its services with a *louis d'or* than to any other manifestation of the feminine psyche. In his decade of fame and prosperity, he could easily have done without prostitutes; however great his sexual appetite, his supply of attractive partners was even greater, and financially unselfish partners they were, for women (and not women only, perhaps) like to be generous towards those not in need of it. But he would take leave from an attractive mistress to pop into a brothel as he would sip a tumblerful of fresh water when his throat got dry between heavy dishes and glasses of vintage wine. Those girls with their uninhibited and unsophisticated gaieties were a refreshment to him, like the river or the sea, like the purring of his cat or the swift flight of a teal over wintry marshes at dawn, as he watched it rifle in hand. Prostitution, like hunting, was part of Nature. The Nature he loved was cruel and amoral, and therefore gay, and ultimately tragic.

There was nothing more beautiful than that icy dawn, in company with Cousin Karl, that 'likeable semi-brute', and his hounds, Pierrot and Plongeon, all eager to kill the wild birds

[1] *Un Sage.*

whose cries and chatter movingly expressed life in the state of awaking. Then he, the narrator, shot a female teal, and Cousin Karl shot the male who had flown to her rescue, and the hounds brought their bodies. 'I put the two bodies, already cold, in the same game-bag . . . and returned, that very day, to Paris.'

With this brief paragraph ends the story *Amour* (1886). It is curious to compare it with another story by Maupassant, *L'Armoire* (1884), no less heart-rending though in a very different way, and also ending with dry brevity.

Both stories are attributed to a narrator in order to make them conversational. *Amour* is supposed to be 'three pages of a hunter's diary'; and *L'Armoire* was told by a friend, 'after dinner, as chatter was going on about *filles*, for what else should men chat about?' 'One evening last winter,' the friend said, 'I was the victim of a sudden attack of desolating lassitude . . .' and so he picked up a *fille*, agreed with her on the price for the whole night and followed her to her room 'in a big, big building, rue des Martyrs' – Maupassant liked to be specific in his topography. After slipping into bed the two of them were talking about the intricacies of her *métier*, and she had just confessed to having a twelve-year-old son somewhere, when there was a crackling in the cupboard and he discovered behind its door 'a pale little boy, trembling, with bewildered and brilliant eyes as he gazed at me'.

'It's not my fault, Mummy,' the boy cried. 'I fell asleep . . .' His mother could not afford to keep him elsewhere; whilst she was away, he could use the bed, but before she entered with a client he had to hide himself in the cupboard. The *fille*, though furious, explained in his defence: 'When a fellow comes for an hour or two, he can well stick it out on a chair inside . . . but if anyone stays for the night, like you . . . I'd jolly well like to know how *you* would manage . . .' So she went on shouting, whilst the boy went on sobbing. And here the story ends:

I, too, felt like crying.
And I went home to sleep.

Maupassant was an addict to light pleasures which he knew were not really light.

The France of the 1880s, that of Maupassant's 'meteoric' career,[1] was marked, more strikingly than any other country and epoch, by the rule of the liberal plutocracy. Everything could be bought for money; and the greatest fortunes were made on the stock exchange. In a sense, it had long been like that, and not in France only. The banker, as the chief social engineer, was no novelty; yet, previously, his influence had been dependent on the consent of kings and emperors, bishops and generals, magnates and squires or, in the spasms of political earthquakes, on that of plebeian leaders, the champions of the *comités* and the barricades. But by the time that Maupassant's rocket had soared high in literature and journalism (with *Boule de Suif* marking the take-off), the hereditary and authoritarian obstacles to the comfort of the (mostly plebeian) rich had been swept away by four revolutions and by the Republican purge, after MacMahon's fall, in the judiciary and the State administration; whereas the efforts to curb big business with socialist measures, notable in 1848–50 and 1871, and smashed both times, were now sufficiently discredited to be kept out of the actual struggle for power. The banker now behaved as he pleased. He often behaved like a cavalry officer, or an ancient landowner or a modern bohemian, but nobody compelled him to do so; his power was only limited by its own nature, the freedom of enterprise, speculation and competition, linked with a free press, the freedom of opinion, the freedom of sophistication and of vulgarity, of education and of blackmail. The French law on the Liberty of the Press, enacted in 1881, opened the sluices, to an extent unparalleled till then, to a flood of most variegated ideas, styles and calumnies; the gossip columnist was to become the architect of public opinion and, indirectly, of national policy. The *échos*,[2] are 'the

[1] 'Je suis entré dans la vie littéraire comme un météore et j'en sortirai comme un coup de foudre', Maupassant once told the poet, José-Maria Heredia (quoted by Pol Neveux, Preface to Maupassant's *Œuvres complètes*.)

[2] Roughly corresponding to 'gossip columns'.

marrow of a newspaper', the press millionaire, M. Walter, explains in *Bel-Ami*; 'it is through them that news is launched, and rumours circulated, it is through them that one influences the public and the revenue'.

This was the world in which Maupassant lived and wrote. Not that he admired it; but it was a world which preferred to be mirrored rather than admired. It was a society that felt it could do without *blagues*, without high-falutin' humbug, without self-embellishment through lip-service in public to myths and virtues mocked at in private. Science and philosophy reduced life, spirit, morality to what appeared their crude cells and blind motors; the universe was reduced to the atom, the human being to the unicellular, the pattern of natural and social history to the 'survival of the fittest', the triumph of a genius to the interplay of 'race, moment, milieu'. In fine arts, ideals had given way to reality, and reality was giving way to impressions. Though the trends of the epoch showed variety rather than unity, most of them converged on the discovery that all ugly or trivial features of life could be made beautiful to look at if mirrored with wit and accuracy. There was no longer need, in consequence, to keep any information, any sensation, barred from the field of human knowledge; all facts, all sensations could be admitted to the biologist's microscope, to the sociologist's recordings, to the painter's canvas, to M. Walter's *échos*. Man was at last able to face himself nakedly; it was not always an exhilarating sight but the discomfort produced was to a large extent offset by the pride of being able to see things as they were, without illusions, without *any* illusions. Hippolyte Taine, a man hardly discussed today but of enormous influence before and during the 1880s, whose doctrine was most typical of the sort of detachment aimed at by the thinkers of that epoch, was conspicuous for discarding all myths and dogmas and rhetorical slogans, romantic as well as classic, revolutionary as well as traditionalist, patriotic as well as religious, democratic as well as authoritarian, and even the beliefs in human values other than those determined and prompted by a multitude of facts beyond man's control. This doctrine sounds like the emanation of a Mephistophelian character, but he was nothing of the kind; he was a decent and dutiful citizen, quite unbearably so, pedantic, industrious, professorial, *Monsieur* Taine to everybody. Moral nihilism had become respectable.

Looking back from a distance of some eighty or ninety years, all that nakedness of facts and features strikes us as rather mild and relative, but at the same time over-simplified in the conclusions drawn from it. Those nudes caught in awkward movements by the Impressionists have since been turned inside out by their successors; those organic cells have been dissected into particles which procreate without actually living; those atoms have been split and fused; and the 'soul' expelled from them all has in a way re-entered in the shape of psychical 'complexes' which overrule physical forces, and of electrons parading with the attributes of 'free will'. This only proves, however, that the discarding of illusions can never be final. Maupassant was intent on doing away with them and was qualified to do so; and we shall soon see the barriers he was running into when he tried, solid barriers even by the standards of his age.

Intellectual fashions and general taste, of course, do not always go hand in hand. An aesthetic plebiscite of hearts today would result in an overwhelming vote in favour of the Albert Memorial and its opposite numbers in other big cities all over the world; and the same would have been the result in the Paris of the 1880s. Very different ideas can thrive side by side without taking notice of each other and yet influence each other. Is it right to mention the factuality pretended by the *échos* of the day, and that aimed at by M. Taine in his analyses, in one breath? Most of the social and political notabilities and the fashionable *vedettes* who figured in the *échos* knew little about M. Taine's theory; the thousands of readers for whom they were devised knew even less; and M. Taine was so taken up by his studies of the 'moments' which shaped history in all times that he could not possibly have spared effort to watching his own. Yet both reflected the same atmosphere; and so did Maupassant whose snappy stories, dry but vivid, truthful but entertaining, were as near to the gossip columns as great art could be. There was at the beginning of his 'meteoric' decade but one thing that divided him from their world: the subject-matter. Taine, who had a very high opinion of his abilities, warned him precisely about this.

I should like you to add to your observations another set of
observations. You have depicted peasants, petty traders and
petty clerks, workmen, students, harlots. You are without
doubt going to depict one day the highly educated classes, the
haute bourgeoisie, engineers, doctors, professors, industrialists
and big business.

As I see it, civilization is a power. A man born in affluence,
the heir of three or four generations entrenched in honesty,
hard work and social standing, has more chance to be reliable,
refined and knowledgeable. Honour and *esprit* are more or less
hothouse plants.

This doctrine may well be aristocratic but it is derived from
experience . . .

Maupassant contradicted his venerable friend,[1] but then to a
large extent followed his advice. His interest in subject-matter
became more and more upper class and cosmopolitan. It was
natural that this should happen. The *salons* of the liberal *haute-
bourgeoisie* were his proper environment. Many denied this,
pointing to what had been and always remained provincial,
uncouth and rock-like in his personality. He was both too good
and too coarse to submerge himself in the world of superficial
sophistication with its smooth murmur of gossip and *mots*
steeped in fashionable literature. He was looked upon as an
eccentric. But his eccentricity was appreciated, and he knew it.
His important, indeed, epoch-making contribution to his age
was to describe, more vividly and cruelly than anybody else,
what he called the 'grandes misères des petites gens'[2] – the surroundings he was so familiar with from his ramblings in Normandy, his boatings on the Seine, his years spent as an office
clerk in Paris. But he found kindred souls who saw things in
the same way as he did in that layer of society which stretched
from MM. Taine and Renan and their disciples to the gossip
columnists, with the boudoirs and drawing-rooms of leisured

[1] Actually, it was Maupassant who published these excerpts from
Taine's letter, in his article 'Réponse à M. Francisque Sarcey', in defence
of his own predilection for writing about prostitutes (*Le Gaulois*, 20 July
1882).

[2] See Chapter 23.

and perfumed ladies in between. He had become their lion and was to become their chronicler.

His first two novels, *Une Vie* and *Bel-Ami*, marked in a way his transition towards this new status. *Une Vie* was the working out of a theme that seems to have gripped his mind ever since his first literary attempts; the projection in a detached narrative of his vision of his mother, in the atmosphere of his own childhood, in 'one of those huge high Norman houses that are at once farm and château'.[1] The persons on whom it centred were not 'petites gens', but were no less parochial than if they had been; they belonged to the impoverished landowning aristocracy. It was Maupassant's most momentous, though indirect, expression of filial tenderness; no wonder Tolstoy loved it.[2] Some found fault with it for being 'too much like a long short story'; linear in composition, a series of sample episodes, nothing else. I feel it speaks in its favour, that with such economy Maupassant still managed to convey the essence of a life as he did. It is curious to compare it with some of his short stories in which he struck a similar note, *Première Neige*, for instance – also about a delicate and frustrated *châtelaine* with a coarse (though less beastly) husband, and also a whole life's development condensed; but though *Première Neige* is shorter, *Une Vie* is more succinct. It is really impeccable, and the limitations of its social vistas are due rather to its undercurrents of snobbery than to its short-story-like composition. Maupassant sees that world of rusting or painfully repolished coats of arms as melancholy and ridiculous; yet he feels it the best, perhaps the sole, fitting background for maternal delicacy. The manor house of Grainville-Ymanville is exactly described,[3] but its erstwhile inhabitants are made somewhat more blue-blooded than they were. Nevertheless, the

[1] See Chapters 10 and 11.

[2] 'The life of a ruined, innocent, amiable woman, disposed to all that is good, and ruined precisely by the same coarse, animal sensuality which in his [Maupassant's] former stories stood to the author as the central and dominant feature of life . . . Perhaps the best French novel after *Les Misérables*' (L. Tolstoy, *Guy de Maupassant*, translated by V. Tchertkoff, Brotherhood Publishing Co., 1898, p. 7).

[3] Though there are several amusing topographical slips, as noted by André Vial in *La Genèse d' 'Une Vie'*, Paris, 1954 (p. 29).

atmosphere is as authentic as are its characters; part of the world Maupassant has been familiar with since childhood. It was published in 1883.

In *Bel-Ami* Maupassant's grasp is wider, but far less perfect. In this novel, conceived at the time of North African war crises and published in 1885, he set out to describe – if not, or not mainly, the 'haute bourgeoisie' recommended by Taine, yet its background in journalism, business, and corruption. As a journalist himself, he did so with commendable frankness and even some sensationalist muck-raking. The hero of this novel, Georges Duroy, is an illiterate but crack journalist who owes his success to women beguiled by his good looks – especially by his moustache which in Maupassant's experience must have been the most irresistible symbol of virility – and to the unscrupulousness with which he exploited them. He is introduced by chance, through the casual kindness of a former army pal, to *La Vie Française* which is selling gossip and patriotism every morning to the masses, blowing the trumpet of war one week and forgetting its martial passions the next, resulting in huge profits on the stock exchange for those informed of the coming move, namely, the newspaper proprietor, a Cabinet minister and their inner circle of partners and contributors. Duroy, thanks to women, enters this circle; one of them writes his articles, another keeps his apartment, whilst a third helps him share in the gains on the stock exchange. He finally elopes with the daughter of the latter, marries her, and so becomes a millionaire and a press lord himself. After his wedding, from the porch of the Madeleine, Baron Georges Du Roy de Cantel (which style he has by then assumed) fixes his eyes on the Chamber of Deputies where he feels assured he will rise as the leader of the nation one day, makes an appointment with a discarded mistress to whom he is still attracted and, moved by the beneficence of fate, 'almost believes in God'.

The best parts of *Bel-Ami* are still those dealing, at least partly, with *petites gens*: Duroy, the petty clerk, in his squalid living-room or in the street wondering whether to buy two glasses of *bock* or a meagre supper; Duroy's strange love–hate relationship with his mistress's young daughter who names him 'Bel-Ami'; Duroy with his first wife visiting his peasant father and mother, in deadly embarrassment. Second best are the bizarre happenings in a newspaper office; and poorest, the glimpses of the *monde*, and of the witches' kitchen where political and stock exchange manœuvres are being concocted. The picture of nation-wide corruption and of a nationalism kept going for big business interests – a vision prompted by the recent adventures of French colonialism in North Africa – is creditably outspoken but naïve in details, a Punch and Judy show with the pretence of a sociological study.

In spite of its deficiencies, or partly because of them, *Bel-Ami* was even better received than Maupassant's previous works or, for that matter, anything he was to publish later. His success now went far beyond those readers generally attracted to 'naturalism'. Brunetière, the conservative editor of the *Revue des Deux Mondes*, a most unrepentant crusader against the trends of the eighteenth and nineteenth centuries, virtually capitulated to Maupassant's power; if such a thing as 'roman strictement et vraiment naturaliste' should exist at all, he wrote, well, then *Bel-Ami* was its 'most remarkable product . . . Everything in it is portrayed with outstanding truthfulness, clarity and accuracy.'

The general public's reactions were even more favourable. Maupassant had become the entertainer of the masses. He was worried lest the recent death of Victor Hugo should have diverted public interest from this novel; this was the reason, he argued, why up to the beginning of July 'only twenty-seven impressions, that is, 13,000 copies' had been placed. This 'coup terrible', however, turned out to be less fatal than he thought; within four months of its publication already thirty-seven impressions were sold.'[1] *Bel-Ami* became a best seller practically all over the world in no time, and its hero's name has since then through the media of film and television grown into a household word, even more perhaps than has 'Boule de Suif'.

Why was it that the 'strict and pure naturalism' of this particular novel penetrated into those circles of traditionalist highbrows and uncommitted lowbrows who up to that time had been impervious to Maupassant's appeal? Because it was far from 'strict and pure'. True enough in its outspokenness about sex,

[1] Cf. Maupassant's letter to his mother, 7 July 1885, and the Introduction to *Bel-Ami* by Gérard Delaisement, in the edition of Garnier Frères, 1959.

which was in the public eye the most important distinguishing
feature of 'naturalism', it did not lag behind *Maison Tellier*;
its description, for instance, of an *accouplement violent et maladroit*
in a railway carriage would certainly have caused a public uproar
and provoked prosecution some ten or twenty years earlier. But
on the whole it was the novel of a glamorous career, however
dismal its glamour – a romantic account of contemporary
wickedness in which the author comforts his readers for the
shock he gives them by adding his own misgivings, at least, by
sardonic implication. The 'little people' are more amused by
such accounts of the 'great' than by encountering the drab
features of their own lives in what they read; and the 'great'
people did not seem to mind appearing diabolic.

There was only one quarter which was somewhat touchy
about Maupassant's descriptions: his colleagues, the newspaper-
men. Does M. de Maupassant really think, they asked, that there
is nothing but such dirt to be found in journalism? Maupassant
answered their reproaches on the lines that could be expected:
he did not mean to generalize . . . And, besides, this Georges
Duroy, or Baron Du Roy de Cantel, was not even a journalist,
he was the very opposite, a typical *pseudo*.[1] Maupassant went so
far in offering amends to all who might feel offended as to enumerate a dozen of the most influential newspapers which, he
respectfully emphasized, could not possibly have served as a
model for his *Vie Française*, adding 'etc., etc.' as a sop to the rest.

It was all very well for Maupassant to say so. It was a hypocritical pretence which any novelist might use in similar circumstances. In fact, all persons and all features of journalism figuring
in *Bel-Ami* were clearly identifiable, from the Jewish press
millionaire, 'M. Walter', to the frustrated eccentrics of the editorial offices, though their political colourings had been blurred
and their love affairs recombined.[2] Maupassant was, no doubt,
ungrateful to that *milieu* which had helped him enormously in
developing his powers as a story-teller, and in popularizing his

[1] 'Bel-Ami devant la Critique,' *Gil Blas*, 7 June 1885.
[2] M. Delaisement, in his above-mentioned Introduction to *Bel-Ami*,
makes a careful and most convincing study of the persons and circumstances alluded to by Maupassant; I feel, however, that his vision of Maupassant as a moral philosopher is grossly idealized.

name. His main excuse should be that gratitude is not a virtue to be expected from a novelist. 'A writer,' as Maupassant's spiritual offspring Somerset Maugham has said, 'is not a gentleman.'

And if Maupassant was unkind to his colleagues and acquaintances, he certainly could not be accused of indulging, at the same time, in self-pity or in an overdose of tenderness towards those nearest to him. 'Bel-Ami' was modelled partly on his brother, Hervé, and partly on himself; like Hervé, Duroy had been an N.C.O. in Algeria and then, like young Guy, an embittered petty clerk in Paris; even his way of entering the newspaper offices bears some resemblance to the author's. The two young men if combined, in looks and nature, did really amount to a Georges Duroy, *minus* of course all that made Guy a man of letters and that doomed poor Hervé to passivity and an early death. Duroy's career had nothing in common with theirs, but it did correspond with their daydreams and gave them away no less than it pilloried the journalists and socialites teeming in and round *La Vie Française*. Maupassant, in a way, admitted this: 'Bel-Ami, c'est moi,' he said. This statement in itself did not mean much; it was an echo of Flaubert's more surprising 'Madame Bovary, c'est moi.' But to Maupassant's credit, this admission was not even necessary to identify him and his brother in some gestures of his repellent hero. There was a bit of masochistic self-mirroring in it without which no literary vivisection can be authentic. Cruelty in literature is a merit if, like charity, it begins at home.

37 · *Making money*

He wrote and he wrote. In his tidy and unsophisticated handwriting, he covered some six pages a day, 1,500 pages a year – so Edouard Maynial estimated. From 1880 to 1890, he published on an average three volumes a year, the peak years being 1884 with four volumes, and 1885 with five. In the meantime, he poured out newspaper articles (not collected in a volume until his death), business letters crammed with figures, calculations, self-assertive and quarrelsome claims, and private letters with renewed ventures, now in sexual pornography, now in *amitié amoureuse* or the like.

He sat at his writing-desk, or paced his study, pen in hand and with a dripping towel over his shoulders after his cold shower-bath, generally from 6.30 or 7 a.m. until noon, and he read proofs late at night or in the small hours, headache or women permitting, before falling asleep. When his eyesight had become very bad he tried to dictate, but found that too 'uncomfortable' to carry on; the very act of writing seems to have been a biological necessity for him. The early morning excursions to the Seine had disappeared from his regular timetable. There were *mondanités* instead in the afternoons and evenings, including exercise such as shooting practice, hunting and visits to the beach at Etretat, with a rich display of his brand-new suits and his muscles which outlived the youthfulness of his heart. There were his visits to the *salons* in Faubourg St-Honoré and there were his travels, particularly along the coasts or across the Mediterranean. He was an ardent socialite, though no less ardent a debunker of socialites, and he got entangled in many an adventure, sportive or amorous. 'My life has no history,' he liked to say, in a coy reflection of the Flaubertian idea that an author only lived through seeing the lives of others. But he was glad to be caught living his own 'history'. He was keen on publicity and money. His love for publicity he liked to disguise; his love for money he put into the show-window.

'I only write for money,' he used to say; and, 'I am an *industriel des lettres*.' Smug remarks like these, supported by his large sales, fixed his image, especially with the young intelligentsia who wrote him off as an 'NC', standing for *notable commerçant*.[1] His defence against disparagement by his juniors consisted in not reading their work; he was not really interested in new talent unless he found one of his lady friends thrilled by it. His attitude towards the bureaucratic Establishment and its distinctions was no less contemptuous. 'I shall never receive any decoration,' he had said as a young man, 'because to do so would mean licking the boots of too many politicians';[2] and when after

[1] *Petit Bottin des lettres et des arts*, 1886.
[2] Quoted by Albert Caim, *Souvenirs sur Maupassant*, ed. Lumbroso, p. 385.

his successes he was approached by some who thought he should be decorated, he declined because 'I have always said that I wanted to stay outside all honours and dignities'.[1] There is no reason to doubt his sincerity on this; he was defending his independence, not his moral virginity. He was widely quoted as saying that 'there are three things unworthy of a writer: the Légion d'honneur, the membership of the Académie Française, and contributing to the *Revue des Deux Mondes*'. Of these three conservative institutions, the third was the only one against which he bore a personal grudge – for its refusal to publish one of his early poems. All the same, it was the only one of them which made him overcome his aversion; as an *arrivé*, he sold his novel, *Notre Cœur*, for serialization in its pages. He had, however, a good reason: it was not for honour, but for money.

He did want money, no doubt; for his costly luxuries and medical treatment, for building his house in Etretat, and to support his mother and brother . . . Yet, one feels, all these needs do not account for his ostentatious passion for making money out of literature. Edmond de Goncourt was shocked by Maupassant's boast that he had 'pocketed 40,000 [francs] for his works in journalism', and felt such young men (Maupassant was then thirty-two) were 'condemned by their love of luxury to nothing but industrialism'.[2] We are also indebted to Goncourt for the information that Maupassant, in 1888, the year of his greatest prosperity, accepted a bribe of 500 francs from the Princess of Monaco, or rather embezzled it from his publisher for whom it had been intended.[3] Goncourt indeed was not an unbiased witness; of his hatred for Maupassant, more later. But they were still on quite friendly terms when Maupassant called on Goncourt with the idea of starting a publishing house to be financed and run by the well-to-do authors themselves. Why let the publishers skim the cream off their incomes? Goncourt objected: 'Then, Zola, Daudet, you and I would have to eat from the same platter as Ponson du Terrail, Fortuné de Boisgo-

[1] Letter, undated, addressee uncertain, found amongst his papers; published in Vol. I, *Œuvres complètes*, 1908, p. cliii.
[2] *Journal*, Vol. III, p. 214. (For a note on the numbering, see Appendix 4.)
[3] *Journal*, Vol. IV, pp. 440–1.

bey, Paul Féval, Georges Ohnet, and other prose-concoctors . . .'
Maupassant did not seem to mind. 'And then,' Goncourt carried
on, 'what will become of the young writers if we let them
down?' Maupassant gave up;[1] he was unable to drive home to his
colleagues what was boiling in him. To his empiricist Norman
mind, money was the token of reality, and the race for bigger
sales was the test of values.

It would be easy to prove that this was not his aesthetical
opinion; he knew the 'deep and delirious joy' which 'comes
from an absolute accord between the expression and the idea, a
sensation of harmony, of secret beauty, which usually escapes the
judgment of the masses'.[2] But his instinctive notions were
anchored in the vulgar mystique of Facts and Figures which
should provide the testimony of that 'secret beauty'; and when
he felt he must stand up for himself as an author, he referred as
proof of his importance to the high fees he was paid and to the
large sales of his books, 'second only to those of Zola's'.[3]

For this very reason he felt it an outrage – not a social injustice, about which he did not care very much, but a personal
offence – that, between the man who wrote and the readers who
paid for his work, there should stand the publishers who actually
owned the books, made fortunes out of them, and whose dupes
the authors were. Was it not an illusion to believe in any literary
success so long as this was the position? 'I would like to ruin
some of the publishers one day,' he used to say jokingly;[4] but
it was not really a joke.

Pestering publishers thus became his lifelong hobby. He
found his ideal target in the person of Victor Havard, a minor
publisher. Maupassant's volume of poetry, as will be remembered, had been published by Charpentier, Flaubert's friend, the
principal publisher of the leading realist authors. After the
success of *Boule de Suif*, however, Havard made an offer to
publish his forthcoming books and Maupassant agreed because,
in the words of an English biographer,[5] 'Norman shrewdness

[1] Billy, *Les Frères Goncourt*, pp. 355–6.
[2] *Gustave Flaubert*, 1884.
[3] Maynial, *La vie et l'œuvre de Guy de Maupassant*, p. 139.
[4] 'J'aimerais à ruiner un jour quelques éditeurs.' Maynial, op. cit., p. 227.
[5] Jackson, *Guy de Maupassant*.

warned him that it might prove more profitable to stand at the head of Havard's list than halfway down that of Charpentier's'. Their business relationship, which might be called a game of cat and mouse, lasted from 1880 to 1891. Havard wrote enthusiastic letters to his 'dear author and friend', lyrical essays about the masterpieces he had the privilege to publish. Maupassant, in reply, urged his 'dear publisher and friend' to be more prompt about accounts, more efficient in promotion, to send him proofs and cash, even to collect for him cash due elsewhere. Havard invited Maupassant to lunch, beseeching him to accept: 'I am absolutely sure you will not regret the few moments spent with me.' Maupassant declined, now because he had 'made an absolute rule of not going out during the day', now for some other reason. He went to other publishers; he returned to Havard; in fact, he made full use of Havard's masochism. Below is one of his letters to Havard, written, presumably, at the end of 1884;[1]

Villa 'Mon Plaisir', Cannes

My dear publisher and friend,

Haven't you received my last letter in which I asked you for news of *Yvette* and warned you that I had drawn up my bill for the 500 francs owing to me from you on 15 January?

I must point out the ill-will of all booksellers in this country towards you:

1. All along the Lyons line, at all railway stations, all copies of *Yvette* have been sold out. Hachette have not supplied any more. Whereas *Les Sœurs Rondoli* can be seen everywhere.

2. In Marseilles, *Les Sœurs Rondoli* is on display everywhere, *Yvette* nowhere; the same is the case in Nice, also in Cannes, save at Vial's. I am speaking of the booksellers in town. In Cannes, the railway bookseller had sold one copy of *Yvette* the very first day and she seemed to be most surprised that no more copies had been forthcoming, as with *Les Sœurs Rondoli*.

[1] To make the references clear: *Yvette* was a collection of Maupassant's short stories, published by Havard; *Les Sœurs Rondoli*, one published by Ollendorf; and the great publishing house, Hachette, was responsible for distributing reading-matter to the kiosks at the railway stations.

I shall return to Paris in a few days but only for a very short time.

Now an extract from Victor Havard's reply, on 14 January 1885:

My dear author,
You are tyrannizing me for your account with unheard-of cruelty. You know what the position was to within a few hundred francs. You cannot thus in all conscience blame your poor publisher who has opened his purse for you! [. . .]

I spent almost 5,000 francs on printing [of *Des Vers* re-published by him], and 2,000 on publicity. I am still far from recovering my expenses. I think you would be well-advised to be a bit more conciliatory and to help me a bit in weathering that little difficulty.[1]

During his last three years, his private crusade against publishers took the shape of a persecution mania. He was no longer himself, it was his disease, one might say; but mental illness is often nothing but a magnified reproduction of what has always acted on the comparatively healthy organism. This was clearly Maupassant's case when, in the autumn of 1891, he turned his full fury on poor Havard. He threatened him with legal action unless he supplied 500 copies of his novel, *La Maison Tellier*, within twenty-four hours. The book was actually out of print, but Havard hastened to have the 500 copies specially printed to save his own peace of mind and to pacify the raging author who was, in spite of these harassments, a good source of income to him.[2] This income was, however, the very thing Maupassant found most insupportable; in his will drafted a short time later, he definitely excluded Havard from the right to publish his posthumous works.[3]

Most resounding of all Maupassant's squabbles with his publishers was that which flared up in the spring of 1890 – just before he became obviously a mental case. This set him against

[1] 'Lettres inédites de Guy de Maupassant', edited by Pierre Borel, in *Les Œuvres Libres*, Paris, April 1958, pp. 27–8; see also 'Documents inédits' in *Souvenirs sur Maupassant*, ed. Lumbroso.

[2] Lumbroso, op. cit., p. 451; Jackson, op. cit., p. 282.

[3] Maynial, *La vie et l'œuvre de Guy de Maupassant*, p. 290.

Charpentier, his old friend of Flaubert's days. Charpentier published a new illustrated edition of the *Médan* anthology, including portraits of all its contributors, Maupassant amongst them, without first asking for his permission. Maupassant protested in a way that was not only petulant but also, unlike him, pompous and hypocritical. In addition to a shower of letters of complaint and threats, he issued in his own handwriting a solemn statement which reads: 'I have made it an absolute rule not to let my portrait be published whenever I could prevent it. Exceptions have only taken place by chance. *Nos œuvres appartiennent au public, mais pas nos figures.*' And this was followed by a signature particularly full of flourishes.

He put in the reference to the 'exceptions' because he knew he could be reproached for having previously allowed his portrait to be published without any fuss.[1] But this much is true that, for a man so keen on publicity and so noted for his fondness for showing off his clothes and his biceps, he was surprisingly seldom portrayed. His own features were, apparently, one of the few things which he did not like to observe.

Towards the end of his career, and at the height of his passion for quarrels and litigation, on 5 December 1891, when pressing his lawyer, Maître Jacob, to sue an American paper for a violation of his author's rights, he added in his own handwriting a *pro memoria* about himself in the third person, so as to stress the magnitude of the damage done.[2] This reads:

M. Guy de Maupassant was the first French writer to revive the national taste of his country for *contes* and short stories.

He published, first in periodicals, then in volumes, all his stories which amount by now to a collection of 21 volumes with an average sale of thirteen thousand copies each, as can be testified from the quarterly accounts of his publishers.

These stories were paid for both by the papers and the publishers at the highest rates reached in France.

[1] Maynial, op. cit., p. 60, mentions that he did not object when Havard, in a new edition of *Des Vers*, 1884, included his portrait. The facsimile of Maupassant's above-quoted statement was published in *Souvenirs sur Maupassant*, ed. Lumbroso.

[2] Lumbroso, op. cit., p. 456.

His six novels: *Une Vie*, *Bel-Ami*, *Mont-Oriol*, *Pierre et Jean*, *Fort comme la Mort*, *Notre Cœur*.

Volumes of short stories: *Les Sœurs Rondoli*, *Monsieur Parent*, *Le Horla*, *La Main gauche*, *La Maison Tellier*, *Mademoiselle Fifi*, *Miss Harriet*, *La Petite Roque*, *Contes de la Bécasse*, *Yvette*, *L'Inutile Beauté*, *Le Rosier de Madame Husson*, *Clair de Lune*.

Books on travel: *La Vie errante*, *Au Soleil*, *Sur l'Eau*.

Theatre: *Musotte*.   Poetry: *Des Vers*.

> 169 thousand copies of short stories
> 180 thousand [copies] of novels
> 24 thousand copies travel books
> ———————
> 373 thousand copies.

His Norman mind worked in figures – under the shadow of lunacy even more than in his youthful sanity. The figures do not always tally. He misses out several volumes of his short stories, though they would have made his numerical record even more impressive; of his three plays performed and published, he only mentions the (by then) last; and it is not quite clear how he reaches the '21 volumes' for he actually enumerates more and had indeed published more than he enumerated. But the picture of a frenzied mass-producer of literature that emerges from these additions is authentic.

Money was his incentive, he felt; what, then, would he have done in a world which does not pay for writing? He would, in all likelihood, have done the same, and invented another excuse. He incessantly thought of his work and never stopped recording what he saw, sometimes, though not very often, in notes jotted down, but always by storing the material systematically in his mind, and with a desire to see it on paper. By his thirties, to borrow again a formula from his English biographer,[1] 'he had so drilled his faculties that his mind's eye seemed to click like a turnstile'. He did not do it with such ease as his prolificacy and the very tone of his writings, especially in the chatty newspaper articles, would suggest; quite a number of erasures and correc-

[1] Jackson, *Guy de Maupassant*, p. 147.

tions can be found in his manuscripts, and pages several times rewritten, for instance in *Une Vie*, which he wrote with particular care; but by Flaubert's standards, he still was a light and rapid worker. And his lightness, like Flaubert's heaviness, stemmed from an inability and unwillingness to let the man of letters in him relax for one single moment. Once he had discovered his own proper style, he really never gave himself any rest, not in his sleep, not in the ecstasy induced by ether, least of all in his recreations. When cruising the Mediterranean, each attempt to get some repose resulted in begetting another book. So long as he saw people and scenes, he could not help observing them; though his faculty of observing was uneven – slipping into the melodramatic and journalese, for instance, at the sight of a Corsican or an Arab – it was incessant. And left alone with the sea, he observed his own mind in the near-schizophrenic cramp of always observing. What he then had to say about it smacked a little of *fin de siècle* self-pity, but was sincere all the same:

Why do I not experience the reality of pleasures, of expectations and of rejoicings?

Because I carry within me that second sight which is the strength and, at the same time, the misery of writers. I write because I understand, I suffer everything that exists, because I know it only too well and mainly because, without being able to savour it, I watch it in myself, in the mirror of my thoughts.

Don't envy us, and don't pity us either; it is just in this that a man of letters differs from others.

For him, there is no simple feeling. Everything he sees, all his joys, his pleasures, his suffering, his despair, become at once subjects for observation. Despite himself, he analyses everything, the hearts, the faces, the gestures, the intonations. He no sooner sees anything, whatever it is, but he must ask Why? He has no single-minded enthusiasm, no urges or kisses, none of those spontaneous acts performed simply because one feels like doing them, without knowing, without deliberating, without understanding and taking notice of what one does.

If he suffers, he records his suffering and classifies it in his memory; he says to himself, when returning from the cemetery where he has left the man or woman he loved best, 'It is strange what I felt, it was like a painful drunkenness,' etc. And then he remembers the details, the attitudes of his neighbours, the false gestures, the false griefs, the false expressions and a thousand little insignificant things; artistic observations come to his mind, he recalls the way an old woman crossed herself whilst leading a child by the hand, and the ray of light in a window, a dog that ran across the procession, the effect of the funeral coach under the tall yew-trees of the cemetery, the undertaker's head and contraction of his features, the effort of the four men who lowered the coffin into the grave, yes, a thousand things which would be unnoticed by any honest man who suffered with his whole heart, his deepest soul, with all his strength.

. . . With the man of letters, the repercussion is livelier and more natural than is the first impulse; the echo is more sonorous than the original sound.

He seems to have two souls, one that records, explains, comments on each sensation of its twin soul, the natural soul which is like everybody else's. . . .[1]

Not even this was enough for his 'second soul'; when not writing for publication he still went on writing – heaven only knows why. In 1884, peak year of his output, he received a letter from a lady who described herself as 'charming', and coyly said she had read him 'almost with delight' and who, whilst unwilling to disclose her identity, offered him the pleasure of a high-minded correspondence. Actually she was Marie Bashkirtseff, intrepid lion-hunter and frail amateur of the arts. Maupassant replied that he had sixty such letters in his mail every morning; that he really could not be expected to answer such letters; and then he went on answering her again and again. It was the worst of Maupassant – sentimentality turned into cynicism – but still valuable as the symptoms of a graphomania which carries on unhampered by denigrating itself. 'I take everything with indifference,' he tells her, 'and I pass two-thirds of my time in

---

[1] *Sur l'Eau*, 1888, a travel diary of the sea, prepared on board his yacht *Bel-Ami*.

profound boredom. I occupy the other third in writing lines that I sell as dear as possible, distressing myself at being obliged to ply this abominable trade which has brought me the honour of being distinguished – morally – by you . . .' And then, 'In truth, I prefer a pretty woman to all the arts. I put a good dinner, a real dinner, almost in the same rank with a pretty woman.'[1]

Why then spend ink and effort on such correspondence? And it was not the only one. This luckily came to a close, but some five years later in Cannes he started another correspondence with another Russian lady – almost a repetition of the abstract flirtation with Marie Bashkirtseff. The tone of letters he wrote to his lady friends, some of them his mistresses, others not even that, make one gasp for air. Marie Kann, object of possibly the most durable of his love affairs, boasted, after his death, that she had received 2,200 letters from him, five a day sometimes;[2] even at a conservative estimate, if he wrote half that number, it must have been an achievement. Perhaps the most high-minded yet sloppy load of letters went to his neighbour in Etretat, Mme Lecomte du Nouÿ, authoress of *Amitié Amoureuse* and *En regardant passer la Vie*, both recollections, in different ways, of the *tendre* Maupassant. His no less voluminous correspondence with Countess Potocka contains interesting passages; but let us quote here only what refers to the driving power behind such letters:

> You ask what I am doing. I am bored. I am unceasingly bored. Everything overwhelms me, the people I see and the similar events that follow one another. There is so little *esprit* in the so-called elegant world, so little intelligence, so little of anything . . .[3]

He certainly could have chosen more intelligent company, or stuck to solitude, but, as dramatically described in *Sur l'Eau*, he was attracted to that 'so-called elegant world' at the same time as he was disgusted with it. He even enjoyed its boredom as he enjoyed, in a masochistic way, the boredom of existence, as a

---

[1] *I Kiss your Hands*. The letters of Guy de Maupassant and Marie Bashkirtseff, Introduction by Ann Hill, The Rodale Press.

[2] Dumesnil, *Guy de Maupassant*, p. 235.

[3] From Cannes, 13 March 1884.

source of inspiration, as the spur to write to the Countess or to write for his tens of thousands of readers.

To believe that he existed, he needed the evidence of his written records, and to believe that these records made sense, he needed the evidence of banknotes in return. If he had a belief at all, it was this.

Paradoxically for a moral nihilist, which in a way he was, Maupassant felt strongly about the standard of integrity to be observed by an author, was indignant about the tampering by publishers or editors with manuscripts, and refused to put up with any censorship or control. He had quite a contempt for what he called 'littérature tarte à la crème' and its champions – though he forgot about his own contempt when planning to run a publishing house with them. 'I have often said I only wrote because I needed money,' he told his valet, François, and added: 'This is not entirely so, there are things I enjoy writing . . .'[1] And, whether he enjoyed it or not, life for him was senseless without it. 'My *métier* of writer . . . I would not exchange it for a throne, not even for the existence of a free, intelligent and enlightened millionaire.'[2]

And paradoxically for a self-avowed 'industriel des lettres', he could become incensed by questions of money cropping up whilst literary values were on the agenda. In 1887, in Cannes, a young woman, introduced to him by the daughter of his friend, Dumas-*fils*, sent him a manuscript, asking for his opinion. It was a *récit* in the nature of 'science fiction', possibly under Jules Verne's influence. Maupassant was in a bad state of health, hardly able to read even printed text; yet in a great effort of courtesy, and with aching eyes, he carefully went through the manuscript and gave Jeannine Dumas his embarrassed, benevolent and cautious opinion. He took refuge in a Flaubertian attitude: he did not dare to encourage the young lady very much, but it was certainly worth her while studying literary examples. 'I don't think one can acquire essential qualities without having well understood and analysed those of others,' he wrote, 'because I doubt any inborn talent unless it be that of a genius.' Jeannine

[1] Tassart, *Souvenirs sur Guy de Maupassant . . .*, p. 262.

[2] Quoted by André Vial, *Maupassant et l'art du roman*, Nizet, Paris, 1954, p. 56.

then confided in him her friend's motives; her marriage was on the point of breaking up and she wondered whether she had any chance of earning some money by writing. No chance whatever, Maupassant answered abruptly; and anyway, 'the moment the idea of making money is mixed with the secret fever which makes ideas sprout, that fever no longer exists. If so, *que cette femme fasse* N'IMPORTE QUOI, *mais pas de la littérature*' – let this woman do *anything on earth* but keep off literature.[1]

Here we have this genius of a graphomaniac, with his conflicting *mots* about the *métier* he cherishes and despises, his confession that he is bored to death if unable to indulge in it, and that he attributes it to a secret fever, his boast that he does it for financial reasons only, his excited observation of the booksellers' kiosks at the railway stations and the quarterly accounts of the publishers. It is no good dismissing any of them just as cracks; though the grimaces behind them are obvious, the contents of all of them were borne out by his labour, struggle and ecstasy. Those figures of sales and returns were indeed his leading stars, but in a rather complicated way; as existence lacked reality for him unless recorded in writing, so also did writing lack reality unless rewarded in hard cash. His was a personality split not into two personalities, as he suggested in *Sur l'Eau*, but into three. There was the man who lived; there was the one who observed the living man; and there was another who marketed the observer. This third was a metaphysicist as well as a *notable commerçant*.

38 · *Spending money*

Maupassant made much money, spent much money and even saved some. His ways of spending were those of a devoted son, of a Norman peasant investor, of a boastful and luxury-loving upstart, and of a sick man addicted to drugs and chasing medical miracles. Generosity also came into this strange mixture, but in thin and erratic trickles only.

[1] Maurice d'Hartoy, *Guy de Maupassant inconnu; ses conseils à une 'Femme de lettres'*, 'Les Amis de Maupassant', Paris, 1957.

From rue Clauzel he moved first to 83 rue Dulong, Batignolles, to have a more comfortable apartment, and, in 1884, to 10 rue Montchanin, to have a more splendid one, occupying the ground floor of an *hôtel* built there by his cousin, the painter Louis Le Poittevin. He devoted much money and labour to furnishing this apartment, as vividly described after his death by his valet;[1] in his lifetime it earned him the reputation of glaring bad taste, although, no doubt, it did attract women, including quite a few of the refined classes. His friend, Georges de Porto-Riche, the poet and playwright, described it, at the time of *Bel-Ami*, as 'simple, crammed with junk in bad taste, very hot, very stuffy, very strongly perfumed',[2] and though one may wonder how that over-richness in scents and colours could be 'simple', one feels that in a way it could . . . This remained Maupassant's Paris headquarters for about five years; then he moved, in quick succession, to 14 avenue Victor Hugo (November 1889), and 24 rue Boccador (April 1890), and the sanatorium of Dr Blanche in Passy, where he died.

But, to quote Porto-Riche[3] again:

> M. de Maupassant spends in Paris as little time as possible. He spends the winter on the Mediterranean coast near his mother. And in summer, when not travelling, he often stays in Etretat. There, on the road to Criquetot, he has built himself a little yellow house which one can see from a distance standing between an orchard and a kitchen garden. He prefers fruit and vegetables to flowers.

To build that house, not far from his mother's, in his boyhood surroundings, had really been his most urgent task as soon as he had money to spare. He planned to name it *La Maison Tellier*, but his mother dissuaded him and to please her, it became 'Little Guy', that is *La Guillette*. It is a two-storey building, still inhabited today. Anybody interested in aesthetic merit may understandably be disappointed with it, but it struck me as quite a pleasant motley of purple and yellow, with a wide spread of terraces in the sunshine. In the large garden, an alley where

[1] Tassart, *Souvenirs sur Guy de Maupassant* . . .
[2] In an essay on Maupassant, reprinted in *Figaro Littéraire* in March 1912, quoted by Dumesnil, Morand, etc.   [3] See footnote to p. 77.

Maupassant used to walk and muse is still intact. He used to rear goldfish, and poultry, and keep hounds, not to mention Piroli, his pet cat, who was at home on his writing-desk in rue Montchanin no less than in *La Guillette*; their spirit, one feels, has survived together with the tribes of apples and cabbages round the house. And so has his taste for the comic. The only conspicuous feature in the back garden is a *caloge*, an old barge turned into a hut, which served for his bathroom as well as for the private villa of his valet. François was at first sight taken aback by the idea, but later got to like it.

François Tassart was engaged by Maupassant in 1883, and in no time became his intimate and *factotum*. They were really sister souls: both were literary-minded but unintellectual; Tassart was a great reader of *belles-lettres* – even of quite high-brow stuff, such as *Salammbô* – more so than Maupassant at that time; but neither of them was good at analysing what they read, and they were glad to talk Piroli, vegetables and social scandals instead. Both had a conservative but irreverent outlook, taking dignities and authorities for granted, but without taking them seriously. Their relationship was paternalistic but pally, as in a seventeenth-century picaresque comedy. What united them particularly was their sense of humour and adventure. The *Souvenirs* by François, published in 1911, not quite twenty years after his master's death, and made ample use of in practically all books on Maupassant written since (including the present one), is a marvel of innocent indiscretion, a goldmine of romanesque and farcical anecdotes; whether actually written by Tassart or a ghost writer, it reveals an ideal literary valet, humble towards his master's genius, sympathetic towards him in his sickness, but sharing with gusto in all his jokes and pranks and, indeed, in his schoolboyish cruelties. François Tassart could be called a good writer. His misfortune, however, was to live too long; he died when ninety-two, in 1949. In a second volume, only published posthumously, he tried to live up to his master in a genuinely literary way, with catastrophic results.[1]

---

[1] François Tassart, *Nouveaux Souvenirs Intimes sur Guy de Maupassant*, Nizet, Paris, 1962. Though on the whole a freak, it also contains some interesting passages, and its editor, M. Pierre Cogny, should be given credit for careful salvaging and annotation.

We know from François how hospitable Maupassant was, and how lavishly he entertained. In vain had he pledged himself strictly to limit his *mondanités*, for 'that's the end for an author'; whether in rue Montchanin or *La Guillette*, in a house fancied and rented on the bank of the Seine or in the villa chosen for his rest in Cannes, there was constant coming and going, the champagne flowing and rich meals carefully prepared, often – when in Etretat – with vegetables handpicked by Monsieur. Already by lunch-time or soon after ladies swarmed in to play bowls, gentlemen to emulate him in range-shooting, and the riotous dinner parties were frequently crowned by Monsieur's favourite hoax which consisted of deceiving his guests about the time and making them miss their train. He then put them up and *La Guillette* was sometimes transformed into a glorified doss-house. He was fondest of entertaining the sort of people described in *Yvette*, those on the borderline between the *monde* and the *demi-monde*, smart adventurers, with florid and phoney titles and just enough money to make women think that they had more. And women who matched them, either as partners or as dupes. 'Voyez, François', Monsieur explained – there had been a handsome Spanish count for dinner, who behaved abominably all the time, and there were two women who cajoled him and left with him – what do you think was the reason? Monsieur had made them believe that that man was rich and wished to marry, though there was no question of it. Fancy them hoping . . . And another night there was a dinner with a *collégien*, an Ephebian beauty, and two stoutish but extremely *chic* women, who were in competition to conquer him. 'Voyez, François,' that youth was really a girl dressed up. Can you imagine what faces the ladies will pull when they find out! Another time François was commissioned to surprise one lady friend with a basketful of frogs, and another one with toy devils which jumped unexpectedly. All came off; Monsieur was priceless.

Of Maupassant's mistresses who turn up in flashes, anonymously, amongst these anecdotes, few are identifiable with certainty. There was one recalled with affection, an American woman novelist,[1] in Etretat, in 1884, who was more worried

[1] Actually she was Blanche Roosevelt Tucker Macchetta, a rich Ohio girl married to a constantly absent Italian, Marquis d'Alligri. Francis

about Maupassant's state of health than about his promiscuity, and who told François she loved his master 'for his good heart, for his extreme loyalty' – actually quoted in English and, of course, with full approval. Other ladies were, at best, funny. There was one who made a habit of chasing Monsieur around with cries and tears, and a revolver, but who, after heated exchanges, and with François's blessing, smilingly agreed that in future they would be 'good friends'. This happened in 1887, apparently a year of great amorous turnover, even by Maupassant's standard. In the spring of that year, 'a young lady in an attractive tight-fitting grey tailored costume with hat to match' called at 10 rue Montchanin, and as Monsieur was away, she just wrote on a slip of paper, COCHON! – and left. This was a *marquise*, Maupassant later explained, the daughter of one of Napoleon's cabinet ministers; he did not wish to see her again, he added, though he admitted that 'she writes well'.[1]

This happy-go-lucky rushing about between changing seacoasts, river-banks and women was a despairing effort to get rid of his two suffocating troubles: boredom, and physical pain. To some extent, the two were interconnected; though the vision of cosmic boredom had always haunted him, it turned from musing melancholia into a raging fury when, apart from writing, he no longer found any spiritual outlet. This was due to his illness; his *migraines* and eye troubles, always worsening, hindered him in reading and contemplation. He dipped erratically into studies which required less sedentary occupation; astronomy one day, ancient Arab relics another. As to books, there was only one sort on which he was able to concentrate: medical books in which he sought a magic remedy for his illness.

Steegmuller in his *Maupassant* (Collins, 1950) gives a vivid portrait of her. She was, it seems, a passionate lion huntress and a dabbler in all the arts – a former opera singer, a former Longfellow biographer and a failure in all such ventures – but a kind and generous character, and of outstanding beauty; 'a tall, well-made blonde with masses of red-gold hair', as Frank Harris wrote. Victor Hugo saw in her 'the beauty and genius of the New World', and Browning said, 'What a pity Raphael is not living to see her! There would be a new Madonna!'
[1] Tassart, *Souvenirs sur Guy de Maupassant . . .*, pp. 24–5, 74, 82.

Like many another hypochondriac unwilling to pay attention to his real disease, he ran from one doctor to another, consulted one textbook after another, tried one drug, one treatment, one sort of shower-bath after another, whilst concealing some of his symptoms even from himself, as was to become apparent in the end. His wish to find a cure was his main reason, if not excuse, for never staying in one place. It was the humidity of the North that was killing him, he discovered one day: that must also be the cause of his mother's pains in the head and stomach; the *Midi* was the answer. He took a villa in Cannes, and his mother in Nice, nearby but not *too* near. No sooner had he settled there than it was time to run back to Normandy or Brittany, so that he would not miss the hunting season, and then again to Paris, and then Italy, and Africa where he felt he excelled in enduring the heat, yes, sunshine was the answer to his medical problems, at any rate for a while . . . He also visited England, invited by the Rothschilds, and saw London and Oxford, and ran back again as if panic-stricken.[1]

He did enjoy much of his travels, he liked to watch strange faces and colourful scenery, but was aware of their being, altogether, a poor substitute for what he was unable to find between four walls. One travelled, he maintained, in the hope of escaping something which one took with oneself, which one was incapable even of defining. 'To move from place to place seems to me a useless and tiring activity,' says one of his heroes[2] who may very well stand for himself:

Nights spent on the railway in the disturbed sleep of the shaking carriage, with pains in the head and cramp in the limbs; waking dog-tired in this box on wheels with the feeling of dirt on the skin, eyes and beard powdered with flying smuts; the smell of coal on which one lives, the appalling dinners in the draughts from the buffet, are to my mind the hateful beginning of a pleasure tour [*partie de plaisir*].

After this introduction on the express we face the sadness of the hotel, a large hotel full of people, yet so empty, the unknown and disturbing bedroom, the suspect bed!

. . . And the hotel dinners, those long dinners with *table*

[1] See pp. 213–4.   [2] In *Les Sœurs Rondoli*.

d'hôte, surrounded by boring or grotesque people, and the frightful solitary dinners at a little table in a restaurant lit by a miserable candle topped by a lampshade.

And the distressing evenings in the unknown city? Do you know anything more lamentable than nightfall in a strange town? . . . The heart feels crushed, the limbs slack, the soul depressed. One walks as if one were trying to escape . . .

Nevertheless, typical of the picaresque Maupassant, that adventure with the Rondoli girl turned out after all to be a *partie de plaisir*. Travel adventures could be funny, but in essence they were depressing, in their psychical background as it were. He knew he couldn't 'escape' through travelling; nor could he escape his temptation to try. What attracted him most was always *l'eau* – if not the Seine, then the sea. He bought the yacht, *Zingara*, had it renovated, renamed *Bel-Ami* and launched in Marseilles, on 18 January 1888.

Bel-Ami had a crew of two seamen, Bernard and Raymond, with whom Maupassant developed a relationship almost as idyllic as with François; he liked them for their racy tongues, and they liked him for being a sturdy companion in seafaring. His eyes were failing, but his muscles were not, and there was bliss in Nature, in the water of the Mediterranean 'limpid and blue', even more so than in Normandy. What to do next? After some cruising among God-forsaken beauty spots, to visit one Casino after another, to stage luxurious displays, to hold uproarious parties on board, with baronesses and duchesses swarming in and out. 'Voyez François,' Monsieur explained, he had to impress the rich, the *chic* world.

For all his love of money, he was no miser; was he also generous? Tassart insists that he was, but the evidence he gives is scanty. They wandered together near Antibes, in the Alpes-Maritimes, at the end of 1886, amongst poor people ruined and made homeless by an earthquake; it was a heart-rending sight, for instance, a mother with her four children crammed on to two straw mattresses joined together. Maupassant was deeply moved and dipped far in his pocket. This is, in fact, the way one would expect him to behave in the circumstances; one is only astonished (as Tassart was) that he did not write an article about them, although engaged in journalism at the time. He gave away some francs willingly when he knocked into the needy, but he did not go out of his way to find them. He was forbearing towards some who made a habit of scrounging on him; old Marte Seize, for example, a depraved *bohémienne* in Etretat, who visited him with threats of suicide and always left with a donation of ten francs. Once she brought back Maupassant's tortoises which had mysteriously strayed; she had found them near her home, she claimed, and, anyway, she was on the brink of suicide. How odd of the tortoises to make a mass exodus to that particular lady! Maupassant was amused and paid the indemnity.[1]

As to helping fellow-writers – he only did so tactfully and in secret, but had not really much to hide. Herewith one of his acts of charity – a paragraph of his letter to Havard, from *Mon Plaisir*, Cannes, 20 February 1885:

> This letter is confidential. René Maizeroy tells me that if I don't lend him 300 francs within four days, he won't have any choice but to disappear. I am answering him that I have 200 francs with you and am authorizing you to remit this sum to him. Kindly pay him 200 francs when he asks you, and charge it to me.[2]

René Maizeroy, author of the volume *Celles qui osent*, published in 1883, with a Preface by Maupassant, was in real life Baron Toussaint, who held a plot of land in the vicinity of Maupassant's house in Etretat. Judging by the Preface, Maupassant did not think much of him as a writer but liked him for liking *risqué* subjects. He was a pal rather than a colleague.

And there was noble and whimsical Villiers de l'Isle-Adam, precious old soul, distinguished symbolist, an aristocrat by blood and spirit but in plebeian penury: 'Tenez, François', Maupassant said, 'here are 100 francs, take them to him but nobody must know . . .' This happened in 1889, shortly before Villiers's death. At the same time, Maupassant told Tassart to make an arrangement for a monthly subscription of twenty francs in support of

[1] Tassart, *Souvenirs sur Guy de Maupassant* . . ., pp. 29–30, 72, 92.
[2] Maupassant's letters published by Pierre Borel, *Les Œuvres Libres*, April 1958, p. 28.

Mallarmé or his literary projects.[1] These were kind gestures; but the sums were paltry when set against what he spent on a good dinner or a bad joke.

One for whom he could never do too much was Laure Le Poittevin de Maupassant. She was beyond all and above all people on earth, whether men or women, friends, colleagues or lovers . . . the only reliable friend he had, the most loving of lovers, and even a colleague: erstwhile his guide and now his voluntary assistant who, for instance, read or re-read Turgenev when he wished to write an essay on him. Were women really nothing but copulating machines, to be appreciated only for the quality of their flesh? Madame de Maupassant put on a slightly shocked expression: 'And what about me?' – 'You are different', was the reply she both expected and received. Maupassant could not claim to be original on the matter; but he was sincere. Laure shook her head with pretended disapproval and a satisfaction she was unable to hide. She did not mind her son using any woman as a machine; it was rather Mme Lecomte du Nouÿ who got on her nerves, the polished lady in Etretat who used to read to him while he was quietly listening with his sore eyes closed . . . And she was quite enraged with an old peasant woman who claimed to have been Guy's wet nurse – 'I alone fed my son'[2] – and wouldn't share him.

Nor did he want her to share him in the deepest and highest emotional spheres, those beneath sexual desires and beyond *salon* talk. It was in her that he had confided when a miserable petty clerk in Paris:

> I feel so lost that I am forced to beg you to send me a few kind lines. Sometimes when I find myself alone at my table with my sad lamp burning before me, I experience moments of such complete sadness that I do not know on whom to throw myself. And I remind myself that you also must suffer such frightful feelings of sadness . . .[3]

[1] Tassart, *Nouveaux Souvenirs* . . ., p. 12.
[2] This happened actually after Guy's death; cf. André Vial, *La Genèse d' 'Une Vie'*, p. 39–40.
[3] 24 September 1873.

He was always worried about her: 'What worries me is the solitude in which you will find yourself this winter.'[1]

In the years of his fame and prosperity, their intimacy continued though he had always more and more to hide from her – namely, the aggravation of his illness. The greater the number of his friends, the more his mother was unique. To call his attitude generosity, or even magnanimity, would be an understatement. For her health, her comfort, her happiness – anything and everything on earth!

And her happiness included Hervé's. This was a problem for them both. Madame de Maupassant, when introducing her fifteen-year-old Guy to Flaubert as Alfred's *alter ego*,[2] had said that the younger one, Hervé, then only nine, was still no more than 'un brave petit paysan'. The trouble was that he had hardly developed beyond that, not, at any rate, mentally. He was an excellent horseman and a swaggering swashbuckler[3] – brave indeed in so far as this went; but with a mind like clay, and though fundamentally not ill-meaning, full of that sneaking malignity which is easily developed in people who feel themselves failures. He seems to have had a genuine liking for the land – the 'peasant' streak in him – and to make his occupation somewhat more intellectual and rewarding, he was to become an 'agronomist'. Guy bought him a little estate in Antibes, where he settled and ran a horticultural establishment; he married and became the father of a daughter – there were still hopes for him, and for his mother.

It did not last long. He was knocked out by syphilis – either congenital or, more likely, contracted when serving in the cavalry. He was in his early thirties when his mental disorder became too bad for him to be left at large. Guy was asked to come and help. It was his sad duty to lure his brother into the hands of the ambulance men. He attended when Hervé was put into the strait-jacket. Hervé struggled in despair: 'Guy, *you* are the madman,' he howled, 'c'est toi le fou de la famille!'[4] He was interned in an asylum in Lyons.

Maupassant visited his brother several times in his internment.

[1] 3 September 1875. [2] Quoted on p. 59.
[3] Jean Lorrain, *Villa Mauresque*, p. 8 (see footnote 1 on p. 67).
[4] Georges Normandy, Introduction to *Villa Mauresque* (note p. 8).

He found him brutal and violent; 'more irritating than pitiable' he once remarked. Next time, however, he only saw a suffering and decaying soul, who hoped desperately to leave that place.

> ... It tore my heart [Guy wrote to Countess Potocka, in 1889] and I have never suffered so much in my life. When I had to leave and when they refused to let him come with me to the station, he began to tremble in such a frightful way that I could not keep from crying as I looked at this man condemned to death, whom Nature is killing, and who will never come out of this prison and never see his mother again. . . . He feels that there is something frightening and unavoidable which has taken hold of him, without knowing what it is. . . . Alas, the poor human body, the poor soul, what a miserable, what a horrible creation it is. If I believed in the God of your religions, what endless horror I should have of him!

His most tormenting thoughts, however, were with his mother:

> ... If my brother were to die before my mother I believe I should go mad myself in thinking of the suffering of this creature. The poor woman, she has been crushed, trodden down and martyred without respite since her marriage!

Shortly afterwards, on 13 November 1889, Hervé died. Guy, by then, was on the brink of the same destiny, and his symptoms suddenly took a graver turn.[1] Hervé's spectre pursued him in his dreams, in his hallucinations. It was now Hervé who appeared dressed up as a bogey and alarmed him, just as Guy had frightened Hervé and his little pals in their childhood. The sight of his decaying brother, together with the thought of their grieving mother, was the greatest emotional tragedy in Guy de Maupassant's life; he could never forgive himself for not loving him.

---

[1] 'C'est de ce moment que les troubles, chez Guy, s'accentuent' (Dumesnil, *Guy de Maupassant*, p. 233).

In several biographies of Maupassant the role of the Villain is meted out to his distinguished elder colleague, Edmond de Goncourt. Goncourt really never harmed Maupassant; he had no power to do so. In his *Journal*, however, he unmistakably gave away his feelings: his envy of Maupassant's success whilst it lasted, his gloating over his sick and dead body later; and all this spiced with anecdotes on his lowness, meanness, perfidy, mendacity, social snobbishness, vulgarity, cruelty and sexomania. A number of his entries are eyewitness accounts; he had known Maupassant since 1874, from Flaubert's circle, and they later met quite frequently in the *salons* and literary cafés – the two top naturalists conspicuous for their *particules*! In addition, Goncourt industriously interviewed everybody likely to supply him with material: Maupassant's lady friends, from the 'velvet-like' beauty, Geneviève Halévy-Bizet-Straus, to the 'Rabelaisienne' actress, Suzanne Lagier; Maupassant's pals and coevals, Céard, Hennique, Huysmans, Alexis, Bourget; Maupassant's business associates such as the theatrical director, Koenig; and even Valentin Simond, editor of *Écho de Paris*, whose source of information was a backstair chat he had just had with Maupassant's 'valet and sort of literary secretary', Tassart . . . It was spirited research, and its presentation was carefully documented. Though biased, no doubt, most of the factual details thus recorded ring true. The *Journal* is a formidable work, nauseating as a self-portrait but outstandingly precious as a collection of contemporary documents. Goncourt composed it, through long decades, with the twin aims of venting his hatred and of securing the survival of his name.[1] He succeeded, but in doing so he cuts a pathetic figure, as does every hater not quite honest about his own motives, and every writer too keen on immortality. Yet no one interested in the world he described will ever be able to dispense with his material. Though a highly educated man, and not without talent, he would have had but a slender chance of

[1] Goncourt's idea was to release the *Journal* gradually, and selected parts were already published during his lifetime and created an uproar.

survival as a scholar or a novelist; with his sniffing and snooping, however, he made himself unforgettable for centuries to come. He should be credited for his shamelessness. It provides an entertaining guide to the notorieties of his country and his epoch, their foibles, their poses, their glamour. As to Maupassant, it would be an exaggeration to say that he emerges in purity out of the mass of mud slung at him – purity was not, after all, one of his virtues – but his sexual savageries, his brain-picking for subject-matter, his passion for money-making and mystification, his conquests and blunders in high society, his bravadoes, his anxieties and the horrid symptoms of his collapse, all recorded with relish in the *Journal*, do help us to sense the lyrical tension behind his neat and cool observation. Surely he fares better with the twentieth century than does his snarling debunker? Goncourt, with the worst of intentions, commendably sacrificed himself in the service of Guy de Maupassant's memory.

Until Flaubert's death and for about a year after, Goncourt would refer to 'le petit Maupassant' with patronizing benevolence, as a master to the disciple of a fellow-master. But as little Maupassant's sales grew bigger, Goncourt's lips became stiffer. By 1882, he was already recording that Maupassant, who had boasted to him about an amorous adventure – a wound inflicted on his fingers, according to his story, by a jealous husband, with a revolver – was 'the greatest liar' ('as Zola said', Goncourt added, and Zola may really have said so, though less snappishly, referring to Guy's bragging and fondness for mystification). So Goncourt's benevolence was fading, and by the end of that very year Maupassant had in his view been eaten up by 'industrialism', and lost to literature.

There was more to it than just Goncourt's jealousy. He rightly considered Maupassant's career, the reflection of the spirit that was ruling in France in the 1880s, and especially in her *salons*. It was a renewed Rococo style, inventive in expressing and dispelling boredom, a spleenish and frolicsome outlook on life, playfully frivolous, generous and cruel. Like its predecessor a hundred years before, it was basically agnostic; with less moral philosophy and geometry in its intellectual ferment, and with chemistry, biology, embryology instead. Its fashionable world

was conscious of being a 'hot-house plant' – and this conscious-
ness again, as under Louis XV and Louis XVI, was a source of
pride and showiness as well as of defeatism and humility. There
were no sacrosanct principles to believe in any more, neither
were Royal crowns nor business returns any longer attributed
to the grace of God: social and financial prominence derived
from 'the survival of the fittest', and the grandsons and great-
granddaughters of the fittest were only more refined than the
rest because they had been bred and brought up to be so. It may
not last for ever, so its credo ran, but it should be enjoyed as long
as it does last.

Goncourt hated all this. And he hated it the more bitterly
that he had no moral ground on which to base his hatred. He
could take pride, as occasionally he did, in being one of its protagonists. He had rediscovered the beauties of eighteenth-
century fine arts for his contemporaries; he had stood up for the
graceful flippancies of the decadent *ancien régime* in face of both
ecclesiastic and republican prudishness. And whilst hoping for
a revival of that charming old world, he was far too intelligent
to think that its ways could ever be repeated. Nor did he really
aim at this. With all his nostalgia for the past, and his speculation on the curiosity of the future, he was very much a man of his
own age, at one with his best contemporaries in detecting the
artistic value of factuality, in daring to record biological symptoms exactly in a novel. He was no conformist; though busy
trying to resurrect time-worn authorities that were slumbering
in their crypts, he was most critical of what had survived of
them: 'Académie' was as dirty a word for him as was 'democratic'. What he had dreamt of as his ideal surrounding was a
powerful neo-Versailles where the highly educated beneficiaries
of leisure should be as familiar with natural sciences and Naturalist arts as those of ancient Versailles had been with the Encyclopaedia. The dream had now materialized; and it was agony to
see what it was like in reality. Goncourt incessantly fulminated
against the *chic* world: how cheap its taste, how phoney its
values, how nauseating its proneness to the appeal of money, its
gullibility to appearances, the journalese stigma of its witti-
cisms, the insipidness of its pastimes. That Mme Straus! She
was a collector of princesses and duchesses; Goncourt had never

yet seen so many blue-blooded aristocrats gathered together as he did at her parties;[1] but as soon as there was a Rothschild in sight, she would drop them all for him – 'il faut qu'elle s'attache à lui', as her bosom friend, Princess Mathilde, cattily remarked.[2] Mme Straus would make an appearance in flesh-coloured stockings, like 'no stockings at all', which, again, according to her bosom friend, was a *cocotte* fashion.[3] And look how she would spend her time. With another highly fashionable lady, Mme Lippmann, they would set out for a journey: first to the 'marchande de mode', then to the 'lingère', and so on and so forth, and end up with the fortune-teller, 'à salons dorés'. Goncourt was exasperated. 'Ça, des femmes du monde? Non! ce sont des fausses cocottes.'[4]

Certainly his anger sounds more biblical than eighteenth century; what was behind it? Sour grapes? No doubt, to a large extent. Goncourt felt he was let down by those who should have acclaimed him. He was admitted, he was respected, but only just. His authority and popularity in the liberal *salons* was nothing when compared with that of Taine and Renan and Zola whom he loathed; the late Flaubert was the only one he was willing to admit as almost his equal. Surely he, Goncourt, was too good for his age, too noble for that adulterated aristocracy which fed on commerce and compromised with the Republic? Princess Mathilde, focal figure of social life in the literary world, was herself too much of a democrat, certainly not exclusive enough for Goncourt's taste; her *salon* in rue de Berri packed with *juiverie*;[5] the stuff she wrote, dull and barely mediocre. 'There are no more princesses today,' Goncourt sighed. He was running down an article by Mathilde Bonaparte on Théophile Gautier, and about this he may have been right; it was just typical of so many charming patronesses of arts who cannot resist the temptation to emulate their own *protégés*. But, to do her justice, she never tried to make people forget about her plebeian background. As to the Great Revolution denigrated by her admirers, 'if it weren't for that', she used to say, 'I'd be selling

---

[1] *Journal*, Vol. III, p. 680.
[3] *Journal*, Vol. III, p. 1129.
[5] *Journal*, Vol. IV, p. 942.

[2] *Journal*, Vol. III, p. 733.
[4] *Journal*, Vol. III, p. 959.

oranges in a street in Ajaccio'. Was her title's attraction *her* responsibility?

The two 'false cocottes' whose tour in Paris was followed by Goncourt with such despair were both wives of rich Jews; one, actually a Jewess herself, *née* Halévy, and married to the lawyer, Emile Straus – a couple who had an important part to play in Maupassant's life; the other, the elder daughter of Dumas-*fils* and of a Russian princess, was married to that most horrid of all the Jewish businessmen as Goncourt saw him, Maurice Lippmann, whose face beamed with pride as if boasting, 'I could get as many marquises as I like for my money . . .'[1] This pointed to the root of the evil. Like many a titled malcontent, Goncourt got used to blaming his torments on the Jews. They were the 'masters of France'; and their wives and lady friends, with their 'esprit de journal', the dictators of taste. It is, he complains, in the *hôtels* dominated by such women in Paris, in Deauville, in Fontainebleau, at the tea-parties from 5 to 7 p.m., that the young men of letters *arrivent*.[2] The Jews, with the 'petitesse de leur race', with their mercenary-mindedness, had defiled France; the debasement and commercialization of arts and letters were their responsibility.

This indeed could be proved; they were the most efficient dealers in art, vulgarizers of ideas, manufacturers of opinion of the *boulevards*. The only trouble was that the opposite could also be proved; they were in the vanguard of any daring venture of art and thought, the patrons of nonconformist literature. Without their assistance, and without that of foreigners who had only just taken root in France, no French man of letters with an independent mind could have set his foot in any of the stately French *hôtels*.[3] Goncourt was aware of this: 'only Jewesses read – and dare to admit it – young talents scorned by the Académie such as Huysmans', he sighed.[4] He was indignant about their 'daring' as well as about others not 'daring'.

Goncourt shared with other anti-Semites the habit of grossly

[1] *Journal*, Vol. III, p. 1085.
[2] *Journal*, Vol. III, p. 140 (7 January 1882).
[3] See Appendix 5.
[4] *Journal*, 25 February 1883.

overestimating the abilities of the Jews and in being intrigued by their entourage. Though an avowed sympathizer with anti-Semitic pamphleteering, he was a keen visitor of 'Jewish'[1] *salons* – which involved him in awkward imbroglios on both sides. Some of his exchanges on the matter, and his accounts of them in the *Journal*, are very funny indeed. In June 1891, for instance, at the peak of a scandal in which his alleged duplicity was being discussed, he met at a party 'le Straus' (as he contemptuously referred to Jews) and after some embarrassed beating about the bush, they discussed the delicate matter amicably. Goncourt, we read, explained that he was indeed 'the theoretical enemy of the Jewish race,' but this did not prevent him from 'being friends with individual Jews'. Though 'le Straus' did not think de Goncourt's proceeding entirely beyond reproach, he understood and they shook hands.[2]

With the smart Jewesses his attitude was even more ambivalent, it was *Hassliebe* undiluted and sparkling. He was fascinated by their 'nonchalance particulière', their movements of 'chatte paresseuse', their languidness and their dark complexion; and when blonde, he added, it was the Titian shimmer of gold through darkness. The curls of Mme Cahen d'Anvers appeared like a nest of snakes . . .[3] And Mme Albert Cahen, and Mme Kann, and again and again Mme Straus who, though not genuine enough for a courtesan according to one of his entries, was a real 'femme d'esprit' in others. . . . Should they be cursed or admired? He could not make up his mind. But he certainly could not remain indifferent about whom *they* liked. And they liked Maupassant more than they liked anybody else. He had become Lion no. 1 of their *salons*.

Goncourt was shocked. He found this a depressing show; but he never decided on whose behalf to find it depressing. Should he be sorry for that gifted young nobleman attracted and mesmerized by such phoney creatures? Or rather for those

[1] They were really a very mixed cosmopolitan circle, racially as well as confessionally, with the rich Jew, who brought his children up as devoted Roman Catholics, as a permanent feature. See Appendix 5.

[2] *Journal*, Vol. IV, pp. 109–10.

[3] *Journal*, Vol. III, p. 66.

polished and graceful *femmes du monde*, impressed and duped by that uncouth Norman literary salesman?

In the first years of Maupassant's success, there were still moments when Goncourt regarded him as a professional accomplice – almost as his own secret agent amongst the smart and uninitiated. Goncourt was the president of the Flaubert Memorial Committee; Maupassant, its secretary. When meeting in this capacity, they talked little Flaubert and much *boudoir*. They were both experts; if Goncourt knew more about Mme de Pompadour and Marie-Antoinette, Maupassant knew more about those Orléans now retired in luxurious privacy on the Côte d'Azur, and Princess Sagan, and Baroness Alphonse Rothschild, at the very peak of the *chic* world of the day. Goncourt was pleased to record that Maupassant, just back from Cannes, had come to see him – about the Memorial – and had recounted to him the amusing intimacies of that circle. Mme de Rothschild, the 'hunting Jewess', taking special exercises in jumping, on a patch of lawn specially watered so as to keep it soft in case she fell! And so forth . . . 'And he [Maupassant] gives me to understand,' Goncourt concludes his entry,[1] 'very exactly and very intelligently, that he finds amongst these people the types of men and women he requires for the novel he is planning about the *monde*, the Paris society and its love affairs.'

Goncourt was also pleased to note Maupassant amongst others attending his 'Grenier' which was to continue Flaubert's Sunday afternoons; and Maupassant published a flattering 'letter' about such a gathering: 'certes . . . ce qu'on peut voir de plus intéressant à Paris, en ce moment'.[2] Until 1886, apparently, Maupassant did not notice Goncourt's hostility.

Nor was Goncourt quite clear yet about his own feelings. In any case, he liked to stress his superiority over Maupassant. He could do so on safe ground when comparing his own expertness in collecting *bibelots* with Maupassant's lush and unselective taste. That famous apartment in 10 rue Montchanin, on

[1] *Journal*, Vol. III, p. 406.
[2] *Journal*, Vol. III, p. 505; *Gil Blas*, 24 November 1885.

which Maupassant had spent so much time and money, was an
ideal butt for Goncourt's barbs. 'Its furniture, like a whore's!'
he triumphed. 'Just imagine, skyblue wainscot in a man's home,
a glass half veiled with a plush curtain above the chimney-piece,
a set of quite turquoise Sèvres porcelain' – the commercial
variety of Sèvres, he explained. 'How unfair of God to have given
such abominable taste to a man of talent!'[1] Goncourt seems to
have been right about Maupassant's taste, but just a bit too
pleased about God's unfairness.

This entry is dated 18 December 1884 – peak moment, as it
were, of Maupassant's prolificacy. From then on Goncourt, in
gossip with his friends, elaborated with gusto on the subject,
and it took a comparatively long time – about two years – before
Maupassant learned, thanks to well-wishing informers, that according to Edmond de Goncourt his cherished 10 rue Montchanin was a 'logis de souteneur caraïbe'.[2] He hit back – slightly
under the belt – on the first occasion which offered, on the Flaubert Memorial Committee.

The committee had planned to erect a Flaubert statue in
Rouen for which 12,000 francs was needed, but, by early 1887,
only 9,000 francs had been collected. Various ideas were broached
to make up the balance. A journalist under the pen-name 'San-
tillane', in *Gil Blas*, reproached Committee members with good
incomes, Goncourt, Maupassant, Zola, Daudet, for toying with
such schemes instead of providing the money themselves. The
article contained a particularly unpleasant reference to Goncourt
who, so the argument ran, had enough money for a future
Académie Goncourt to immortalize himself, but not for a
monument to his great friend. . . . Maupassant promptly replied to the paper, expressing his approval and announcing his
readiness to contribute 1,000 francs. A generous gesture – except
that it ignored the personal attack on his friend and President of
the Committee. Goncourt, offended, handed in his resignation
of the presidency, with a subscription of 500 francs. Maupassant
offered his apologies, asserting that he had overlooked the special
reference to Goncourt; which was either true or not . . . Where-

---

[1] *Journal*, Vol. III, p. 406.

[2] Cf. Dumesnil, *Guy de Maupassant*, p. 227, referring to an unpublished
letter of Henry Céard.

upon Goncourt withdrew his resignation, reconciled, at any rate, on the surface; but not in the *Journal.*

There were really two things Goncourt could not forgive Maupassant; that he was accepted as a real gentleman, not just as a writer; and that he was accepted as a real writer, not just as a gentleman.

Soon after the Memorial squabble had been patched up, they met at Princess Mathilde's where Goncourt felt he found the exact definition of what Maupassant was like: 'the image and type of the young Norman horsetrader'.[1] He had never seen any gentleman of fashion with a more red complexion, common features and low-class appearance, and one who wore clothes that looked as if they came from a cheap off-the-peg store and hats stuck back as far as his ears. Could such a man be a real *de* Maupassant? But if only people were content to treat him as such! Almost immediately after the above-quoted entry, Goncourt wondered: 'Why is it that, in many people's eyes, Edmond de Goncourt is a gentleman, an amateur, an aristocrat just toying with literature, yet Guy de Maupassant is a real man of letters? Why, I should like to know.'[2]

Because de Maupassant was the better author – this would be the obvious answer; but not the pertinent answer. Goncourt, as an author, could hold his own. What did and does make him look amateurish and, indeed, silly was precisely his solemnity in professionalism, his posterity-mindedness, his gate-crashing into the Pantheon. Maupassant could always beat him with his deeper sense of futility.

Maupassant had a well-known inferiority complex, mistaken by many for pride,[3] *orgueil*: he was shy of 'talking literature'. He knew he was no good at theorizing, either verbally or in writing, and would get quite panic-stricken if interviewed on 'literary trends'.[4] Once he braced himself to expound his views *Sur le Roman,* and this ominous essay, badly cut by the editor

[1] *Journal*, Vol. III, p. 641.   [2] *Journal*, Vol. III, p. 659.
[3] Cf. Paul Léautaud's accounts, quoted on p. 98.
[4] As reported, *inter alia*, by Jules Huret in his *Enquête sur l'Evolution Littéraire,* Paris, 1891.

of the *Figaro Littéraire*, was then restored and corrected by him and published in full as a Preface to his novel, *Pierre et Jean*,[1] in January 1888. On the whole it was a defence of the novelist's right to write as he pleased; and particularly of Guy de Maupassant's right to write 'objective' novels. And slightly out of context, it contained this sentence:

> There is no need for that bizarre, involved, numerous and fanciful ['Chinese'] vocabulary which is nowadays imposed upon us as *artistic writing* ['*écriture artiste*'] in order to express all the subtleties of thought. [. . .] The French language is a clear stream which artificial writers have never been able and will never be able to disturb . . .'[2]

For reasons difficult to understand today this was read at that time as a broad hint at Goncourt, and smacked of some slyness as innuendoes usually do. Maupassant, probably to relieve his conscience, made a clumsy gesture: ignoring his attack but simultaneously with its publication, he sent a letter by post to Goncourt (according to the *Journal*) 'assuring me of his admiration and attachment. This compels me to think him a very Norman Norman. Incidentally [Goncourt repeats] Zola told me that he was the king of liars . . .' As to the question of style, Maupassant may be an 'adroit *novelliere*', but he is

> no writer, and he has his own reasons to disparage *écriture artiste*. The writer, since La Bruyère, Bossuet, Saint-Simon, and continuing through Chateaubriand and finishing with Flaubert, has always 'signed' his sentences and made them identifiable to the *lettrés* without his signature, and without this there can be no great writer; well, if a page of Maupassant is not signed, it is just a good copy of current stuff and might have been written by anybody. – Guichet, last Sunday, made the best remark on his indisputable and, at the same time, second-rate talent: he said that his books *se lisaient, mais ne se relisaient pas* [would get themselves read but not re-read].[3]

[1] See pp. 104–5 and 107 and 112.
[2] *La langue française est une eau pure que les écrivains maniérés n'ont jamais pu et ne pourront jamais troubler . . .*
[3] *Journal*, Vol. III, p. 740.

Goncourt had something here, but he certainly missed the point. The strongest argument against Maupassant's simple and hollow theory is Maupassant's ingenious and sophisticated practice. Pages and pages of his writings, whole volumes perhaps, read like anybody else's work and then a character or a scene comes to life in his own inimitable way; and a searcher for the clues to this legerdemain, when analysing his sentences and paragraphs, will come across a most involved pattern showing the marks left on French style by a great variety of *écrivains maniérés*, stretching from epochs earlier than La Bruyère's to influences more recent than Flaubert's. His 'objective' sentences, usually short, dry, frequently recalling the rhythm of a Stop Press column in a daily paper, alternate with paragraphs of a vibrating, impressionist lyricism, akin to the poetry of his contemporaries, Verlaine and Mallarmé.[1] He made his peasants talk in a Norman dialect which could be enjoyed even by those who did not understand every word; was that not 'Chinese'? He was not at all particular about neologisms and barbarisms; in spite of his ignorance of the English language – or, maybe, because of it – some of his passages read like an early sample of what is today ridiculed as *Franglais*: the use in current French writing of the expression 'high-life', for instance, is supposed to be his innovation which, for good or evil, certainly does not strike one as a molecule of 'l'eau pure'. There is no pure water in nature, and no pure language in literature; there is distilled water in the laboratory, and there are words reduced to semantic symbols – but it was certainly not such pure substances Maupassant was seeking. Anatole France wrote about him that his three main virtues were 'clarity; and clarity; and, again, clarity'.

[1] This has been most carefully demonstrated by André Vial in his *Guy de Maupassant et l'Art du Roman*. About Maupassant's ways of applying the Norman dialect, cf. *Les parlers populaires dans l'œuvre de Guy de Maupassant*, by Anthony Butler (1962), and *Explication de Maupassant*, by Charles Bruneau (1941), dealing mainly with the idiomatic expressions in the short story, *Le Petit Fût*. M. Bruneau demonstrates the authenticity of the peasants' dialogue in Maupassant's stories and emphasizes that Maupassant's own language, unlike theirs, was essentially a *written* one. René Dumesnil, in his works several times quoted in the course of this book, has also interesting observations on Maupassant's use of idiomatic phrases, e.g. in his stories, *Une Vente* and *Le Père Milon*.

This in a way was true; for he had the gift to draw from any stream of language just as much as he needed to make his meaning clear, his text easily readable, his sentences appearing as a natural flow. It was a combination of *manières*, and a *manière* itself; a most engaging and often unnoticeable style – but why should it be the only permissible one? Maupassant himself did not really think it should be; Rabelais, whom he (and Flaubert!) so infinitely admired, excelled in a vocabulary as 'bizarre' and 'Chinese' as anybody's. But, to quote Anatole France once again, Maupassant when he explained why he wrote as he did was like a lion expounding the theory of courage; and, on this occasion, it was an offended lion, apparently unable to forget that his den had been compared to a 'logis de souteneur caraïbe'.

Nevertheless, had Goncourt come out into the open with his arguments, quite an interesting literary debate might have developed. Nothing like this happened. Goncourt gritted his teeth; he was obsessed with hatred. His proper platform was, he felt, the *Journal*; in its pages, he appealed to posterity for a just verdict in his litigation with Maupassant's spectre. As to the exhibits produced, very few referred to the merits and/or demerits of the *écriture artiste*; rather he concentrates on personal detail, for instance, only one month after the above-quoted entry he noted:

> Sunday, February 5th – Huysmans talked to me of the way Maupassant liked to surprise people, men and women, when he received them in intimacy: by painting a 'con' on his navel, with figurations of hair and large and small lips, and by painting his 'verge' vermillion with huge cankers on it: farces of a filth-loving commercial traveller.[1]

And so on, and so forth.

There was never an open clash between Goncourt and Maupassant. They remained on cool and civil terms; when they met now they shook hands but did not talk, not even *boudoir*.

They met at the unveiling of Flaubert's monument, ten years after his death. Goncourt, in his speech, invoked Maupassant by name, correctly, as one of those nearest to the late master. On

[1] Vol. III, p. 748.

his return, he noted in his *Journal* that he had found Maupassant haggard and with staring eyes, 'less vulgar than usual'.[1]

About one year after Maupassant's death,[2] Goncourt made reference, *en passant* as it were, to 'the oblivion into which Maupassant is supposed to have fallen'; and from then on the paragraphs on Maupassant in the *Journal* became, if not more tender, at any rate much rarer.

So much for the relations between the two novelists. But this is only a fraction of the information supplied on Maupassant in the *Journal*. We shall occasionally return to this source, mainly to share with Goncourt in the glimpses he gave of Maupassant's *monde* and some of its most picturesque hostesses.

40 · Cruelty and compassion

Maupassant's third novel, *Mont-Oriol*, published between *Bel-Ami* and *Pierre et Jean*, in 1887, definitely dealt with the *haute bourgeoisie* which by then had absorbed the worldly part of the ancient aristocracy. There is in it a Jewish banker who turns everything into gold through cheating and speculation; a peasant landowner who turns everything into gold through avarice and usury; a nice but spineless marquis who admires these efficient or sturdy money-makers and is glad to see his family intermarried with theirs. As to the younger generations, the son of the marquis is a spendthrift masher, born to be a pimp if anything; and he has a bosom friend, a rich trader's son, more sympathetic, more poetically minded, who knows some Baudelaire by heart, but does not differ from the rest in essentials, and is carried away by their ways. It was noted by the critics that Maupassant's *impassibilité* in this novel gave way to some extent to lyrical compassion – towards the marquis's daughter, a frail and delicate but empty-minded woman. She is married to the plump, rich banker for whom she does not care, not even to the extent of being disgusted with him; she commits adultery with

[1] Vol. III, p. 951, on 29 March 1889.
[2] Vol. IV, p. 625, on 15 August 1894.

the Baudelairian *amoroso* because it is in her nature to yield rather than for any other reason; she only falls in love with her seducer when she realizes she is with child by him. Her tragedy is that this rather revolts her lover:

> She did not appreciate that this man belonged to the race of lovers and not at all to the race of fathers. As soon as he learnt that she was pregnant, he turned away from her, feeling disgusted with her in spite of himself. He had often repeated formerly that a woman was no longer worthy of love once she undertook the function of reproduction. What he admired in the female body was Venus, whose sacred thighs ought always to preserve the pure form of sterility. The idea of a little being who was his own offspring, a human larva moving within the body and already making it defiled and ugly, produced in him an almost insuperable feeling of repulsion. Maternity made an animal of this woman.

Her heart is almost broken, then, when her lover marries one of the two daughters of the rich peasant, whilst her brother marries the other. But everybody survives, there is a happy ending for all, mainly due to the genius of the Jewish banker who launches a legend about the miraculous healing properties of the springs of 'Mont-Oriol' and establishes a spa with fascinating prospects of business returns. Participating in the deal are his wife's father and brother and lover, the rich peasant and some society doctors of high reputation who act as expert quacks. And so also does a tramp who knows what is behind the legend of the miraculous springs and successfully blackmails the spa-creating banker. But on a smaller scale, all the inhabitants of the district profit from the establishment; general welfare thrives on cheating.

All this is about rich men and their associates; the *petites gens* only come into it as background characters or as the funny villain, the tramp who tricked the rich as the rich tricked the world. This distribution of roles according to social status might well have been modelled on a Shakespeare comedy, however modern its setting. Taine's forecast was now entirely fulfilled, though with results very different from those expected by him: Maupassant focused his camera on the upper classes, but instead of discovering in those 'hot-house' plants 'honour and *esprit*', divulged an opulent vegetation of lies and stupidities. There was no implied protest in his doing so. Unlike Zola and even the smooth Dumas-*fils*, or later Bourget or Anatole France for that matter, Maupassant did not add any note of moral or social criticism to his observations; not, in any case, in his novels and short stories. When it came to individuals, his *impassibilité* now and then softened, but not with communities and their problems. War, as will be remembered, was the sole exception, but this did not come into the picture in *Mont-Oriol*.

At the beginning of the decade, in a satirical story[1] he had made a wise-cracker profess to have three political principles:

Principle No. 1: Government by one man is a monstrosity.
Principle No. 2: Restricted suffrage is an injustice.
Principle No. 3: Universal suffrage is stupidity.

This might well be taken as Maupassant's political credo. He tended, in the meantime, towards vesting his hopes in the emergence of a new and liberal *élite*, a technocracy selected from schools and business, of persons skilled in engineering all sorts of machinery, including that of the modern State. Until that came about, there was nothing better than the free and comparatively peaceful interplay of corruption, with hard-boiled money-grubbers as its heroes. These got the rewards they deserved, one, like the banker in *Mont-Oriol*, by being cuckolded, and the other, like the greedy great farmer, by marrying his daughter to a pimp. Actually poetic retribution in both these forms had been meted out to the Monsieur Walter of *Bel-Ami*, the cleverest racketeer of them all.

Mont-Oriol is a second-rate novel[2] but with beautiful patches and in many ways it is revealing. It showed Maupassant's revulsion for maternity. This did not prevent him from adoring it in his own mother; nor from describing maternal attachment most tenderly, in a sturdy, rustic peasant maid (*Histoire d'une Fille de Ferme*), no less than in the aristocratic heroine of *Une Vie*.

[1] *Les Dimanches d'un bourgeois de Paris*, 1880.
[2] Tolstoy loathed it as much as he loved *Une Vie*.

Whilst agreeing, on the whole, with his hero in *Mont-Oriol* that a beautiful body should not be allowed to be deformed by pregnancy, he could be moved by motherhood and even by its ugly trivialities; but, as an author, he did not extend this tenderness to children. Human beings, under the age of sexual maturity, are, by the testimony of his writings, a nuisance if anything. *Le Papa de Simon* (1879), his early story of an illegitimate child, which is highly thought of by many, does express compassion but is really a sloppy piece of writing; whereas *L'Armoire* which is the very opposite of sloppy[1] evokes compassion for a prostitute's son and for his conditions of life, but hardly touches on his character. What did he feel when conceiving and writing *Le Mal d'André*? This describes the way a brutish young captain tortures baby André into silence so as to be able to make love to his mother undisturbed. The baby is half dead and all the other *dramatis personae* – father, mother, nurse – are sufferers; the officer alone is happy. As Jules Lemaître remarked, we feel that it is wrong to be amused by the story and yet it is terribly funny. We really should not laugh, but cannot help it.

Did Guy Maupassant never feel like playing with children? Did he never enjoy their babblings and find interest in watching their development? If he did, he must have considered it a weakness and managed to hide it more carefully than anything else – certainly more than his lust for money and sexual orgies. He does, in fact, seem to have had a hidden life where he indulged his paternal feelings in secret just as some exemplary fathers would keep their illicit loves in dark corners. Amongst his many mistresses, there was a young lady of Strasbourg who bore him three children – in 1883, 1884 and 1887 – and he visited them frequently. Nothing was known about these children in his life-time; the first article pointing towards their existence was published in 1903, ten years after his death; and, strangely enough, since then, hardly any notice has been taken of this whole affair by the Maupassant biographers. Surely it rings a too romantic note to be easily believed; but so conscientious a scholar as René Dumesnil has quoted its source[2] without ex-

[1] See Chapter 35.

[2] *Guy de Maupassant*, note, p. 194, referring, *inter alia*, to an account by A. Nardy, in *Mercure de France*, 1 January 1927.

pressing any doubt about its reliability. What, then, was Maupassant's reason for keeping so carefully silent about his illegitimate children? A dozen guesses may sound credible; but there was in his relationship with them something that he was never able to express articulately, a despotic feeling he was never able to come to terms with, and which was to become manifest in the outbursts of his lunatic obsessions.

A picnic party in *Mont-Oriol*, including the delicate heroine, is proceeding by coach, and then:

> Suddenly in the middle of a little pine forest the landau stopped and the coachman began to swear; an old ass was barring the way.
>
> Everyone wanted to see and so they got out. The ass was stretched out, a dark patch in the grey dust, and so thin that its skin, from which the bones stuck out, would have been split by them, if the beast had not drawn its last breath. The whole of the carcase could be seen defined under the mangy skin of its sides, and its head appeared enormous, a poor head with eyes closed, tranquil on its bed of crushed stones, so tranquil, so dead that it seemed happy and surprised at this novel repose. Its large ears, still soft, lay like rags. Two open wounds on its hocks spoke of frequent falls that day before it collapsed for the last time, and another wound on its flank showed where for years and years its master had pricked it with an iron-pointed stick to make it hasten its slow steps.
>
> The coachman, taking it by the hind legs, dragged it towards the ditch, and the neck stretched out as if to bray again to utter its last note of protest. When it had been pulled on to the grass, the man, now furious, muttered, 'What brutes to leave that in the middle of the road.'
>
> No one else spoke; everyone got back into the carriage.

It is this spectacle which makes the heroine of the novel, that 'hot-house' plant, realize for the first time what 'la misère des créatures esclaves' is like – but whatever one's judgment of her character and of the novel as a whole, the life and death of a toiling animal cannot be visualized more perfectly than it is in these snapshots of a donkey's corpse. It is the finest compound of Maupassant's styles: *impassibilité*, objective observation, as the basic attitude; the action or situation described in short and dry sentences; the 'Naturalist' interest in the anatomical and visual details; 'Impressionist' lyricism flowing in longer sentences, with the throbs of a panting breast, with the repetition of nouns and adjectives – 'sa tête . . . cette pauvre tête; . . . tranquille . . . si tranquille' – when a new shade of sentiment can be added by it: the sentiment of compassion this time which, in line with the basic attitude, must stop short of taking up the cause of harassed and exploited creatures, either as a kind of a R.S.P.C.A. or Trade Union advocate. There is also irony in the description; and some cruelty in making use of it.

Maupassant often seems callous. His friend, Porto-Riche, called him a 'moral impotent'. Indeed, his lack of commitment makes one shudder now and then; it is magnificent but inhuman. 'His indifference,' Anatole France wrote,[1] 'equals that of nature; it astonishes me, it irritates me. I should like to know what that pitiless, robust and good man really believes and feels in his heart of hearts.' Does he really not suffer, Anatole France wonders, when describing wretched people so perfectly and so entertainingly? Pol Neveux says Maupassant simply conjures people to life, without any *arrière-pensée*, as a real conjurer would. These are tremendous shortcomings, but they stem from his tremendous powers; it is no good ignoring them. Why should he be like any honest man? Why should a stone-faced god turn out to have a quivering heart like the frail mortals struck with awe by his imperturbability?

Yet, however naïve it may be to defend Maupassant against moral accusations, it would be no less naïve to think that they contain the final truth about his character. His callousness was genuine; but, like his style, most complicated in substance. Active cruelty no doubt came into it; and so, even more, did pity. Pol Neveux, while fascinated by the playful 'conjurer' in him, also detects universal pity as the main characteristic of his mind.[2] Maupassant found pleasure in cruel farce, and yet was overwhelmed by compassion. In his best pages there is evidence

[1] *La Vie littéraire*, Vol. I, p. 56.
[2] 'Sa compassion est infinie pour tout ce qui vit misérablement', Preface to *Œuvres complètes*.

of both, though in unequal proportions; about children, he could write best when in a cruel mood, and about animals, when compassionate. Baby André suffering under the brutal pinches of a stranger was funny; the dog left to the mercy of stronger dogs, and the bird under the shotgun,[1] and the donkey under the stick were tragic. All, of course, were both funny and tragic; but about his relationship with animals, he had less to hide.

41 · Bourget

Next to Maupassant, the brightest and most irritating young literary star in those cursed 'Jewish' *salons*, as Goncourt saw it, was Paul Bourget. Indeed, Maupassant and Bourget shone as twin stars at that time, with analogies and contrasts in their characters of which both were only too conscious. Today, Bourget has for at least thirty years been the most forgotten of erstwhile famous authors, and there is no reason to rediscover him either as a thinker or as an artist; but as a case history of intellectual success, his career deserves comment.

He was a many-sided and devoted reader, extremely sensitive of the values which an intelligent young man was supposed to cherish. Son of a provincial university professor of mathematics, he had hesitated between the medical profession and literature until he – or rather, his father – decided for the Sorbonne and the humanities. He started early by publishing poetry and literary criticism, often in the same papers as Maupassant; and then essays with a view to illustrating 'la Psychologie contemporaine', initially under the influence of Taine whose spirit fluttered above him rather like Flaubert's above Maupassant. The two young men – Bourget was actually Maupassant's younger by two years – met frequently in Zola's entourage, both mixing readily with the modern novelists whilst conspicuously differing from them: Maupassant in being more of a savage oarsman than the rest, and Bourget in being more of a scholar, priestly though by no means bigoted. Both had their reservations towards the Natural-

[1] *Pierrot* and *Amour*.

ist school: Maupassant because it was, after all, a school; and Bourget, because it was not sufficiently spiritual.

Bourget's most important essays in 'contemporary psychology' were erudite and polished portraits of the great writers of his country and century, some by then dead, others still alive, but all substantially his elders and already recognized as masters. His other valuable achievement consisted of popularizing English life and literature, traditions and fashions, which he profoundly admired and carefully studied.

All this would amply account for his kindly reception as an essayist; but why, one wonders, that eruptive interest in him, far beyond the usual circle of literary scholarship? The reason is that he was fundamentally a politician, a 'politician of culture' as he would be termed in some countries today. As to daily politics, he was at that time no more and no less interested in them than most of his colleagues; his ideal was the Perennial. But, like many another lofty soul, he was mainly concerned with selling the perennial values to temporal powers; and, in addition, with selling himself. To do so successfully, he had to please two establishments: the traditionalist and the millionaire. One was the world of the Church, the Army, the Académie Française and the ancient châteaux which went on inspiring French literature though no longer supplying readers; the other, that of the liberal *salons*, in Faubourg Saint-Honoré, in Cannes, in Deauville, one-third Jewish, one-third *métèque*, one-third Imperial and bohemian *à la* Princesse Mathilde. In literary criticism, the former had its most popular chronicler in Sarcey, and its most spirited crusader in Brunetière; the latter, its most sophisticated spokesmen in the 'Impressionist' critics, Lemaître and Anatole France. In practical matters, the dividing line between these two ruling sets often dwindled; they were united in business interests, in social gatherings, in loveless marriages and extramarital love affairs; (cf. amongst other documents, *Bel-Ami* and *Mont-Oriol*). But on the plane of ideas, the irreconcilable had still to be reconciled. For this task, Bourget was the chosen man. With his reverence for everything Great – a bishop, a banker, an author – he touched on the keyword under which all gods could be satisfied without even the appearance of hesitating between their cults. This keyword was 'psychology'.

To see how he turned this one key in all locks which he felt worth opening, let us have a glance at his handling of Baudelaire – the 'Satanist' poet of *l'Art pour l'Art*, raved over by the polished ladies of the plutocracy, frowned upon by the upholders of public morality. Bourget diagnosed in him 'les mornes ivresses de la Vénus vulgaire'; appreciated him as an artist representative of his epoch which he viewed with apprehension. 'The murderous rage of the conspirators of St Petersburg, the books of Schopenhauer, the furious flames of the Commune, and the passionate misanthropy of the Naturalist novelists . . . reveal the same *esprit de négation*.' The lady who sighed about the futility of life in her villa in Cannes could agree, and so could the priest who sighed about the immorality of that lady. In fact, Baudelaire would have been quite happy to read this appreciation, in his somewhat adolescent pride on producing the 'flowers of Evil'. And, to do Bourget justice, it was quite a competent portrayal; there was just a shade of superfluous unctuousness in his verbiage – which was, from his point of view, not superfluous at all: for it was this which made his admiration for naughty masters go down with those shocked by the masters themselves. He had the genius of conformism. He knew how much to dare and when to stop. Though an enthusiastic admirer of Zola in the cafés, he did not include him in the series of essays on his colleagues because, he argued, Zola happened to be some years younger than the others. On the other hand, he tried his best to build up an image of a Renan acceptable to the Roman Catholics. This was too ambitious a diplomatic venture to succeed, but was not altogether futile: in reward, Bourget's ideas were embraced simultaneously by Christian devotees and Jewish baronesses. The latter did not always limit themselves to his psyche; his amour with Mme Cahen d'Anvers – actually a countess – was a well-known feature of French literary life.[1]

In his middle-thirties, Bourget took to fiction-writing, and

[1] Provided that the Mme Cahen d'Anvers, mentioned for example in *Anatole France par lui-même*, by Jacques Suffel, Seuil, 1957, as being known for 'se consacrant au triomphe de Paul Bourget' (p. 30) was the same as the lady registered by the annotator of the unexpurgated *Journal des Goncourt* as 'Comtesse Louis Cahen d'Anvers'.

his star rose even higher. It was agreed that his style was poor, but, again, there was the merit of striking a balance between traditionalist and Naturalist ways and presenting the outcome not as a compromise but as a new venture. And, again, it was 'psychology': observation, yes, but focused on souls rather than bodies and objects, even at the cost of lengthiness. He was encouraged to take this course by his favourite author, Balzac; and today he seems vindicated in his belief that it was worth trying the reader's patience with detailed descriptions of mental processes – Proust, amongst others, provided the proof. So much for his flair as a cultural politician; but as a novelist, he was simply dull and highbrow. All the same, he was acclaimed as an innovating genius and grew to be a *complex* with practically all his colleagues, both old and young.

With Goncourt, this complex took the shape of contemptuous chilliness. Envy and peevishness immunized him against being duped; he did not give in for a moment to the Bourget fashion and, with laudable lack of gratitude, refused to be impressed by Bourget's numerous gestures of reverence towards himself. Nor was he willing to consider Bourget as a kindred soul in their horror of the democratic trends of the century: 'Yes, I did stand for refinement,' he noted, 'but it was a different sort of refinement.'[1] Bourget, the middle-class snob of the aristocracy, the well-groomed climber, who made up to the priests and the Jews, the Académie Française and the bankers, who raved with the same awe about the one and a half million francs dowry of a Rothschild girl as about the saints of Roman Catholicism or the architectural marvels of Oxford, was, wherever he stood, whomever he courted, the embodiment of that commercialized society which they both professed to despise. If he, Goncourt, condescended to talk to Bourget at all, he only did it to serve posterity – that is, to gather intimate notes (*inter alia* about Maupassant) for his *Journal*; and Bourget, as we shall come to see, was willing to oblige.

Bourget's finest hour came with the publication of his most memorable novel, *Le Disciple*, in 1889. In this *roman à thèse*, he made it clear that when a choice was called for between tradition and liberalism, he opted for tradition. With his excellent

[1] *Journal*, Vol. III, p. 1174.

sense of timing, he saw the light just at the moment when the *salons* of the liberal plutocracy were themselves starting to get tired of liberalism and horrified by its prospects. The hero of this novel was a young intellectual turned by the scientific trends of his time, such as determinism and the theory of *milieu*, into a moral nihilist, with tragic results to others and himself. This sounded like the knell of the two preceding centuries of Enlightenment, and the bugle call of youth that was to reinstall, in a modern, 'psychological' setting, the beliefs and hierarchies discarded by the philosophers. There could be no doubt about who the master of the disciple was: Bourget's own master, Hippolyte Taine. Taine was shattered when he read it; not for fear that his theory would really have had such melodramatic effects on the love affairs of the youth, but because he felt he had lost his hold on the coming generation. 'I can only conclude one thing,' he wrote in a most melancholy letter to Bourget, 'that the general taste has changed, that my generation is finished . . .'

By the time of the controversy over *Le Disciple*, Maupassant's powers were already failing; we shall have to return to earlier years to see what his association with Bourget meant to him. But before doing so, let us have a look at the development of Bourget's further career. He outlived Taine, Goncourt and Maupassant, and indeed most of his contemporaries, including himself. He quickly achieved all the honours available to a French man of letters and, in the twentieth century, grew into a living statue of distinguished dullness. His top hat and impeccable *redingote* were an institution in the literary world. He went on reading and writing and selling himself to newspapers, and publishers, and academies, with unflagging industry and without a flaw in his unexciting gifts; as a matter of fact, his character became nicer as it mellowed and scaled off the pretence of originality. He remained faithful to his ideals and loyal to his colleagues, particularly to those masters whom he had disavowed at the time of his zenith; no one agitated more vigorously than he did for a statue for Taine . . . From 1914, his interests became more strictly political. His two bugbears were the Germans and socialism. His arguments were those of a scholarly Colonel Blimp. Yet, history might have helped him; after Hitler and Stalin, some of his idiosyncrasies would have seemed less ludicrous today than they did to the progressive intelligentsia in the inter-war period. He firmly believed that nationalism was a noble ideal in France and Britain, but must be wicked in Germany; when Germany lay prostrate, and her economy seemed to be falling to pieces, he was alarmed by the aggressive militarism detectable in the nebulous utterances of some Teutonic professor. Was there some prophetic wisdom in this single-track-mindedness? Perhaps; yet, the way the prophecy was fulfilled, some twenty years later, was substantially different from the way Bourget saw it approaching. Many of his fellow Christian and patriotic Germanophobes were only too glad to capitulate to the national arch-enemy; whereas others decided for a handshake with the Reds rather than submission to Hitler. Bourget was spared this agonizing dilemma; he was saved, as he had always been, by his perfect sense of timing, for he died in 1935, without a slur on his *redingote*.

Young Maupassant and young Bourget entered the *chic* world arm-in-arm as it were, shifting at about the same time the main field of their social activities from the literary cafés to the *salons*. They were both dandies, quite mad about clothes and discussed dress in great detail; allegedly, Maupassant chose his tailor on Bourget's advice. They were equally keen on impeccable underwear, though not in the same style; Bourget ordered special shirts buttoned at the back to prevent creasing of the front, whereas Maupassant was more concerned with the impression he would make when undressed. Their choice of apartments also revealed their different concepts of smartness; Maupassant, with his marquis coronet, moved right into 'Saint-Honoré',[1] seeking *bourgeois* comfort and luxury; whereas Bourget, with his unspectacular middle-class background,[2] built up his fortress of bookcases in the Faubourg Saint-Germain, the

[1] The erstwhile rue de Montchanin – today rue Jacques Bingen – as Michel Chrestien kindly informs me, is in the Arrondissement 17ᵉ, on the Plaine Monceaux, running from the rue Legendre into the Place Malesherbes. It was a new district in Maupassant's time, and socially an appendage of the Faubourg Saint-Honoré. Maupassant's two Paris apartments in his last years of activity were also situated in modern districts.

[2] His grandfather had been a peasant farmer; his father, a provincial professor of mathematics (see p. 195).

impoverished stronghold of the ancient aristocracy. Yet, Bourget's career was even more of the 'Saint-Honoré' brand than Maupassant's; as a 'genius', he was the invention of 'high-life' Jewesses, thirsty for something celestial in flavour, feudal in reminiscence, and slightly anti-Semitic.

Maupassant liked Bourget as a good and loyal friend, a meek and gentle fellow, somewhat girlish, shy and over-refined – the ideal target for pally teasing. And what was all that 'psychology' about? Maupassant wondered; there must be something in it if their mutual lady friends thought so, for, whatever he wrote about women as an inferior species, it was the reactions of women – *femmes du monde* – which mattered most to Maupassant. Bourget thus became for him not only a paler *alter ego* which he wore as his shadow but also an intriguing puzzle to attack. Not much came out of their academic discussions; Maupassant quickly tired of them. Bourget tried to get him interested in England, and showed him round some churches and museums when they met in Italy, but the anecdote most revealing of Maupassant's attitude towards him is attached to another sort of sight-seeing. In Rome, ciceroned by their friend, Count Joseph Prioli, they visited a brothel together one night, and Maupassant made a quick disappearance with a girl of the establishment. When, after a short while, he returned, he found his friend 'sitting in a corner, sheepishly [*tout penaud*]', as Baron Lumbroso later reported,[1] 'in the same corner and the same posture as when he had left him. Then, the Norman writer shouts at him gaily: '*Now, my dear fellow, I understand your psychology!*'

At the time when Maupassant was nearing his death, at Dr Blanche's clinic, Bourget, in the course of a casual chat, told Goncourt[2] about a more dramatic sex excursion he had had with Maupassant. One day, so the story goes, Maupassant, 'without any other preamble' told Bourget:

'I'd like to have you *baiser* my mistress.'
'O-ah!'
'Yes ... Well, she'll be masked ... Oh! she is pretty ...

---

[1] *Souvenirs sur Maupassant*, p. 507 – adding: '*Bien entendu*, this happened before M. Bourget's marriage.'
[2] *Journal*, Vol. IV, p. 324.

but she belongs to respectable society . . . She doesn't want to be known.'

The idea appealed to Bourget. The lady, as he found out, was the wife of a *gros universitaire*! The three met as planned, in Maupassant's apartment, that notorious 10 rue de Montchanin. At the moment of prospected fulfilment, there she stood with the two young men, naked except for her mask and a pair of pink cotton stockings which 'gave away her middle-class background'. It should have been Bourget's turn; but her nervous quivering, the cold sweat on her bosom and, particularly, the sight of her legs in middle-class pink disabled him. Whereupon the woman threw herself on Maupassant with the cry, 'A moi, mon faune!' as befitted the wife of an *universitaire*.

As Bourget had failed, Maupassant recruited Catulle Mendès. Mendès was prepared, provided that his own mistress could also join in. This 'foursome' went quite well until one day the university nymph, in a fit of hysteria, picked up Maupassant's revolver and shot at both him and Mendès – the possible origin, Goncourt suggests, of that wound on Maupassant's fingers . . .[1]

42 · Marie Kann

At a time when he was still on smooth gossiping terms with Maupassant, 7 December 1885, Goncourt noted:[2]

> Dinner with Mme Marie Kann.
>
> Three servants stationed up the staircase, the height of the double doors, the vastness of the rooms, the succession of *salons* with walls covered in silk, will tell you that you are in a dwelling of the Israelite Bank. Unfortunately for the eye of the collector, in all this luxury, in the midst of all these splendours, the eye lights on Japanese screens worth only seventy-five francs, on shelves running round the mirrors in

[1] See previous excerpts from the *Journal*. This, or a similar, wound is also referred to, with other explanations, in Tassart's *Souvenirs sur Guy de Maupassant* . . .

[2] *Journal*, Vol. III, p. 510.

the German style, and little china pots which one sees in wooden bowls at the doors of merchants of cheap Chinese wares.

Relaxed on a sofa, Mme Kann is sitting with her great round eyes full of the languor of the brunette, a complexion like a tea rose, a dark beauty spot on her cheek, her mouth pursed in mockery, her dress cut low to show the whiteness of her lymphatic throat, her indolent and broken gestures which sometimes show a mounting fever. This woman has a charm at the same time moribund and ironic to a singular degree, in which is combined the peculiar seductiveness of the Russians, an intellectual perversity of the eyes and a guileless chirping voice. And from time to time her frail person with its languid grace is shaken by a dry little cough.

Really she appeals to amorous curiosity, this woman, and yet if I were still young, still in search of love affairs, I should not want from her anything more than a flirtation; it would seem to me that if she gave herself to me I should taste death on her lips. Now and then she stiffens her arms, which makes me think of a swathed corpse in a coffin.

The conversation, I don't know how, switched from Palermo and its catacombs to the morgue and its drowned bodies, and Maupassant, who was dining with me, spoke at length of fishing up bodies from the Seine, of his taste for the *macchabées*[1] of the Parisian river on account of the primitive ugliness which invests them. He expatiated at length on the horrible pulp, like *papier mâché*, the loathsomeness of these corpses, with the intention – it was plain to see – of affecting the minds of the young ladies who were there and of enhancing his reputation as a terrifying teller of nightmarish stories.

While we discussed death and morgues in the *salon*, Mme Kann was sitting on one side, at the threshold of the *little salon*, in between the doors, her chin leaning on the back of a chair, withdrawn, smiling yet scared, adorably strung to breaking point [*crevarde*], standing out from a background entirely filled with her great full-length portrait –

[1] Used here to mean 'corpses' (or 'ghouls', according to George D. Painter in *Marcel Proust*, (Chatto and Windus, 1959).

a portrait Goncourt debunks as a poor imitation of Rembrandt, and he adds that he would like to see one adequately portraying this 'delightfully morbid' creature.

This Marie Kann, according to some, attracted Maupassant more and, according to others,[1] tired or annoyed him more than anybody else; in a way, both allegations may be true. Others again attributed to her the powers of a pernicious demon. The novelist, Jean Lorrain for instance, hinted at her when he wrote:

> It was in this Jewish high society that Maupassant was to meet that woman, so capricious and bored, whose fierce fantasy helped to unhinge the mind of the unfortunate great writer. It is to this society woman that literature owes the disappearance of Maupassant's talent.

Lorrain, a gifted but stranded and frustrated writer, childhood friend of Hervé de Maupassant, was a Norman local patriot with a sort of hate–love for Guy to whom he would refer as 'great' on one occasion and as nothing but a breed of the 'Flaubert–Zola stud' on another; he particularly resented Guy's desertion (as he saw it) of Normandy for the cosmopolitan *salons* of Faubourg Saint-Honoré; his demonology applied to Maupassant should therefore be taken with a pinch of salt. Surely the *spirochaeta pallida* had more to do with both the rapid incandescence and equally rapid exhaustion of Maupassant's powers than Marie Kann or any other partner in 'macchabéen' and 'crevard' parlour-games could possibly have had? Yet it is true to say that Maupassant's later development should be seen against this social background – leisured and elegant women in a spleenish search for happiness, with morbid allures and eschatological jokes as a fashion. To this world belonged the two Warchawska sisters (remembered in France today as the aunts of the actress Ida Rubinstein, a close friend of André Gide, a well-known figure in the artistic life of the twentieth century). In the 1880s, one of them, Lulia, who married the music composer, Albert Cahen – and was thus sister-in-law to Countess Louis Cahen d'Anvers – was, according to Goncourt,[2] who referred to her as *la petite perfection*, a member of

[1] His doctors, Voivenel and Lagriffe, quoted by Morand, *Vie de Guy de Maupassant*, p. 170.   [2] *Journal*, Vol. III, p. 140.

the female brains trust that determined literary careers; and the other, Marie, the demoniac character known to us as Mme Kann. If Goncourt and his informer, Hervieu, can be trusted,[1] Marie Kann had for a time been shared between Maupassant and Bourget; but 'le Kann' found this too much. He gave his wife a coarse ultimatum that she must choose between his purse and M. Bourget's charms; and Madame chose the purse. Bourget thus was dismissed, but with Maupassant the affair was still going on; the husband was too scared of Maupassant to risk such a show-down with him, and, in reward, Maupassant treated him like dirt.

Whatever the truth,[2] Maupassant would not have objected to this being the case. He was always prepared to share his mistresses, especially with Bourget, whom he considered as his own complementary character. 'A thousand kisses,' he wrote to Gisèle d'Estoc.[3] 'One half on Department Bourget (head), the other on Department Maupassant ("con").' It was the idyllic comradeship between a faunal and a cerebral talent, and one may only deplore that, in this special case, the 'head' was of so much poorer quality than the body it was supposed to match. The 'head' who could have fitted that 'body' was Anatole France.

43 · Pater incertus

Maupassant had a strong sense of jealousy in matters of sex and love; but the claim to exclusiveness did not come into it. In any love affair, as he saw it, the man was bound to get tired sooner than the woman; so he should be only too glad if somebody cropped up to relieve him of his burden altogether, or at least, to share it with him. The *cocu* was ridiculous because he had no idea of what was going on behind his back[4] or because he

---

[1] *Journal*, Vol. III, p. 1221.

[2] Steegmuller (in *Maupassant*) quotes a relative of the Warchawska sisters according to whom Marie Kann was not, in fact, sexually promiscuous and may not even have had an affair with Maupassant. She was, however, like Maupassant, a drug addict.

[3] Pierre Borel, *Maupassant et l'Androgyne*, p. 125. See Appendix 8.

[4] A typical example, amongst the many, is the short story *Décoré!*

thought he had married an innocent virgin who had in fact been a most entertaining lover before.[1] This was merely the punishment for a philistine obsession with respectability and had little to do with love. Maupassant simply did not believe that any man could worry about his wife or mistress going to bed with another if it were not for the sake of vanity. Sound and wise men could get over this vanity; they took the polyandry of their partners for granted and lived happily ever after – until trapped again by another unhappy, passionate affair. *L'art de rompre*,[2] for a man, was a skill no less important than was *l'art de séduire*; the fickleness of a wife or mistress was a free gift from Heaven.

How and why could a man with such an outlook still be devoured by jealousy? There were special situations when he could; and there were two which seem to have haunted Maupassant particularly. One was jealousy of the *former* man; not because of his precedence in time – this was a philistine worry – but because he might go on dominating the woman even when she was lying in *your* bed; because he may have taken possession of her for good; because you may be nothing but a substitute for him . . . 'Bel-Ami' found it quite convenient to ignore his (first) wife's lovers, and only made a row about one of them when his interest demanded; but the resemblance between his own position and that of her former husband tortured him all the time. The spectre of a dead husband was much more difficult to be reconciled with than the existence of a live seducer.

And Maupassant knew one thing that made the worry about conjugal unfaithfulness understandable and human and, indeed, sensible, even when manifest in mad outbursts: the *uncertainty about the real father*. There was nothing more grotesque than an unsuspecting husband cuddling somebody else's baby as his own,[3] and nothing more tormenting than doubts about the father's identity – doubts on the part of the man who was supposed to be the father, but also of his wife, and most of all the children. Why was Maupassant so tormented by this subject? Some suspected a secret about his three alleged children. Others

---

[1] Cf. the short story *Ce Cochon de Morin*, with a husband affectionately thanking his wife's former lover for having behaved tactfully and chivalrously with her in a delicate situation.

[2] A newspaper article.　　　　　[3] The banker in *Mont-Oriol*.

thought that he must have had doubts about the identity of his own father; the gossip about his mother and Flaubert may have reached him. This was an obvious assumption, but there was nothing to substantiate it; nothing except, perhaps, the fact that when Jean Lorrain referred to him as to one of the 'Flaubert–Zola stud', he reacted in a pathological way – preparing to challenge Lorrain to a pistol duel[1] one day, and running away from the whole problem on another in a state of lethargic depression. It was a rude remark, no doubt, but why should he have taken it to heart more than he did any other abuse by unsuccessful colleagues? Was it because the word 'stud', when applied to Flaubert, may have alluded to biological links? All these are guesses. The fact is that his writings in which the problem of hidden or mistaken paternity is touched upon are innumerable; the industrious *Maupassantien*, Dr Pierre Cogny, advised by his elders, MM. Vial and Dumesnil, enumerated some forty short stories relevant to the subject, but added that his list was far from complete.[2] Disguised or not, a feeling of *alarm* about such a possibility seems to be ubiquitous in his works. And the book in which he exposed it most fully was his fourth novel, published early in 1888, *Pierre et Jean*.

Pierre and Jean are brothers; the former a penniless doctor, the latter a penniless lawyer, in Le Havre. With meagre parental support, they manage somehow; the modest and monotonous pleasures of provincial middle-class youth keep them going. Unexpectedly, the younger, Jean, inherits a large fortune from an old friend of the family. This should make them all happy; Jean is a good boy, he will certainly be generous with his close relatives, including Pierre who has dreamt much of touring far-away countries, entertaining glamorous women ... Pierre cannot really feel that he has been deprived of anything since he has never claimed or counted on even a fraction of that money. Yet, as he went out for a stroll:

> He felt uneasy, oppressed, discontented, as when one has received disturbing news. Yet it was not any precise thought

[1] *Inter alia* Goncourt's *Journal*, Vol. III, p. 576.
[2] Preface to the 1959 edition (Garnier Frères) of *Pierre et Jean*, pp. xliv–xlv.

that afflicted him. . . . [And after a while] he began to ask himself the question: 'Ought this to be Jean's inheritance?' Yes, it was possible after all.

This fraternal jealousy was followed by an alarming suspicion of his mother: and this suspicion turned out to be true. The mother confessed. It was shattering, but had to be endured; they suddenly sensed the frustrated woman that their mother had been; could they condemn her for what little colour had mixed in her drab life? And, anyway, what could they do? Money was money; besides Jean was engaged to a pretty mercenary-minded little bourgeoise, who found it natural to take stock of incomes and expenses at the peak moments of amorous scenes. Understanding, horror of complications and a desire for comfort decided the course to be taken.

Pierre et Jean is a beautiful novel. Maupassant was at grips with the trend of 'psychology' when writing it. He had always had an aversion to analysing souls directly; the art of the novelist should, he urged, rather consist in making the 'intimacy of souls' *visible*.[1] In his essay attached to *Pierre et Jean*, in defiance of the fashion symbolized by his friend, Bourget, he reiterated this point; but in the novel itself, he allowed himself to be more 'psychological' than he had been before – as he himself emphasized in an article he wrote later. The novel was not like Bourget in any way; it was his own, lyrical and self-tormenting 'intimacy' breaking through the 'visible' crust under which he liked to hide it; but the encouragement to loosen up came from the climate of the fashion which he contradicted. His giving in did not amount to more than a deep breath; the story is undistorted Maupassant, made even more touching by some slight weakness.

This novel was based, as his fictions had always been, on a true story, partly read, it seems, in the *faits-divers* and partly heard from Mme Hermine Lecomte du Nouÿ.[2] As to its *milieu*, this was once again the middle classes of Normandy with which

[1] In a private letter quoted by Pol Neveux, Preface, *Œuvres complètes*, p. xliv.

[2] Maupassant, in his letter to Edouard Estaunié, from the *Bel-Ami*, on 2 February 1888, referred to a newspaper; Tassart, in *Nouveaux souvenirs . . .*, p. 180, referred to the lady.

he had always been familiar; but a spark of what he had picked up in the *salons* helped him to broaden his sight of their 'great miseries'. It was not his most perfect work; the admirable terseness of his style had to some extent to be sacrificed in this excursion towards the 'souls'; but it was an excursion well worth taking. His love of factuality did not abandon him; nor his fondness for topographical accuracy, strangely dissolved in his meditative visions, for instance, when describing Pierre's evening stroll:

> After taking a few steps he stopped to gaze at the harbour. On his right above Sainte-Adresse the two electric beacons on the headland of la Hève, like two monstrous twin cyclops, cast their long and powerful beams on the sea. Projected from the two neighbouring sources, the two parallel rays descended like the tails of two giant comets, following a straight and immeasurable path from the summit of the cliff to the depth of the horizon. Then on the two jetties two other fires, offspring of these colossi, indicated the entrance to le Havre; and beyond, on the other side of the Seine, one could see still more, many more, fixed or winking, with flashing or dimmed lights, opening and closing like eyes, the eyes of the ports, yellow, red and green, keeping a look-out on the darkened sea covered with ships, living eyes of the hospitable earth saying merely by the regular and invariable mechanical movement of their eye-lids: 'It is I. I am Trouville, I am Honfleur, I am the river of Pont-Audemer.'

How many names of localities which cannot possibly mean anything to most readers! Who knows Sainte-Adresse, who knows the river of Pont-Audemer? One would expect a mass of such names to strike one as senseless and tiresome. Far from it – they grow into poetry, acquire the radiation of mythological figures. There seems to be some truth in the belief of Naturalist writers that no fact, however trivial, is ultimately unimportant; its authenticity exerts a magic even on those unable to check it.

Of Maupassant's *amitiés amoureuses* in high society, the most platonic was that with Mme Lecomte du Nouÿ,[1] and most *amoureuse* that with Mme Kann; the flirtatious flippancies and musings with Mme Straus and Countess Potocka were halfway between the two. The two latter counted as outstandingly beautiful and witty women, and their different styles met in the cult of playful morbidness. Maupassant besieged them both with his amorous approaches and seems to have been, at heart, quite glad to be refused by both; they suited him as partners in sensually tinged drolleries and reveries more than they would have done as mistresses. His friendships with them were really love affairs kept unconsummated for additional fun.

Countess Emmanuela Potocka, of ducal origin, half Italian, half Polish,[2] made her greatest impact on the *fin de siècle* society as the patroness of the *Macchabées* – men who were supposed to have 'died' for her or be ready to do so at any moment. Their badge which they received from her if qualified was a sapphire jewel with the inscription 'A la vie, à la mort', and they wore it when entertained by her for dinner, on Friday evenings. Maupassant was the staunchest of the *Macchabées* – this was, apparently the only sort of association whose statutes he was prepared to observe! It was a fairly large body comprising mostly authors and artists of standing, and some bankers, philosophers and diplomats, the British Ambassador, Lord Lytton, for instance; Bourget, as could be expected, also made his regular appearance though in a rather passive role. Mme Potocka, according to Marcel Proust who knew her later and wrote about her in an article for the *Figaro*, had 'Roman majesty, Florentine

---

[1] At any rate, in tone; in the meantime, they are likely to have had an affair.

[2] According to the notes in the full edition of Goncourt's *Journal*, wife of Count Nicolas Potocki, daughter of Duke di Regina; according to Morand, *Vie de Guy de Maupassant*, p. 157, 'Italienne par sa mère, la princesse di Regina, et Polonaise par son père.' According to Steegmuller, *Maupassant*, p. 187, *née* Pignatelli.

grace, Parisian wit'. Many, so Jacques-Emile Blanche said, thought her a virgin; she struck people with her beauty as of an 'indifferent Artemis' though a passionately bawd-loving Artemis at that.[1]

Her refusal to be Maupassant's mistress, and all the things Maupassant had to do to console himself for her cruelty, was a constant subject of his letters to her. Had she an idea what she had been missing! Once she sent him six perfumed dolls as a joke – tokens, as it were, of the women she was planning to entertain in his company. Maupassant stuffed the dolls so as to make them look pregnant and returned them to her with this text: 'All in one night!' Then, he apologized to her[2] though, needless to say, she was not at all hurt. He always apologized to her, in one playful way or another; once in a *madrigal*, for dreaming that she appeared to him as the Holy Virgin,[3] but more often for having quite different thoughts of her. He was not sure whether he should not have insisted on going to bed with her after all. But what he wanted most of her was *partnership*!

> I have a tremendous desire to go on a journey and I curse the social conventions which prevent me from asking you to accompany me. It would be a dream of a journey with you. I do not speak of the charm of your person, which I can enjoy here, and of the pleasure of looking at you, which is as great in Paris as elsewhere, but I know of no woman who can evoke as you do the idea of an ideal travelling companion. I may add that if you said 'yes' tomorrow, I would perhaps reply 'no', for I should leap as I climbed the misty slopes with you . . . a danger so lively that prudence would counsel me to avoid it. . . .[4]

The play went on as long as it could. Countess Potocka was a good sport, besides being extremely good-looking. She survived Maupassant by many years, and died in misery; her corpse was found in a dingy room, gnawed by rats.

[1] Steegmuller, *Maupassant*, pp. 188 ff.
[2] Letter from Cannes, 13 March 1884.
[3] Morand, *Vie de Guy de Maupassant*, p. 158.
[4] Letter, probably end of 1888.

Mme Geneviève Straus, daughter of the composer Fromental Halévy, had first been married to the composer, Georges Bizet, by whom she had a son, Jacques. She became a widow in 1875, and married the rich lawyer, Emile Straus. One of Goncourt's standing jokes in his *Journal* was to go on talking about her as Mme Bizet, and then occasionally to correct himself. In his entry of 28 March 1882,[1] he described her thus:

She was dressed in a billowing dressing-gown of pale soft silk, trimmed from top to bottom with large French knots. She was stretched out lazily in a deep armchair. Only her soft velvety black eyes moved feverishly with the coquettishness of feigned sickness. On her lap she had a little black poodle, *Vivette*, with paws as tiny as the claws of a bird.

The lady's environment was charming. On a panel facing her was a splendid Nattier representing a grand Regency lady in the floating costume of a naiad, rising out of a forest of reeds; and over the chimney-piece, against the marble of which the mistress of the house sometimes pressed her brow, was poised an elegant statuette in white marble attributed to Coysevox . . .

Mme Bizet, or rather Straus, spoke of love with a kind of bitterness, saying that after its culmination it is rare for two lovers to love each other with equal force, and that this inequality in love of the one for the other makes a lame partnership which cannot keep in step. And all the while she spoke her words seemed to regret their own softness. At one moment she even rejoiced in her good fortune in being alone in life, which was a surprising revelation, and when I said that a house or a large apartment was very empty with only one person in it, she let slip the remark that when in the house or large apartment there were two beings who did not get on together [*ne s'emboîtaient pas*] then it was even more sad.

Then leaving her dissertation on love, Mme Bizet came back to her poodle, to a recital of its habits, and spoke of one of its predecessors which had a horror of baths and which, when it knew that a bath was being prepared, produced the

[1] Vol. III, p. 659.

most excellent imitation of a running cold in the head that
one could imagine.

Maupassant had already been a lion of the *salons* for quite a
long time when his closer association with Geneviève Straus
started. In the summer of 1886, he besought her to receive him
tête-à-tête, and promised not to be encouraged by this favour to
'claim the privileges of intimacy'. It was typically the kind of
letter that Maupassant would have found most ridiculous had it
not been written by himself – or maybe he found it ridiculous
even when writing it. It was solely 'la nature de votre esprit'
which he was so keen on enjoying undisturbed by the presence
of others! In a way he was sincere, in spite of himself as it were;
feminine *esprit* did appeal to him. This he expected and obtained
from her; she was a social friend, fascinating him by her social
splendour, and their intimacy consisted in discussing illnesses,
cosmetics and adultery. He certainly liked her company, and
when distance prevented him from going to see her he went on
writing to her long letters couched in the terms of socialite devotion which may or may not convey a real attachment. From
Cannes, in 1888, for instance:

> Madame,
>   Do you remember me? There was last year in Paris a man
> of thirty-eight, with the rather clumsy and harsh air of a cap-
> tain of infantry, who was somewhat peevish. This man, who
> was merely a merchant of prose, disappeared towards the
> autumn and no one knows what has happened to him.
>   He used to dine with you often and found great pleasure
> in doing so. This pleasure he has certainly not forgotten. . . .

A few weeks after his entreaty for a *tête-à-tête* he wrote to her from
England, recommending hair tonics to her, reporting on the way
the Duchess de Richelieu used them. He was staying with the
Rothschilds whose name appealed to them both. In their home,
he had met the Prince of Wales. But England as a whole did not
appeal to him; 'men do not interest me very much', he wrote,
'and the women here lack the charm of ours'.

English women readers may draw some comfort from learning that this complaint may be taken as 'sour grapes'. Maupassant had come to London with an introduction from Bourget

to Henry James, as the sole man in this island who would know about 'Gallo-Roman' ways. According to an anecdote heard by Vincent O'Sullivan from Oscar Wilde, and quoted by Steegmuller in full,[1] James took Maupassant out for dinner in an Earls Court restaurant where Maupassant spotted some good-looking women and asked his host to 'get' one of them for him. James was horrified, and Maupassant disappointed by his refusal; what on earth did Bourget and James mean by 'Gallo-Roman' style if it was not this sort of thing? 'If I only knew English!' he sighed. Steegmuller refers to the whole anecdote with due reservation; Maupassant, he suggests, may not even have made use of Bourget's introductory letter. But so much can clearly be seen from Maupassant's utterances – including his letter to Mme Straus – that he felt totally lost and helpless in England where he had arrived in a bad state of nerves, and bad weather. Blanche Roosevelt was with him at least through part of the journey – the American gold-red-blonde Marquesa, François's favourite amongst his master's mistresses – a live evidence of the charm that could be enjoyed if not exactly in English, at any rate, in Anglo-Saxon females. It was with her that he visited Oxford, mainly to satisfy Bourget, who urged on him that it would be unforgivable to miss such an opportunity; Oxford 'is the only medieval town in the world'. Oxford was drenched in rain, Maupassant was cold and longing for Africa. Cutting his journey short, he returned to France, practically running away from his friends. This was the first and last time that he saw England.[2]

Another letter by Maupassant to Mme Straus, written not long afterwards, is equally typical but from a different point of view:

Madame,

I am sick as I never was before. Migraine and ether have produced in me just now two hours of absolute madness. I cannot leave my bed. I beg your pardon a thousand times and I kiss your hand with respect.

[1] *Maupassant*, pp. 224–5.

[2] In 1886, according to Steegmuller, op. cit., p. 228. According to Schmidt, *Maupassant par lui-même*, p. 190, he had a brief sojourn in England in April 1890.

This was one of several apologies for being unable to attend
a party: but what we know of Maupassant's state of health confirms what he said in it. Maupassant, in the meantime, made
friends with her husband; he was one of Maupassant's lawyers,
to whom he was to complain in a torrent of letters about the
infringements of his author's rights, and it was on Emile Straus's
advice that he ultimately dropped the case against Charpentier
for publishing his portrait without authorization.

All this would indicate that the friendship between Geneviève
Straus and Guy de Maupassant had shrunk to merely conventional cordiality, without any deeper mark on either of them.
Again, we are indebted mainly to Edmond de Goncourt's nosi-
ness for learning that this was not the case. In Maupassant's
last two novels, *Fort comme la Mort* (1889) and *Notre Cœur*
(1890), both dealing with the love affairs of the *chic* world, and
in his stories and plays and fragments of novel which conveyed
the same atmosphere of boredom, luxury and eroticism, Mme
Straus was one of his guides and inspirers, possibly the most
competent in this capacity. She was supposed to be the live
model of Michèle de Burne, in *Notre Cœur*, who, when setting
out to see her lover, in her coach stuffed with a fabulous variety
of little drawers for comfort and cosmetics, only feels a pang of
conscience because she does not really enjoy her vice. What
makes her carry on 'is not the rapture of being possessed, but the
pride in being generous and the satisfaction of making someone
happy'. Mme Straus, Goncourt says, had the reputation of
being 'like a man' in love, that is, taking and leaving men according to her whims and only anxious not to be bound by their
spell.[1] What shocked Goncourt most was that she was quite
proud of having served as a model for that heartless Michèle.
Really, people asked her, was there 'si peu de tendresse' in her?
Her answer was that men did not deserve anything better. She
was an *allumeuse sans cœur*, generous in her own way because,
in her words, 'it is difficult to refuse the demands of a man for
whom you do not care'.[2] For Maupassant she did care. It is not
in this same entry that Goncourt made this clear but some five
years later[3] when Maupassant was no longer alive. Goncourt at

---

[1] *Journal*, Vol. III, p. 636. [2] *Journal*, Vol. III, p. 1197 (5 July 1890).
[3] *Journal*, Vol. IV, p. 725 (28 January 1895).

the Princess's *salon* found Mme Strauss 'in beauty' as usual, but learned from her friends that she was *souffrante*, had just had a nervous crisis and had hardly eaten anything for a fortnight. She was a woman who 'only loved love'. There had been, however, one moment in her life when 'if Maupassant had asked her to follow him, she would have left everything'. Or else she may have felt for him what he felt for Countess Potocka: 'If you say *oui*, I may say *non* . . .', the danger of a monogamous attachment was too great; one was obliged to save the solitary pride of promiscuity.

Geneviève Halévy-Bizet-Straus's impact on French art and letters continued deep into the twentieth century. Her son, Jacques, was a friend of young Marcel Proust, and introduced him in their *salon*; and her wit echoed years after in that of 'la duchesse de Guermantes'.

According to other sources – or rumours – the heroines of both *Fort comme la Mort* and *Notre Cœur* were modelled mainly on Marie Kann; the actress Lagier, too, was amused to recognize some of her own words in *Fort comme la Mort*.[1] The subject of this novel is the falling in love of a middle-aged bachelor, an established and fashionable painter, with the daughter of a countess who has been his mistress for long years – years first of passion and then of friendly affection and routine. The countess, when she notices his infatuation with her daughter, looks upon him with forbearing sadness; she feels he is not really unfaithful to her – it is not another person but *her* youth, *their* youth which he loves. He, however, is less philosophical; unable to face his own feelings, he allows himself to become the victim of a fatal accident.

The origin of this subject seems to have been a true story which went round in 'St-Honoré'. Bourget was planning to write a novel about it; he mentioned it to a 'dame du grand monde israélite' (who may or may not have been Mme Kann), and this lady then offered it as her own idea for a subject to Maupassant, 'to please him'. Bourget 'did not learn of the reason until he read his colleague's book. There was nothing he could do about it and he had to draw on the deflowered subject for

[1] Goncourt, *Journal*, Vol. IV, p. 225.

the theme of *La Duchesse bleue*, which was a very mediocre novel.'[1]

Tassart notes[2] that his master whilst preparing *Fort comme la Mort* told a 'very pretty woman': 'I shall make you a countess'. This, again, may or may not have been Mme Kann; nor is it clear whether Maupassant actually hinted at the middle-aged countess heroine of his novel or at her daughter who may colloquially also have been referred to as a 'comtesse'. One thing is certain: that the women whose words and features he reproduced were in real life if no less of the *monde*, yet, on the whole, less of the ancient nobility than they appeared in the novel.

This also applies to *Notre Cœur*. The ways and manners of that proud and impregnable erotomaniac, love-seeking, loveless, slightly lesbian, Michèle de Burne, and the rituals of her *salon*, frolicsome and macabre: what sort of environment do they recall? The present-day *Maupassantien*, after carefully comparing various sources, claims, surmises and recently published documents,[3] concludes that the main inspirer was 'without any doubt' Marie Kann,[4] with hints, however, of Mme Halévy-Bizet-Straus, and the two Cahen d'Anvers, the Lippmanns, the Rothschilds, Countess Potocka and Mme Lecomte du Nouÿ, and even perhaps of the crazy prophetess of hermaphroditism, Gisèle d'Estoc, who, according to one writer on the subject, was Maupassant's 'most beloved one' and, according to another, did not exist at all.[5] In a word, most of the women were Jewesses; and none representative of the French nobility of the old stock.

[1] 'I have been told this anecdote by M. Paléologue,' says M. Morand (*Vie de Guy de Maupassant*, p. 156). It seems to be true in essence, but not in all details. However little Maupassant talked about his literary projects, it is most unlikely that in that period of his life he would not have mentioned, at any rate briefly, the subject of his forthcoming novel to Bourget — unless he concealed it purposely. So either he must have been privy to the 'treason' or Bourget could not have been surprised to see the novel in print.

[2] *Nouveaux Souvenirs* . . .

[3] Pierre Cogny, in the Introduction to a new edition of *Notre Cœur* Librairie Marcel Dédier, Paris, 1962.

[4] As suggested already by Edouard Maynial.

[5] See Appendix 8.

The last two finished novels by Maupassant differ from those written earlier in so far as they only deal with smart society and only concentrate on its love affairs; both, and more markedly *Notre Cœur*, depict the vegetation of luxury, sensualism, boredom and artificial pastimes in a 'hot-house', without taking notice of what is going on beyond its glass walls. In their tone, as well as in their subject matter, they are typical of the 'late' Maupassant, affected by the *monde* and the current of 'psychology'; the crispness of his style, particularly effective in visualizing the awkwardness of the *petites gens*, has been softened into waves of wistfulness and spleen, with now and then a facetious grimace and with the undertones of sentimentality. Some of his lyrical sentences now sound like a languorous sigh from Mme Kann or Mme Straus – Princess Mathilde's 'two intimate Jewesses', as Goncourt called them.[1]

His development from lower-class to upper-class subjects, from dry staccato to lyrical undulations, from fact-recording to soul-searching was not uniform; in his short sketches, he mostly tended to be snappy, whether recording the bedroom adventure of a 'petite comtesse' or the practical jokes of peasants and tramps; whereas in his long short stories, travel diaries, and novels, he was always inclined to make the dramatic dialogue alternate with musing and descriptive paragraphs of a softer rhythm. Yet, from a bird's-eye view, he would seem to have moved from a stale *bistro* where he watched the various types with implacable detachment, to a perfumed *salon* where he was quite glad to see the barriers melt away between himself and some of the types he was observing. He shared not only in their lives but also in their wishful thoughts; though denouncing and debunking 'the world called elegant', he did so in terms which themselves smacked of 'elegant' people, in their moods of self-pity and misanthropy. He was convinced that the finest short story he had ever written was *L'Inutile Beauté*, published in 1890.[2] This longish story reads indeed like a compressed montage of the idiosyncrasies he developed in the second half of the eighties and of what could be fitted into them from his former

[1] *Journal*, Vol. IV, p. 255.
[2] As he told the publisher Havard in a letter about the time of its publication.

self. These idiosyncrasies are apparent in features such as: female beauty debased by maternity; maternal attachment; anxieties about paternity; frustration of a noble soul bound to a selfish and coarse husband; her ivory complexion; her diadem; her tragic glances; her soundless tears; worldly gossip between two gentlemen in the interval at the Opera; melodramatic exchanges between Count and Countess in a superb victoria, driving through the Bois de Boulogne, and in a smart church; and the moral of the story, which the husband does not recognize, until it is too late, that his wife is 'not simply a woman destined to perpetuate the race but the bizarre and mysterious product of all our complicated desires, accumulated through centuries, diverted from their primordial and divine course towards a mystic beauty, glimpsed but indefinable'.

Maupassant, the farce-maker, fell into his own trap. He had discarded all illusions. He had always been on the alert to eschew all sorts of duperies. He resisted the temptation to accept any faith or idea, any 'commitment' as it would be called today. His most sympathetic accomplices in this posture of playful disenchantment were the ladies of the fashionable *salons* with whom he discussed death and *morgue* and *Macchabées* and futility. And whilst doing so, he slipped into a lyricism which, by the very choice of its words, expressed the belief in a myth, in the supernatural radiation of a woman for no other reason than that she was good-looking, well-dressed, well-bred, rich, titled and unhappy. *L'Inutile Beauté*, more typical from this point of view than even *Fort comme la Mort* and *Notre Cœur*, is not simply a poor story; it is heartfelt, clever, but sloppy. Comparing it with his short long stories of some ten years before, *Boule de Suif* and *Maison Tellier*, one's first reaction is to regret that he should ever have turned his attention from the 'bawdy-house' to the 'hot-house'. Some of his old friends and lately converted admirers, Bourget, Brunetière, the circle of the *Revue des Deux Mondes*, were delighted to see his development. Their satisfaction was inspired by their half-conscious dogma that an author's literary standing increased in proportion to the social standing of his characters. Maupassant in their view was turning into an author eligible for the membership of the Académie Française and for veneration by the upholders of traditional

Christian morality. One wonders why? In fact, Maupassant's outlook had not become less sensual; only his sensualism had become more pompous. Tolstoy was utterly disgusted with the sensual licentiousness sympathetically described in *Notre Cœur*. One may not share his indignation at such literature; but he certainly knew what he was writing about. The accomplished scholars of the *Revue* really failed to see the sense of what they read; the moral message (or its absence) impressed them less than did the fact that the smell of stale food and stale bed-linen was now, in Maupassant's writings, to a large extent replaced by the fragrance of high-class ladies. What captivated them in Maupassant, ever since *Bel-Ami*, was what was second-rate in him.

Yet, it would be wrong to dismiss the 'late' Maupassant as nothing but the decline of the 'early' one. The perfect master was indeed the implacable observer; but a reader truly appreciative of that perfection cannot fail to be moved by Maupassant's surrender to the magic of sentimental self-revelation, his vesture in refined weakness. Without this, the whole man and the whole *œuvre* would have been poorer. It is worth quoting what Pol Neveux had to say on the matter, in his essay regarded as 'magistral' by René Dumesnil, and referred to several times in the course of this book.[1]

> In certain troubled hours our secret preferences, in spite of ourselves, lean towards *Fort comme la Mort* and *Notre Cœur* although the writer does not follow the man in his refinement. When he loses his *impassibilité* he loses his genius; there remains only a smart and catchy virtuosity. Why is it that this epoch of his talent, which corresponds with the most intelligent, most delicate and most noble of his intimate life, should remain from the literary point of view the least arresting?

Perhaps it is not entirely accurate to say that it was the loss of *impassibilité* which eclipsed his genius. *Sur l'Eau*, his meditative travel diary, written on board *Bel-Ami*, was certainly a beautiful book; Tolstoy, with his very vivid sense of Maupassant's gifts (a sense only distorted by some puritanical schoolmastership) thought it the best he had ever written. *Sur l'Eau*

[1] Preface to *Œuvres complètes de Maupassant*, Conard, Paris, 1908, p. lxxxiii.

was even more lyrical and, as to its mental climate, hardly less sex-ridden and sensual than *Fort comme la Mort* and *Notre Cœur*; yet, the travel diary can be enjoyed without a bad after-taste, whereas these novels, however entertaining, even impressive they are, leave the reader with an impression of hollowness, phoneyness, nausea. All were typically by the 'late' Maupassant. What was the decisive difference between them? To put it simply it was that, in *Sur l'Eau*, if Maupassant meant the Princess of Monaco or the Rothschilds he said the Princess of Monaco or the Rothschilds, and when he meant commercial travellers in an inn he said commercial travellers in an inn; in *Fort comme la Mort* and *Notre Cœur*, when he meant Mme Kann he said Comtesse de Guilleroy, and when he meant Mme Straus he said Michèle de Burne. In doing so, Maupassant was not trying to dissociate himself from his lady friends but rather to fall in with their own fancies of themselves. Those women of the *salons juives et métèques* of the liberal plutocratic era did not mind seeing themselves portrayed as fickle, or heartless, loose or frail; all this had its glamour; but to make it look glamorous, their surroundings had to be replete with the hackneyed requisites of a world that no longer existed – if it had ever existed at all. The *clichés* of that *littérature tarte à la crème*, so very much despised by Maupassant, had to be made use of, not in depicting love or marriage, but in describing their social ornaments. The names, of course, are only one example; so is Jewishness; and, to be fair, most of Maupassant's cosmopolitan high-class friends were too intelligent, and too proud, to dissimulate or be shy of their origins. But *clichés* of dignity in imagination outlive reality, even among intelligent people. When Mme Straus was asked, 'Si peu de tendresse?' she was able to answer with a teasingly affirmative smile: why not? 'Mme de Burne' rang true all right; but had it been a 'Mme Schlésinger', she might have winced. And Maupassant instinctively conformed with this order of symbols. The interesting Jew, for him, was a great money-maker (maybe a fascinatingly inventive one); the interesting Jewess, a hot-blooded whore (maybe a melodramatic and patriotic one); the fairy of the *salons* must appear fairy-like and feudal.

Was Maupassant a snob? Slightly less so than the average; but even this amounts to quite a good deal. Malignant rumours were being circulated about his susceptibility to social distinction and his passion for appearances. These should be taken with a pinch of salt. The most assiduous rumour-monger was his outstanding senior co-snob, Edmond de Goncourt. Maupassant, he noted,[1] was interested in nothing but the *chic* world, and kept *Bel-Ami* not to sail but only to receive Princess Sagan and her like on board . . . Maupassant only read the *Almanach of Gotha*, this was his whole spiritual food . . . [2] The picture Goncourt intended to convey is false. For one thing, Maupassant was too much of a hedonist, and too fond of money, to feel like this; his pleasure in seafaring was certainly not a fake; and the cult of titles for their own sake was in his eyes the most pathetic of human self-deceptions. He may have felt glamour in coronets but only when of gold.

Goncourt was anxious to record how the two *gandins de lettres*, 'literary fops', Maupassant and Bourget,[3] were ultimately being duped and made fun of by their makers, the smart Jewesses. A story that went round as typical was that they had been invited to dinner by Mme Louis Cahen d'Anvers and been told that all gentlemen would appear in red tailcoats. The two *gandins* then really turned up at the dinner dressed up as English foxhunters, but they were the only ones to do so – 'to the great amusement of Jewry', so Goncourt was told by Jean Lorrain . . . Bourget when he was asked about this by Dumesnil, many years after Maupassant and Goncourt had died, answered that not one word of the story was true.[4] It does sound like an invention, but characteristic of the atmosphere. Maupassant, in his oversensitiveness to worldly splendour, like Bourget in his zealous pan-snobbery, laid himself open to the sneers both of those who envied him for his status of 'lion' and those responsible for it.

Steegmuller, American *Maupassantien* of our times, says that *Fort comme la Mort*, though on the whole a good novel, suffers from Maupassant's 'over-estimation of the characters and world

[1] *Journal*, Vol. III, p. 1161.
[2] *Journal*, Vol. IV, p. 178. This entry was made in 1892 after Maupassant's collapse and attempt at suicide; but with the implication that this had always been his real interest.
[3] *Journal*, Vol. IV, p. 125.
[4] Dumesnil, *Guy de Maupassant*, p. 224.

that he portrays'.[1] This is paradoxically true; Maupassant does not utter opinions that betray this 'over-estimation' but when, for instance, the hero of the novel, the *arrivé* artist, driving through the *Bois* with young Any de Guilleroy, is trying to impress her by gossiping about the passers-by, one has the impression that the author is equally proud of his familiarity with that society of coach-owners. He may disparage the 'world called elegant', but the kick he gets out of being able to disparage it from inside gives him away.

Maupassant's disillusioned philosophy provided him with no sure defence against fascination by appearances and social glamour: this shortcoming of his realism can be traced throughout his novels, from *Une Vie* to *Notre Cœur* and to the few fragments of the two major works he started when his end was approaching. He was willing to see all human failings in all social classes; and yet, there were some conventional aristocratic symbols which he could not do without when tempted to invest female characters with an aura of dignity. The women he was attached to he ennobled. He also dyed their hair. Both Laure Le Poittevin and Marie Warchawska (Kann) acquired a fairer complexion, as well as a more feudal pedigree, when identifiable in his novels. A high-class beauty, in Maupassant's fancies, was a 'blonde', but as it happened, his live models on record were more often dark or of auburn touch.[2]

Obviously these alterations in themselves did not matter; but the core of sentimental snobbery behind them did. Or was it lack of sociological perspective which made him submerge himself in the imagery of a society about whose values he professed to be most sceptical? His imperviousness to general ideas proved to be overdone; he paid for it by allowing passage to some of their unchecked reflections. Beyond the reach of his senses, his mind faltered. He was graceful in faltering so long as he had the strength to finish a novel, but as his mind became deranged his writing became fragmentary, and he became entangled in metaphysics, in battles with weird demons which he could no longer control.

---

[1] *Maupassant*, p. 278.   [2] See Appendix 6.

Maupassant was to die before he was forty-three of syphilis developing into lunacy. It was a disease which carried off very many in Europe up to the 1920s, and affected artists more than other social categories. Up to now I have deliberately avoided making too many references to his illness. The development of his attitude to nature, people, and his 'métier', should, I felt, be followed without constantly reverting to description of his pains, manias and treatments which, if frequent, were only part of the background of his life's drama and of his *œuvre*. From 1890 this is no longer possible. As he came to the end of his thirties, the shadow of his approaching death became so overwhelming that it could not be ignored for a single moment. 'Vivre, c'est en fin mourir,' he wrote; as an aphorism, it was far from subtle, but as the sad motto of his last three years it is perfect.

When did his illness start and what was its origin? A tremendous amount has been written about this: gossip started in his lifetime and echoed in the daily press when news of his collapse spread; and recollections and treatises on the subject, medical and psychological, followed in quick succession after his death.[1] All this was insufficient to give a firm and definite answer to certain basic questions; partly because Maupassant, although an exhibitionist, liked to mystify his friends, mistresses and doctors about his illness; and partly because medical opinion of the nature of the *spirochaeta pallida* has changed since his lifetime. Moreover, the nature of the germ itself seems to have undergone several waves of change during this period. The data are conflicting, yet, from their multiplicity, a fairly clear picture emerges both of Maupassant's family background and of his personal character.

Both Guy and Hervé de Maupassant died in early middle-age,[2] after showing unmistakable signs of lunacy ascribable to

[1] See Appendix 7.
[2] It will be remembered that Hervé was actually thirty-three.

luetic infection. Their disease may have been congenital[1] or it may have been contracted, or it may even have been congenital *and* contracted. From what we know about both the Maupassant and the Le Poittevin ancestry and the way of life of the two brothers, none of these possibilities can be ruled out. Gustave de Maupassant and his separated wife insisted that the tragedy of their two sons had nothing to do with their ancestry. This is possibly true. According to Mme de Maupassant, Hervé's derangement of mind had been caused by a sort of sunstroke, and not by infection which could have been passed on to his little orphan daughter, Simone; as to her elder son, Guy, she attributed his collapse mainly to *surmenage*, overstrain, and maintained that it could not have been a long-standing illness, for he had until his very last years 'enjoyed an admirable equilibrium both physically and morally'.[2]

Part of this is obviously false: both Guy and Hervé were textbook cases of what *The British Medical Dictionary* (1961) defines as 'general paralysis of the insane, found in late stages of syphilis',[3] which cannot develop overnight, and certainly not without the contribution of *spirochaeta*. But as to their paternal and maternal ancestries, however eccentric they had been, there is nothing to prove that the syphilitic infection had come from them.

Gustave de Maupassant was a passionate *coureur de femmes*, and his son's forerunner in sexual over-potency; in his old age, he showed signs of a paralysis which may have been akin to the 'progressive' variety that had killed his sons; hence the idea that he may have been the *spirochaeta* carrier. But he lived on the whole in good health until his death at seventy-eight – which seems to speak against the suspicion.

[1] According to prevailing biological findings today, there is, strictly speaking, no 'inherited' syphilis, as the genes are not affected by it; but 'congenital' syphilis does exist, owing to the infection being passed on to the embryo in the uterus. From the point of view of genetics, this is, of course, a most important distinction; yet, the infection and some symptoms of behaviour seemingly connected with it may be referred to as a 'family heritage'.

[2] '. . . il jouissait, au physique et au moral, d'un admirable équilibre' (*Souvenirs sur Maupassant*, ed. Lumbroso, p. 148).

[3] In the words of Dr Louis Thomas (op. cit.) 'cas type de la paralysie générale'.

More can hardly be said with certainty about the maternal ancestry. There were the two *enfants terribles* (in Cocteau's sense) Alfred and Laure Le Poittevin. Alfred, with his passion for self-annihilation in ecstasy – his addiction to the idea of addiction – may be regarded as a foreshadowing of Guy de Maupassant's life;[1] but it seems far-fetched (though not completely absurd) to assume that this similarity was due to an infection traceable back to Guy de Maupassant's maternal grandfather, if not earlier.

With Laure, the pros and cons are even more paradoxical. She was the maddest of the lot and yet in the end proved to be the most vigorous, and most tenacious of them all. She had always had nervous fits, and after her two sons started to grow up, her symptoms conspicuously resembled theirs. She suffered from tapeworm like Hervé, and from eye troubles like Guy. In 1878, when Guy's eyes started aching, Mme de Maupassant was reported to be unable to see the light 'without crying out in pain';[2] and her readiness to resort to drugs also suggests both Alfred's and Guy's dispositions. In January 1892, soon after Guy's internment, she complained: 'I am old and very ill, and the narcotics which I drink by the glassful only result in drying up my mind.'[3] Previously, for almost a decade, the doctor used to come and see her every day, for reasons which are not quite clear. No wonder the collapse in quick succession of her two sons pushed her into extremity; she took her bitterness out on anyone within reach, maltreated and drove away her widowed daughter-in-law and raged the whole day, gulping down glasses of laudanum. Her separated husband complained in a letter to the family lawyer:[4] 'Mme de Maupassant really ought to be given an attendant or we should arrange for her to be cared for in a *maison de santé* as she herself asks . . .'

After such tribulations and attacks, Laure de Maupassant lived another twelve years and died in Nice on 8 December 1904

---

[1] In the words of Georges Normandy (*La Fin de Maupassant*, p. 26) 'la vie obscure d'Alfred Le Poittevin apparait comme *une esquisse fidèle* de la vie glorieuse de Maupassant . . .'.

[2] Georges Normandy, *La Fin de Maupassant*, p. 36.

[3] Fragment of a letter, quoted by Georges Normandy, op. cit., p. 39.

[4] Letter to Maître Jacob, 29 March, 1892; quoted by Lumbroso, Thomas, Normandy (op. cit., pp. 52–4).

– at the age of eighty-three. She had remained erratic and bad-tempered all the time, but surprised her callers with the unflagging command of her intellectual faculties; she wrote letters correctly, and chatted in several languages fluently, and was quick in repartee, practically till her last moment. Is it possible that the hidden germ would have allowed her to carry on like this? Was the astounding similarity between her symptoms and those of her sons only due to hysteria? Scientists would differ on this – which leaves the layman free to make his own guesses. My guess is that Guy de Maupassant inherited his morbid over-sensitiveness but not his fatal disease, and that he contracted syphilis some time between his twentieth and twenty-fifth year. At the time when his genius for fiction-like fact-recording, or factual story-writing, became manifest, the spirochaeta had already been active in him for years.

I feel that his most phoney mistress, Gisèle d'Estoc, and her discoverer (or as some would say, inventor), M. Pierre Borel, can on the whole be trusted in their description of the way in which Guy de Maupassant reacted to the infection.[1] Maupassant, she writes, had confided to her that the microbe carrier had been a 'ravishing frog-girl', *grenouille* (meaning strumpet), picked up on the Seine like the heroine of *Mouche*. Having discovered his illness, he alternately boasted facetiously about it, and concealed it even from himself. Noticing one day that his hair was falling out, he ran to a doctor, but when his turn came to go into the consulting-room, he ran away in panic. Explaining this to Gisèle, he said he had been unable to overcome his reluctance to show himself naked to a stranger, even to a doctor. Yet it was his frequent boast that in physical matters he was completely without *pudeur*, a boast amply borne out by his exhibitionist pranks and performances. Indeed, one of his tasteless jests in this category consisted of parading as a syphilitic amongst intimate friends of both sexes;[2] he lied the truth as it were, he wrapped

[1] *Cahier d'Amour* (pp. 89–90) by an 'Admiratrice inconnue de Maupassant', see Appendix 8. See also Maupassant's correspondence with his boating partners (mainly Pinchon and Fontaine); with his doctors (mainly Dr Henry Cazalis, a poet under the pen-name Jean Lahor), Maupassant, *Lettres à son médecin*, 'Les Œuvres Libres', Nouvelle Série 166, Paris, 1960; and the books quoted in Appendix 7.

[2] Cf. Goncourt, *Journal*, Vol. III, p. 748; quoted on p. 188 of this book.

into farce his alarmed admission of his condition, which generally he pretended to ignore.

Looking back on the first symptoms of his illness, amongst which eye troubles had always played an outstanding part, one would be tempted to assume that he (and also his mother) suffered from exophthalmic goitre (or Graves' disease, or Basedow's disease). The second most frequently recurring symptom was the fits of migraine; and ultimately his whole nervous and secretive system began to be upset and paralysed. He blamed it on a great number of causes, ranging from the humid air of Normandy to overstraining himself whilst boating as a young man.[1] He experimented with various 'cures', from the hot sun of the Sahara to a strange variety of ice-cold shower-baths, with fantastic diets and with a dazzling multitude of drugs. He not only succeeded in blinding himself about his real illness; he drove himself into a state of hypochondria on account of imaginary or overstressed symptoms. His terror of death became apparent and a source of amusement to those who were jealous of him. Some time in 1889 Goncourt – or perhaps Mirbeau, who was his informer – was quite amused by the way an author in Spezia, who for some reason was offended by Maupassant, took his revenge; he had glanced through the pages of a medical book on eye troubles which Maupassant had been studying, and subsequently, at dinner, talked about people who had died of such diseases. The joke came off, 'Maupassant's nose literally fell into his plate'.[2]

Both from his pains and his anxieties there was, in moments of crisis, no relief except resort to narcotics, hashish, ether, morphia and cocaine[3] – especially ether, which with its illusion of a 'superior lucidity' was his guide whilst he wrote *Pierre et Jean*: 'When I am under its influence,' he said, 'it seems strange to me to be what I am, that is, to be somebody.'[4]

Ether became a secret cult for which he proselytized. He recruited Gisèle d'Estoc who recalls: '*Ether*. Ah, to feel oneself

---

[1] Goncourt, *Journal*, Vol. III, p. 1263.

[2] *Journal*, Vol. III, pp. 989–90, '. . . ce qui avait fait tomber littéralement le nez de Maupassant dans son assiette'.

[3] *Souvenirs sur Maupassant*, ed. Lumbroso, pp. 101–2.

[4] Georges Normandy, *Maupassant intime*, 1927.

carried away into that marvellous region where suffering is unknown, where the most outrageous dreams become reality!
On his recommendation I took a whiff from his golden phial.'[1]

Madame Gisèle was a boyish beauty, stiff collar, short hair,
all nerves and muscles, proud of her 'intersex' character and
promiscuity. Dressed as a man, she would bring to Maupassant's
special abode in Bezons, on the Seine, the girls she had seduced
under Lesbian rituals, preferably well-cushioned blondes, with
round buttocks and broad thighs that glittered as they lay about,
half-naked and doped. He liked to share girls, or couples of
girls, with pals; he is supposed to have shared a couple of
Lesbians even with his father for a short while.[2] This hobby of
collective love-making contains, of course, an element of converted homosexuality; and it was exciting to transpose it further,
by finding a male partner in a female. He may have had similar
ties with Mme Kann, Mme Straus, Countess Potocka, but less
uninhibitedly. 'You are the woman of my flesh,' he whispered in
Gisèle's ear;[3] she noted a selection of other compliments, too,
but I quote only the most pertinent.

Was Maupassant a genius because of his illness, or in spite of
it? It is trite to think *because*; but truth, I am afraid, is often on
the side of triteness. Whether his erstwhile famous contemporary, Césare Lombroso, was right or wrong when maintaining
that genius was nothing but the 'effervescence' of mental disease,
Maupassant's example does seem to prove his point. What he
had to say, the way he saw the world – his 'matrices' as Arthur
Koestler would call them – can be deduced from what any
reasonably well-educated young man brought up in his surroundings, with his family background and personal ties, could
have acquired through reading and even more by conversation,
without adding the slightest personal touch to it. He had
always been a good observer, no doubt; but with no signs of
this leading him anywhere in art and letters until his thirties.
He had not excelled in anything except in his appetite for exercise
in the open air, for farce and for sex, an excellence that may have
or may not have been pathological at first, but became definitely

[1] *Cahier d'Amour*, p. 83.   [2] Steegmuller, *Maupassant*.
[3] *Cahier d'Amour*, p. 73.

so when, in his late twenties, part of his physical energy was transformed into graphomania. From then on, he wrote as if in panic; the *spirochaeta* whipped a pleasant, ebullient and unimportant upper middle-class young man into the creativeness of genius.

There are indeed flashes of mind that strike us as coming from a genius because they are so utterly different from what an average man could produce, even with the best equipment of common sense and professional skill. Koestler argues – and is certainly able to support his contention with an impressive series of examples – that scientific inventions as well as artistic visions can psychologically be traced back to moments when the mind is submerged in dreams, in images that make no sense in the light of everyday wakefulness.[1] Behind Pythagoras's $a^2 + b^2 = c^2$, behind Einstein's $e = mc^2$, there was initially their dreamland. How much more so, one would be tempted to believe, behind a work of art! An artist of genius is expected to create a dreamland that competes in hypnotic power with reality, that surprises an appreciative audience with the extraordinary imagination it reveals.

But Maupassant's feat was just the opposite: it showed the *non plus ultra* of what a man of common sense could produce when skilled in the art of story-telling. The stories that established his reputation were marked by a lucidity and sense of balance which we are accustomed to associate with good health, sound nerves and mediocrity. This was the reason why some of his admirers refused to admit any causal link between his abilities and his disease;[2] and this also was the reason why many others, though appreciative of his gifts, thought it most unstylish to call him a 'genius' – his writing was too limpid and elegant, and showed too much clever craftsmanship to be granted the touch

[1] *The Act of Creation*, Hutchinson, 1964.
[2] Let me quote a particularly shattering judgment on people holding views like mine: 'Parmi les critiques, certains sont allés jusqu' à prétendre que la maladie de Maupassant conditionnait son œuvre littéraire. La définition de Lombroso, "le génie est une effervescence de la folie", était alors en vogue. Vogue encouragée, bien entendu, par les philistins qui, faute de génie, entendaient se réserver le monopole du bon sens' (Suzanne Pairault, reviewing a new edition of Maupassant's stories, in *La Guilde du Livre*, Lausanne, September 1962, p. 321).

of genius. Perhaps the neatest (and not, by any means, the most deprecatory) expression of this view came from M. André Maurois – himself a craftsman *par excellence* – who thought that Maupassant 'had too much talent to be a genius'.[1]

The truth is that Maupassant *was* a genius if this word makes sense at all; it was his 'healthy' works, lucid, balanced, matter-of-fact, which revealed this genius in full strength; but this genius was the product of an illness, and inconceivable without it.

The madman reported with intensified lucidity on what could be seen by the sane man; but, occasionally, he had glimpses of his own insanity, that is, of his nature. If he had not ended up a lunatic, his excursions into occultism and the phantom world would not even strike us as pathological; we would just say that as a good Norman he was both intrigued by phantasmagoria and amused by their farcical potentialities. He was as interested in the abnormal as any normal person might be, and he handed in his visiting card as a writer of ghost stories as early as 1875, in the middle of his unspectacular Civil Service career, with a feeble little short story,[2] under the pen-name Joseph Prunier, dealing with the weird souvenir he had received from Swinburne. Then from 1880 to 1890 his fascination by the 'Macchabées' must take its place amongst the spurs which kept his observant mind moving;[3] the swing of his imagination into the melo-dramatic would result in terrifying visions;[4] and a number of his short stories can be read as accounts of his hallucinations and forebodings of his approaching end.[5]

To what extent did Maupassant believe in the ghost-like appearances he described? He is unlikely to have known the

[1] Artine Artinian, *Maupassant Criticism in France*, King's Crown Press New York, 1941. (Maurois really made use of a crack that used to be current about Lamartine: 'he is too much of a genius to have talent'. The reverse, Maurois suggested, should apply to Guy de Maupassant.)

[2] *La Main d'écorché.*

[3] His short story *Sur l'Eau*, admirably written, is perhaps most typical.

[4] *Le Champ d'Olivier*, written towards the end of his career (published February 1890) was his most important work to this effect. It is not his most perfect story but one can well understand Taine preferring it to all and calling it 'Aeschylean'.

[5] *La Peur; Lui?; L'Auberge;* two versions of *Le Horla; Qui sait?* etc.

answer. He did not believe in the supernatural; nor did he sub-scribe to any rational denial of the supernatural. If he believed in anything it was in his senses; and if his senses took him for a ride to the kingdom of spectres and demons he thought his findings no more and no less worth recording than any down-to-earth observation made whilst watching the peasants in the Goderville market-place or his colleagues at the Ministry of Marine. 'A marvellous thing,' Marcel Prévost noted; 'he [Maupassant] brought to the observation of these phantoms the same lucidity that he brought to reality. . . . His dilated eyes faithfully photo-graphed the phantoms.' [1] Whether this is really so 'marvellous', as Marcel Prévost thought, may be open to argument; other readers may rather feel their spirits drooping before phantoms as trivial as Maupassant's; but for good or evil, it was character-istic of Maupassant's inability to be obscure even when reflecting shadows. And though he did not rank very high as a writer of phantasmagoria, *Le Horla*, written, rewritten and published in 1886, at the zenith of his career, is a remarkable piece both for the fine descriptive passages it contains and for the psychological process to which it points. The story is about a middle-aged man unable to get rid of a ghost who is in possession of his house. He never actually sees the ghost, but he sees its movements, he sees the pages of the book on his desk turned by the ghost, he sees a flower held in the air by the ghost's invisible fingers. The ghost penetrates his walls and flutters about unseen as befits ghosts, but drinks his water and milk like human beings, though rather temperance-minded ones. In the first version of the story, it was a 'patient' who, invited by his psychiatrist to talk, told his story to a select audience; the second and longer version took the form of a journal, interrupted by the diarist's apparent catastrophe. He could no longer bear the ghost's presence; he locked and burned down his house to annihilate the ghost; but, then he is struck by panic: 'No . . . no . . . without doubt . . .

---

[1] 'Chose merveilleuse: il apportait à l'observation de ces fantômes la même lucidité qu'au réel. En plein dans le domaine de la chimère et de l'hallucination, son œil dilaté photographiait fidèlement les fantômes.' Preface by M. Prévost to Maupassant's *Contes Choisis, Édition pour la Jeunesse*, Albin Michel, Paris, 1959, p. 15. (I am indebted to Mrs Stella Apperley for drawing my attention to this piece.)

without any doubt ... he is not dead ... Then ... then ... there is nothing left for me but to kill myself.' So the story ends. Is it the hallucination of a madman? Or the appearance of a being from another plane of existence? The hero of the story does suspect himself of madness; but he has the visible, the tangible proofs of the ghost's existence. Is it possible that he has sensed a new type or being that may appear as an illness today and may be the dominant animal of the earth tomorrow? 'A new kind of being! Why not? Assuredly it must happen! Why should we be the last comers!' He feels his energies drained; could it not be that the ghost, coming master of the globe, is exploiting man, as man has been exploiting horse and cattle? It is the madman who asks these questions; the author lets him ask, and does not answer.

Six years after the publication of this story, Maupassant literally believed in phenomena far more fantastic than those described in *Le Horla*; in reading it one may, therefore, assume that he recorded his own phantasmagoria as realities. This indeed may have been the case; but it did not prevent him from making use of the 'subjects' given him by others and then turning the frightening experience into a farce. According to Edmond de Goncourt, Maupassant got the subject from Georges de Porto-Riche; according to Georges de Porto-Riche, he got it from Edmond de Goncourt;[1] according to René Dumesnil, he got it from Léon Hennique; and anyway, the man from whom he had got it is supposed to have said, 'If this story is by a madman, then it is I who am mad.'[2] According to Gisèle d'Estoc, Maupassant made a similar remark himself: ' "I have just finished *Le Horla* [he told her]. Everybody will say I am mad!" And he gave a strange, cracked laugh ... Guy ... never gave a better proof of his mental equilibrium than in writing this novel.'[3]

He may have worked with iron assiduity on writing down his hallucinations: this was not out of tune with his character. Though his words were as clear as words can be, he lived in a

[1] Unless Morand (*Vie de Guy de Maupassant*, p. 197) mistook the identity of the two authors.

[2] Quoted by Dumesnil, *Guy de Maupassant*, pp. 204–5. ('Si cette nouvelle est d'un fou, c'est moi qui suis de fou.')

[3] *Cahier d'Amour*, p. 74.

constant penumbra, never quite sure when he was joking and when performing in deadly earnest something that might be taken for a schoolboy's prank. Some discovered the symptoms of lunacy in his behaviour at an early stage. Anatole France, for instance, is recorded as having told the following story to his secretary:

> Long before *Le Horla* appeared I realized that Maupassant's mind was deranged. One evening I called on him, thinking he would be alone, but found he had guests. I met him in the hall, and excused myself.
>
> 'Why won't you stay?' he asked me.
>
> 'You can see I am not in evening dress.'
>
> 'Is that all? All right, have mine.'
>
> To my great stupefaction, he begins to unbutton his waistcoat and his braces, in that hall packed with women. He repeated:
>
> 'I'll give you my trousers and my tailcoat.'
>
> I had all the trouble in the world to get away from this madman . . .[1]

The queer side of this story is that it is so very much like the healthy and sturdy Maupassant, with his wild practical jokes. The madman was not a new man in him; it was himself, intensified to the extent of inarticulateness. In *Le Horla* he had reached an intermediate stage: he talked of inarticulateness articulately. Whoever gave him the 'subject', from then on he stuck to it like a maniac, as he stuck to its title. 'Horla' was his coinage; he may or may not have thought of *hors* (outside) and *là* (there), and *horreur*, and *hurler* (to howl) and a number of other words linked through onomatopoeic associations, but the name once conceived became a reality. He transposed the ghost into a technological mechanism. He joined the Aeronautical Society and assisted its engineers in constructing a balloon which then was stylishly christened 'Le Horla'. He did not pilot it, but two of his flights on board 'Le Horla' are on record, together with an interesting piece of reportage from this pioneer epoch of flying[2]

[1] J. J. Brousson, *Anatole France en pantoufles*, Crès et Co., Paris, 1924, pp. 131–2.

[2] *Le Voyage du Horla*, July 1887. It figures in some collections of his short stories though it is really a newspaper report.

and with quarrelsome letters a few years later in which he protested that it had not been his idea to call the balloon 'Le Horla'; he disliked such publicity stunts . . .[1]

From 1885, if not earlier, Maupassant was constantly haunted by his imaginary *alter ego*, 'Le Horla'. From 1888, his megalomania and persecution mania became unmistakable. By 1890 he was utterly sick, and his state went on deteriorating rapidly; he looked haggard, distraught and as if disintegrating. In the summer of 1891 he tried, in quick succession, treatment at Divonne-les-Bains and Champel-les-Bains, near Geneva. At the end of that year, in December, he put his will in order.

46 · Between madness and death

Amongst his letters there is one quoted by Pol Neveux[2] – addressee and date uncertain, but typical of the tragic moods of his last years:

> If only I could bring myself to speak of it, I should reveal all that I feel deep in my heart, thoughts unexplored, tumultuous and desolate. I feel them swelling and poisoning me like bile in the bilious. But if I could one day spew them out, then perhaps they would evaporate, and I should find my heart light and joyous again – who knows? Thinking becomes an abominable torment when the brain is like an open wound. There are so many contusions in my head that my ideas cannot move without making me want to howl with pain. Why? why? Dumas would say I have a bad stomach. I believe rather that I have a poor heart, at once proud and ashamed, a very human heart, this old human heart at which one laughs, but which can be moved and can ache. In my head, too, I have the Latin spirit which is very worn out. . . . People doubtless think me to be one of those who are completely indifferent to the world. I am a sceptic, but that is not the same thing; I am a sceptic because I have clear eyes. And my eyes

[1] Steegmuller, *Maupassant*, p. 234.   [2] *Œuvres complètes*, p. lxxiii.

tell my heart, 'hide yourself away, old fellow, for you are grotesque', and so it hides.

His Schopenhauer had logically demonstrated that to exist was tantamount to suffering. Maupassant's state of mind was now a vivid illustration of this philosophy. The more he suffered the more he felt the idea of death unbearable. The more futile existence was the more difficult it seemed to leave it without doing anything about its futility. He had hitherto resisted the natural temptation of man to try and defeat death by producing masterpieces, begetting children or making common cause with hoped-for supernatural beings. He could resist it no longer. When his mind had become an open wound and he felt like howling and moaning with pain, he at last gave in and started writing for posterity.

He made a decision never again to write short stories.[1] He would concentrate on novels, on larger schemes, on more ambitious subjects. In spite of his (justified) pride in having revived the 'French national taste for *contes et nouvelles*', he was now carried away by the vision of monumentality, as are many who cannot completely dissociate value from magnitude. This would not have mattered; concentration on larger plans (as Flaubert rightly sensed) was a rewarding exercise in 'originality' even for those more gifted in shorter genres. Great efforts are as a rule failures if measured by what they have been aiming at; but successful in sensitizing the brains of those who have failed. They show minds torn up, in a fertile chaos. Maupassant's subsequent two failures, the two fragments of novels started by him in the last period of his life, *L'Ame étrangère* and *L'Angélus*

---

[1] He had several times decided not to write plays either – and yet, his play *Musotte*, written in partnership with Jacques Normand and produced by Koenig in the Gymnase in March of 1891, was his first real theatrical success; the second and last one was *La Paix du Ménage*, with a first night in the Théâtre Français on 6 March 1893, that is after his internment. The former was very favourably reviewed (*inter alia* by Lemaître, Sarcey, Wolff); the latter with more tact than enthusiasm; but the audience liked both. After Maupassant's death a fragment of a play he had started writing (presumably in 1891) based on his story, *Yvette*, was found amongst his manuscripts. The stage thus never stopped attracting him; but it was not the media through which his originality revealed itself.

are strikingly different. As pieces of narrative prose, both are quite interesting to read; but their real drama lies in the fact that they are unfinished and that their author was unable to round them off.

L'Ame étrangère – 'Strange Soul' – or 'Estranged'? 'Alien' or 'Alienated'? it may mean all of them – with a *casino* as the jumping-off board of its narrative, seems to lead us once again into the realm of opulent homelessness, both metaphorically and literally speaking: with an atmosphere no less sensual, luxurious and *blasé*, and more markedly cosmopolitan, than *Notre Cœur*. It is dominated by an admiration (which Maupassant did not admit) for that world where 'opinions change with the fashion, concerning aesthetics no less than clothes', that 'bizarre free-masonry of high-class society, unique and without country'. And there is a woman (modelled, apparently, after a notoriously polyandrist Russian princess),[1] 'a sort of slave of love, charming, complaisant, devoted, and venal . . .'. His elegance of style is unblemished; his devices, unaltered. M. Vial notes one of his favourite *finesses*, that of coupling two contrasting adjectives with 'and' instead of 'but'; the unobtrusive *pointe* of the sentence ending with 'dévouée et payée' is a typical example. He still knew his job; but was this enough to express what he sensed with 'his brain like an open wound'? No wonder he felt it inadequate and ran away from it.

He started *L'Angélus* forthwith, in 1890, and continued working on it in the early part of 1891. He did so with a quasi-religious zeal and a hatred for God which had not previously been noticeable amongst his incentives. This novel, he told François, was going to be the *couronnement de ma carrière*. He was in a solemn mood, more of a believer in the sense of his work than he had ever admitted to be, whilst at the same time, more raging than ever against the senselessness of life and that suffering which he saw as its essence. This work was an attempt to besiege the universe. He was to condense in it what he felt most horrible and, therefore, most significant in this world. Like his first important story and some others of the early 1880s, it revived the memory of the Prussian War, but without the comfort to be found in the charm or the patriotism of a French *cocotte*, or in

[1] Tassart, *Souvenirs sur Guy de Maupassant*, p. 232.

the mishaps or jitters of the arrogant Prussians.[1] A *châtelaine*, pregnant at the time of the invasion, is brutalized by the Prussian soldiers and gives birth to a boy with a broken leg, who is to be a cripple for life. Did Maupassant have his mother in mind as when writing *Une Vie*? And his late brother, with his crippled soul? It seems likely; this little Henri in *L'Angélus*, just like little Hervé in life, had a brother, four years his elder, who unwittingly made his life even more tragic. Maupassant's plan was to describe the misery and loneliness of this helpless being living with his mother, whose compassion does not relieve him. He falls in love with a girl; and this girl falls in love with his happy brother.

Maupassant had often described tragedies stemming from callousness; in *L'Angélus*, it is rather the pointlessness and tyranny of devotion which seem to have haunted his mind. With a clear hint at his own predicament – his embarrassment with the mother, not dispelled, but rather strengthened by the sincerity of their mutual affection – he described a doctor who was sacrificing his scientific career in order to live in the country with his mother . . . The universe as he saw it was changing its character; it had become God-ridden without improving. Maupassant had never been a believer though he was too little speculative by character to be a non-believer proper; he had simply laughed at religion, and considered any belief in life after death a 'faiblesse indigne'.[2] In *L'Angélus* God emerges as a positively malevolent spirit; and Christian love is no longer laughable. It is an *abbé* in this novel who declares:

> Christ was destined to be also a victim of God. He had received from him a false mission, that of misleading us with a new religion. But the divine ambassador perfected his mission as a union so beautiful, so magnificent, that he has assumed in our minds the place of his inspirer.

Maupassant was delirious with joy about this work. 'It is my *chef d'œuvre*,' he kept repeating, 'I roam about in it as in a room.' He felt he had lighted upon something he had been looking for all his life. He kept the manuscript with him day and night, he would not part with it. And he would read it to his friends. This

[1] Cf. Chapters 20, 32 and 35.
[2] *Souvenirs sur Maupassant*, ed. Lumbroso, pp. 293–4.

had not been his habit since the days of Médan; as an 'industriel des lettres', he would not discuss literature with his friends, and certainly not tear himself open as an author by reading his unfinished works to them; but with *L'Angélus* he could no longer keep up his detachment. Whilst reading it aloud he burst into tears about that brutalized mother, that crippled baby.

He wrote fifty pages, was unable to carry on, and raged with bitterness about his inability. It was in this state of alternating exhilaration over the *chef d'œuvre*, emotion over its subject, and despair over his failing powers that he was found by the poet, Auguste Dorchain [1] and his wife, who met him in the summer of 1891, in the Swiss spa, Champel. Maupassant took out a batch of manuscripts from his briefcase and showed them the fifty pages. 'For a year I have been unable to write another page,' he said. 'If in three months' time I have not finished this book, I shall kill myself.'

He talked ceaselessly. If it was not about this novel, then it was about his illness and cures and doctors and adventures. He had been chased away from his villa in Divonne by a fantastic inundation. And he had been unable to get the shower-bath on which he was particularly keen, 'la douche à la Charcot' that had a powerful jet, so powerful that only the toughest kind of men could stand it, but he, Maupassant, could. . . . He would not leave the Dorchains alone, except for a few hours when he visited Geneva. He returned in high spirits; because, so one gathers from Tassart's recollections, he had seen Cazalis. But to Dorchain he gave a different account whispering in his ear that he had just seduced a *petite femme* – 'I was brilliant, I am cured!' – and he had also had time to see a Rothschild who gave him a 'quasi-Royal' reception. His pride in love-making and his fascination for money-making triggered off his lunatic fantasies. 'See this umbrella?' He showed an umbrella which was like anybody else's. 'Strange? Only obtainable in a certain shop in Faubourg Sainte-Honoré [he gave the exact address]. I have ordered more than fifty through the entourage of Princess Mathilde.' And next day: 'See this stick? With this stick I

---

[1] Most of what is known about the background of *L'Angélus* and of Maupassant's behaviour in Champel comes from Dorchain (*Les Annales*, 3 June 1900; Normandy, *La Fin de Maupassant*, pp. 113–19).

defended myself one day against three pimps in front and three mad dogs behind me.' Dorchain became bewildered and exhausted; he wished he had never run into this mad genius. He could not follow Maupassant in his laughter; but he joined him in his tears over the manuscript of *L'Angélus*.

In one corner of his brain, Maupassant knew exactly what was wrong with him, he knew better than anyone else. 'Don't you think,' he asked Dr Frémy, 'that I am going insane? . . . If so, I should be told. Between madness and death, there is no question of hesitation; my choice is made.' In a letter to Heredia, at the end of 1890, he had already made clear that he was ready to die, 'I don't want to survive myself.'

He wrote, presumably in 1891, the letter to 'Madame X . . .'[1] which defined his state of mind most precisely:

> Those dogs which howl express very well my present state. It is this lamentable wail – addressed to the void, which goes nowhere and tells nothing, but hurls into the night a cry of fettered anguish – which I wish I could utter. If I could moan like them, I would go away sometimes, often, into a wide open plain or the depths of a wood, and I should howl like that for hours on end in the darkness.

Back in Paris from Switzerland, he discovers announcements of his insanity in the press. He hurries to his mother, in Nice, to reassure her. From Cannes in December he writes letters to his doctors and lawyers warning them of his end. Herewith some fragments:

To Dr Georges Daremberg:

> . . . my throat and all my mucous membrane are on fire. I can no longer use any perfume . . . all alcoholic emanations affect my brain. . . . I am ravenous for morphine as for salt. . . . But whatever you do, do not repeat to anyone that these ladies came to see me. That would compromise them terribly. Besides all their family is here, and I am sure they would not have come without them. I am in a pitiable state. . . . Yesterday my whole body, all my flesh and skin was impregnated with salt . . . I have no more saliva . . . the salt has dried it

[1] Quoted by Pol Neveux in his Preface to *Œuvres complètes*.

all up. . . . My headaches are so strong that I have to hold my head in my hands and it feels like the head of a corpse.

To Maître Jacob, 26 December: 'I am dying. I think I shall be dead in two days time.'

During this last week of December, Maupassant was shuttling between the *deux dames* (mentioned to Dr Daremberg) in Cannes, and his mother in Nice. He was under the public eye, watched by doctors, spied on by reporters; yet, accounts of these days are conflicting. It is not even absolutely sure who the *deux dames* were, though it seems likely that it was Marie Kann with her sister, Mme Albert Cahen d'Anvers. (François in his *Souvenirs* refers with puzzling horror to a 'lady in grey' who had free access to his master in his last months spent in Paris and who was suspected by many to be Marie Kann, though it is unlikely). Madame de Maupassant, in Nice, was terror-stricken to think of the ladies in Cannes – whether on account of maternal jealousy or because she really believed that they would do some harm to her son. Of this, her words did not give any indication. Guy went to see her on 1 January; they had a meal together (accounts vary as to which part of the day); and, as Mme de Maupassant later recalled:

> Despite my prayers, my tears, instead of resting, he wanted to leave immediately to return to Cannes.
>
> 'Don't go, my son,' I cried, 'don't go.' I clung to him, I begged him, I dragged my helpless old age on my knees to him. . . .

All in vain, Guy returned. In his house, 'Chalet de l'Isère', François bled him and served him with camomile tea, then later grapes. At about eleven, Maupassant retired. Late at night, a telegram arrived from 'a country in the Orient'[1] – the last message he received from 'the lady in grey'. François took it over, his master was fast asleep; his revolver was lying about but empty; some days before, after seeing him fire through the window at an imaginary enemy, François had secretly taken out the bullets.

At 1.45 a.m. François was woken up by a noise. He found his master with his throat bleeding.

[1] Normandy, *La Fin de Maupassant*, p. 142.

Look what I have done, François. I have cut my throat . . .
There is no doubt that I am going insane.

Raymond, the seaman, and Dr de Valcourt came to the rescue.
On 7 January 1892 Guy de Maupassant was interned in the
maison de santé of Dr Blanche at Passy.

47 · Death

Whilst still in Cannes, before leaving for Passy, François and
the two seamen did what they could for their master who mostly
lay about lethargically. Leaning on their arms, Maupassant
walked to the sea to cast a glance of farewell at his *Bel-Ami*.
One night, he got suddenly excited: 'François, are you ready?
. . . War has been declared.' Tassart answered that they were
going to leave on the following day. Maupassant retorted in-
dignantly: 'What? You want us to put off our departure though
you know how urgent it is? . . . It has always been agreed that
for the *revanche*, we are to march together! You know well this
must be so . . .'[1]

On 6 January he was taken by train to Paris by Tassart and a
male nurse sent for him by Dr Blanche. From the Gare de Lyon
Dr Cazalis and Ollendorff, the publisher, saw him to the mental
sanatorium in Passy, where Dr Blanche, attended by Dr Meuriot
and Dr Franklin-Grout, took charge of him.

It was a stately and comfortable lunatic asylum, with a beautiful park; as pleasant as the most luxurious of prisons could be.
François was allowed to look after him, and he could receive
friends but (as arranged by Mme de Maupassant) no women;
Mme Lecomte du Nouÿ alone was able to penetrate through the
bar. At first he could feed himself, then had to be fed; his physical
functions, one after another, cut out.

How do you expect a madman to behave? He just carries on;
the weirdest of his symptoms is their resemblance to what the
sane man used to be.

[1] See end of Chapter 20.

When on his arrival at Dr Blanche's a member of the medical staff asked Maupassant how he was, he answered, 'Very well, Doctor, very well, I get my erection very well indeed,' and he uncovered himself to prove he was telling the truth.[1] He had always boasted, more or less jokingly, about his sexual faculties.[2]

His second lifelong obsession was money. He had always been scared, to quite a pathological extent, of being cheated – a sickish inclination that made him an efficient businessman, as sickish priapism made him a robust bedfellow – and with the aggravating state of his nerves, his fear had grown into a persecution mania, particularly manifest in his quarrels with his publishers. At Dr Blanche's, he also turned his fury on his faithful François: François had plagiarized his works, François had embezzled his money: 'You are a thief, François, you are sacked!'[3] He first only mentioned some hundred francs, but the sum grew rapidly into millions and milliards. In August 1892, that is, six months after his internment, a benevolent rumour had it that he was improving. At the same time, Goncourt, in a roundabout way, learned that this was not the case and that Maupassant, in his hallucinations, was talking to bankers about huge business deals.[4] Just like that mercenary-minded *novelliere*!

The two obsessions – sex and treasure – appropriately fused in his concentration on his bladder. He withheld his urine deliberately with a persistence that recalled his ability to control his sex glands. When he had not emptied his bladder for some thirty-six hours, he violently protested against the use of a catheter: 'The Director of this house is a pederast who will ruin my brains with his *sonde* . . .' And about his urine: 'It is diamonds! Put them into the safe!' And: 'This can't go into the pot. . . . I mustn't piss: my urine is all jewels. It is with these that I went to the *femmes du monde*.'[5]

Another obsession, his personal quarrel with God (which had started, as far as can be traced, at the time when he wrote

---

[1] 'Le médecin lui demandait comment il allait. "Je vais très bien, Docteur. Je vais très bien. Je bande toujours très bien." Il se découvrait et montrait sa verge qui se dressait progressivement' (Paul Léautaud, 'Journal Littéraire', Vol. VIII, pp. 270–1, *Mecure de France*, 1960; quoting Claude Berton).

[2] See Appendix 9.

[3] Normandy, op. cit., p. 222.

[4] *Journal*, Vol. IV, pp. 295–6.

[5] Normandy, op. cit.

L'Angélus) continued in outbursts even more personal. It was God who conspired with François to deprive him of his millions. Both God and François had tried to estrange the Rothschilds from him. Havard and Ollendorff had also somehow been involved. God, you 'stupide vieillard!' he shouted. 'God, you are nothing but a monster!' on other occasions. 'I shall have the whole world . . . You know that the heathen gods love me.'

Or else he found another personal contact: God had proclaimed, from the Eiffel Tower, yesterday afternoon *à tout Paris*, that Monsieur de Maupassant was the son of God and of Jesus Christ.' Another vision: 'Devils alone are eternal. . . . I am stronger than God! . . . The French Army is disgraceful, and in a lamentable state . . .' And his megalomania fusing with his deepest erotic attachment: 'Jesus Christ slept with my mother: I am God's son.'

He called 'Hervé, Hervé!' to come to the rescue. 'My brother is alive in his tomb.'

In turn he felt he was God, he was the devil, he was Nature. In spring, he pushed green branches in the soil and told François, 'Let us plant these and next year we shall find little Maupassants.'

And his desire to 'howl like those dogs' did at last find an outlet. He did howl, he even licked the wall of his room. 'Maupassant only talks to the walls,' Goncourt notes;[1] and then, on 30 January 1893, he describes how at the Princess's he met Dr Blanche who 'laisse entendre qu'il [Maupassant] est en train de *s'animaliser*'.[2]

Maupassant's main obsessions in the glorified madhouse are traceable back to the healthy, the sturdy, the vigorous Maupassant, to the 'young bull at large' or to the efficient and triumphant *notable commerçant* which he had been during his 'meteoric' career. When at the peak of his creative powers he knew there was a madman in him, it was then that he wrote *Le Horla*. He went on knowing the madman in himself, even when mad in the very narrowest medical sense, when he was at Dr Blanche's. 'Hurry up and leave me,' he told his friend, Albert Cahen d'Anvers, who had called on him, 'for in a moment's time

[1] *Journal*, Vol. IV, p. 221.   [2] *Journal*, Vol. IV, p. 357.

I shall no longer be myself'. Then he rang the bell and asked for the strait-jacket.

He died on 6 July 1893 (this seems the likely date though the death certificate puts it on the 7th) and was buried on the 8th,[1] in the 26th section of the Montparnasse cemetery. His mother was unable to attend, presumably, on account of her illness. His father in Sainte-Maxime only learned of the event from the newspaper. It was, none the less, an impressive funeral, the procession including a great number of friends, mistresses, admirers, sniffers and even colleagues such as Roujon, Mendès, Joseph Reinach, Alexis, Marcel Prévost and Henry Céard, who delivered a moving address. M. Morand thinks it conspicuous that neither official literature nor literary youth was represented[2] and I am sorry to have to agree with him.

Zola bade Maupassant farewell at his tomb, recalling first his early literary triumphs:

> The thing which struck us [he continued], those of us who followed Maupassant with all our sympathy, was his immediate conquest of hearts. He had only to appear and recount his stories, and all the tenderness of the great public was immediately extended towards him. . . . Certainly I do not know of another example of a beginning so happy, of success so rapid and unanimous; he appealed to all types of intelligence, he touched all types of sensibility, and so we have the extraordinary spectacle of a frank and robust talent, which conceded nothing, and which at a stroke secured the admiration, even the affection of the reading public, that public which ordinarily makes new artists pay so dearly for the right to develop in their own way. If he was understood and loved from the first, it was because the French soul found in him the gifts and qualities that have created its finest achievements. He . . . had clarity, simplicity, moderation and strength.

> We must not, of course, attempt to set limits to art; we must accept the complicated, the precious and the obscure, but it

[1] On the 9th, according to *Souvenirs sur Maupassant*, ed. Lumbroso, pp. 98–9; but *Le Figaro* on 9 July 1893 published a detailed account of the funeral saying it had taken place 'hier' and it is 8 July in the records of the Montparnasse cemetery.

[2] *Vie de Guy de Maupassant*, p. 232.

seems to me that these are but the excesses, or, as one might say, the feast of the moment, and that we must always return to the simple and the clear, as we return to our daily bread which nourishes us without satiety.

'Apart from his glory as a writer,' Zola concluded, 'Maupassant will always remain one of the happiest, and one of the unhappiest men the world has ever known.'

48 · In retrospect

'One of the happiest, one of the unhappiest.' It is clear why one of the happiest.

Why one of the unhappiest? The answer, again, seems obvious: syphilis. His brother's early death, his own pains and decay, his mother's griefs for her sons, reflected in his own griefs, all were cause enough for unhappiness, but surely his dark outlook on life did not stem from his disease? This may or may not have been 'congenital'; but his pessimism certainly was. The experiences of his ancestry, both in their family history and in literary history, amply accounted for his deep-seated conviction that life was a tiresome and senseless affair. Maybe this was but a superficial opinion, which did not penetrate his reflexes, until the germs attacked his brain. Maybe it was his illness that sensitized his mind and enabled it to convey in articulate observations what had only been his lyrical visions of a drab and aching universe. He may have owed his creative power to his sufferings – the intensity of his happiness to the intensity of his unhappiness. But the blueprint of that unhappiness is discernible in the happy-go-lucky loiterer, *flâneur*, that he was before his migraines and his graphomania developed, simultaneously, during the years 1878–80. His style had matured but his outlook had not changed when he succeeded in projecting 'The Great Miseries of the Little People'.[1]

He possessed a rare mixture of abilities: humility and impertinence. He watched facts humbly and took notice of them impertinently; he became their recorder, definitely without

[1] See footnote 2 on p. 93.

illusions. There were many poets, thinkers and authors before and after him, including his own Flaubert, who professed to be disgusted with life and contemptuous of human beings. Were they absolutely sincere? Some of them may have been; but not those of whom we know. Anyone able to draw the logical conclusions of such a conviction would kill himself without bothering to explain his reasons for doing so. To express boredom with life is a contradiction in terms. Flaubert performed that contradiction more beautifully than anybody else. After a torrent of misanthropic exclamations he would jubilantly congratulate his disciple on a masterpiece because *ça restera* – that is, it was going to make a lasting mark in that atrocious world which was not worth entering at all! Maupassant, unlike his master, was not duped by such lofty substitute illusions. He doubted not only the value of survival of the writer in his works but also its possibility. A name mispronounced, thoughts misunderstood, were the utmost that could be passed on to coming generations. He found it childish to worry about posterity: 'We can hardly understand Villon,' he said, 'and the speech of the Ile de France in the twelfth century is another language to us . . .'[1]

Creativeness without any illusions as a working hypothesis: Maupassant came as near to this state of mind as possible. He obeyed a driving power which he attributed to the 'industriel des lettres' in him; this was, until his middle thirties, the utmost he did in the nature of trying to find a common denominator for his efforts and observations. He kept his eyes open and pretended to do it only for trifling or non-existent reasons. It was a posture bound to drive him mad. It would have driven anybody mad. His particular madness started, simultaneously, with mythicizing the sensualism of the *salons* and with searching for the Superman in the invisible features of a milk-drinking ghost. It ended up, after all and in spite of all, in an application for immortality. God ceased for him to be non-existent, He became alternately a pal and an enemy. Procreation ceased to be senseless; if impossible, or unsafe, to perform it through children, one may as well do it through plants. Using all his art as a writer, he suddenly started aiming at survival. He had intended to step

[1] Frank Harris, *My Life and Adventures*, Bestseller Library, London, 1958, p. 235.

into immortality through *L'Angélus*; and when he faltered he knew he must die.

This in a nutshell is his life's drama. It is, of course, a de-naturalized nutshell: the medical factor has been removed. In fact, one may argue, it was not his dark outlook on life that drove him mad but the *spirochaeta pallida*. Behind all those ghosts and countesses, behind those occult forces and occult nymphomaniacs, those sobs in the course of reading *L'Angélus*, that urine consisting of diamonds, that God who had slept with Laure Le Poittevin and conspired with François Tassart, there was the disease which would have resulted in similar obsessions, whatever his outlook, his art or his work had been. This is true; except that without the disease that turned him into a grapho-maniac, he could never have devoted himself to an art in which he did not believe, by recording the details of a life not worth either living or recording. We cannot have it both ways: we have either to recognize the pathological strain in the soundest and clearest written records of human life or assume that this very soundness and clarity led into spiritualism and obscurantism and, ultimately, lunacy. This is not to prove that Maupassant was wrong in what he recorded; only that if he was right, he should logically have killed himself long before he first tried to do so, and certainly should not have sacrificed himself in order to pass his observations on to his fellow-men. Without that paradox, there would be no Maupassant.

The Médan group in which Maupassant emerged has often been referred to as the Literary Left of its time. This denomina-tion is, on the whole, justified; as a pointer to the underlying affinity between non-conformity and leftishness. To belong to the Left meant originally an assertion of one's right to dissent. Zola and his young men made full use of this right; they set out to challenge the fundamental lies of the order in which they lived. They defied convention. But they were, as a group, revolu-tionaries neither of artistic form nor of political creed. They were not, or for a passing moment only, what would be called today the *avant-garde*; if Zola had ever been *avant-garde* it was before he became a naturalist best-seller in the 1860s, when he was poor and skinny and young and fought as an art critic for the ridiculed *Salon des refusés*. By the 1880s the appreciation of impressionist art had become a polished half-commonplace to which Maupassant gracefully subscribed; though he, perhaps more than any of his colleagues in the Médan group, preserved his predilection for the conventionally showy, both in painting and in junk. In 1887 he joined a group of writers – Coppée, Leconte de Lisle, Sully Prudhomme, Sardou amongst others – in protesting against the Eiffel Tower, built for the World Fair of 1889. And his travel diary *La Vie errante* (1890) starts with a scene in which 'I leave Paris and even France because I can no longer bear the Eiffel Tower'. True enough, he wrote it in the mood when he loved to be quarrelsome, and appear to be one of the smart set. His further outbursts against that tower indicated an obsession with its monster-like appearance rather than aesthetic distaste. Anyway, before escaping from Paris on its account, he liked to meet friends in its restaurant. His association with the old Parnassian and Romantic poets and with playwright *boulevardiers* in the defence of the conventional architecture of the city serves only to indicate that his Literary Left was not committed to modern taste in other forms of art.

Even less were the young men of Médan wedded to the political Left. Most of the elder artists and scholars whom they regarded as their masters or pioneers were, to say the least, sceptical about democratic and socialist ideas; not to mention Edmond de Goncourt with his coy yearning for old Versailles and his envious hissing against his contemporaries and their Republic: even Renan and Flaubert, though they had scandalized the conservatives with their outspokenness about flesh and God, were in many a way themselves conservative; and the rigorous Monsieur Taine shocked people more by stripping the Revolution of its myth than by his equally agnostic approach to Christianity. The barricade had by this time become as myth-ridden as the throne had been; no wonder a Literary Left with determination to abolish myths had to challenge the slogans urging progress as much as those warning against it. Zola at the head of the Literary Left (unlike, for instance, Courbet or, in his own fickle way, Verlaine) felt no sympathy for the Commune, least of all for its patriotic heroism of despair. And as to Anatole

France, regarded today with reason as a socialist classic, he did not at that time belong even to the Literary Left; he was as averse to Zola as he had been to the Communards – it was his taste and sense of justice polished on Latin and classic French traditions, which later drove him, almost against himself, into the camp of dissenters and reformers and protestors.

The intellectual *élite* of Maupassant's time was, no doubt, a fringe ornament of the *haute-bourgeoisie*; to most of the intellectuals, crusading for the elevation of the masses, with its outworn slogans, seemed pathetically old-fashioned as well as dangerously subversive. And yet there was a 'Literary Left', in which the liberals of Taine's 'hot-house' joined hands with the socialists of the miserable suburbs. They came together subconsciously in opposing the interests and passions that encouraged national intolerance, isolation and war.

The predominance of the Médan group in literature, and of the cosmopolitan *haute-bourgeosie* in social life, coincided with a shift in emphasis of militant national feeling, by which the emotional fuel of the Left was to become the ammunition of the Right. In Robespierre's time, a 'good patriot' was a zealous Republican, one inclined in his most naïve mood to blame the misery of his people on the spendthrift habits of the *Autrichienne*; yet by the 1920s and 1930s, *L'Action française*, the daily of the political sect most determined to restore the Monarchy, consistently referred to the Republic as *l'Anti-France* and carried as its motto a statement of the Pretender: 'Tout ce qui est national est nôtre.' This change was, of course, a long and complicated process, and by no means unidirectional; the Republican patriots of the eighteenth century were in a way internationalists, standing up for the Rights of Man and not only for those of Frenchmen; and as late as 1940, there could once again be seen peaceful *collaboration* on the Right, and national *resistance* on the Left. Yet, with every allowance for varieties old and new, the transformation in the Western World of nationalism from a revolutionary to a retrograde slogan has been the dominant feature of recent history; and, in France, the turning-point was prepared and immediately preceded by the decade which started with the publication of *Boule de Suif* and ended with the mental collapse of its author. It was the decade of the Panama scandal.

It was that of the political adventure nicknamed the *Boulange* which wellnigh cost the Republic her life.

Maupassant, when preparing for the publication of *Les Soirées de Médan*, admitted, as will be remembered, to having one quasi-political aim in this purely literary venture: to counter *le chauvinisme à la Déroulède*. Paul Déroulède, famous for his soap-box poetry devoted to the cause of the *revanche*, ranked at that time with the Left. His rhetoricism fed on the reminiscences of a revolutionary tricolour. Nobody could have guessed that he would end up as a leader of the extreme Right, plotting with inveterate Royalists and Ultramontane Catholics to overthrow the Republic. But, whatever the changes he underwent during his career, his soap-box nationalism with its zeal for *la revanche* and the Army did not change. It was not he and his comrades but the political tendency implicit in unqualified nationalism that underwent the essential transformation. And so, necessarily, did the refusal to brook that nationalism. The Literary Left of the early 1880s acquired and performed the function of a moderate but definite and effective political Left.

This, of course, was not in the mind of thirty-five-year-old Guy de Maupassant when he was talking *macchabées* to Marie Kann and her smart girl guests, and giving old Goncourt the creeps. It was just a cosy and morbid world, with plenty of jewels and drugs, frustrated by its overflow of leisure, but quite happy to toy with its frustration. It was a hot-house, amongst other things, of political intrigues as *salons* had always been, since time immemorial; but without a desire for what Sartre would call *engagement*. It was liberal, quite naturally, for it had sprung of liberty and obeyed its own nature by carrying on. It was embedded in riches as the luxury of sophistication always is; and it was cosmopolitan as the rich always are until they feel they must encourage parochial or national isolation so as to assert their privileges and keep their servants from mixing too easily with people outside their realm. It was Maupassant's world, with its thrill for the truth without the urge for a message, with its fancy for outspokenness as a high-class parlour-game.

It was not to last long. It was crumbling already in Maupassant's lifetime. Whilst socialist and anarchist visions made widening inroads on the intelligentsia, a wave of traditionalist obscurantism spread over the *salons*, together with the hope of a Roman Catholic revival which was then combined with Royalist leanings, and a nationalism reshaped for retrograde use, smacking of what would be called *Blut und Boden* today. Polarization then continued, and events occurred that made it obvious that it was absurd to claim freedom for the individual without accepting the risks it entails to the prestige of privileged army officers and to the properties they are supposed to be defending.

The year after Maupassant's death, a member of the army corps of the Republic, known as a valiant fighter, a polyglot gossip and a pleasant dandy, Count Major Ferdinand Walsin Esterhazy, passed some information on to the military authorities of the German Reich, with the hope of extricating himself from his suffocating debts. Attached to the information was a *bordereau*, which later fell into the hands of the French counter-espionage; and a Jewish officer, considered too keen to be a dutiful and patriotic Frenchman, Captain Alfred Dreyfus, was accused of being its author. Dreyfus was cashiered and gaoled. It was a miscarriage of justice, even on formal grounds; in fact, it was the illegalities of the proceedings which first disturbed some who were satisfied about the guilt of the ex-Captain. A revision of the case was demanded. As it happened, the vociferous champions of Revision had in some way been associated with Maupassant in his lifetime; Zola, Reinach, Clemenceau.[1] ... But this did not apply to all his friends, either literary or social. Most of them, including some courtiers of sumptuous Jewish hostesses, were horrified by the idea that the judgment of a military court should be questioned. Maupassant's world divided: Zola was for Revision but, of his old friends, Daudet uneasily, and Coppée irritatedly against; Anatole France for; Lemaître against; Monet for; Degas against; Mirbeau and Marcel Prévost for; Bourget against ... Edmond de Goncourt, *au-dessus de la mêlée*, maintained a peevish neutrality; however repelled he was by Dreyfus and the Jews, the mob shouting against them, and the journalists anxious to please that mob,

---

[1] When, in 1883, the Hachette publishing house which had the monopoly of supplying railway stations with books refused, on grounds of sex morality, to include *Une Vie*, Clemenceau in the Chamber intervened on behalf of Maupassant.

repelled him even more.[1] He died, incidentally, in July 1896, before the deployment of forces had been completed. On 13 January 1898 Zola's open letter to the President of the Republic, *J'Accuse!*, published in Clemenceau's paper, *L'Aurore*, acted as a watershed. From then until Dreyfus's rehabilitation in 1906, *l'Affaire* with implications far beyond its original scope dominated the French scene from wherever one watched it.[2] There was a dividing line that could not be ignored.

Where would Maupassant have stood? On the side of frailty against priggishness, and on that of civic courage against conformist pompousness. He would have liked Walsin Esterhazy, especially if convinced of his guilt. That picturesque and fool-hardy adventurer would have found more sympathy with him than would the boring Dreyfus with his exemplary conduct. Vice rewarded and virtue punished would have served as the subject of a funny story for him, to be treated with a mischievous smile. But once freedom of speech was in the balance, and Zola prosecuted for telling the truth in face of sly threats and public uproar, he could not have followed his preference for taking it all as a joke. He would have refused, as he always did, the dictate of the *épaulette* over the pen; and he would have opened his mouth, if only to show to Mme Straus, the lady patroness of the *dreyfusard* intellectuals,[3] that he had guts.

This at least is my guess. Crusading for Justice would have been out of tune for Maupassant; but to shun facts would have been even more so. An undiluted Maupassant was no longer possible in the late 1890s or indeed since.

Guy de Maupassant's place in world literature is obvious. He was the finest author of short stories – if by a short story we mean the form of *conte* which developed in his century, that is a snapshot of life in the frame of a prose narrative which is to some extent photographic. No one equalled him in that. Amongst

[1] *Journal*, Vol. IV, pp. 710–11. Entry of 6 January 1895.

[2] The literature on the question is enormous; the reader can find a readable summing up in *Captain Dreyfus, The Story of a Mass Hysteria*, Nicholas Halasz, Simon and Schuster, New York, 1955.

[3] Painter, *Marcel Proust*, cf. particularly pp. 227 ff.

his immediate predecessors in that genre, there was Prosper Mérimée to whom he was often compared with some reason; but Maupassant surpassed him in both the genuineness of his characters, and the sharpness of their outlines; the schooling of Croisset, of Médan and of the modern newspaper trade helped him to improve on the amorous and romantic story. Outside his own country, the only realistic story-tellers comparable to him in the art had a warmer and heavier touch; the Swiss German, Gottfried Keller, for instance. This contrast is less marked but no less essential when comparing him, and French Realists in general, with their Russian counterparts. From Gogol's *Overcoat* through Tolstoy down to Chekhov and Gorki, there flourished the beautiful craft of taking poetic shots of drab corners of life, a flow of short stories that might well have been collected under Maupassant's own title, 'The Great Miseries of the Little People'.[1] Some of these stories may in some ways have been better than Maupassant's; but certainly they were less snappy and less *impassible*. Chekhov, only ten years younger than Maupassant, provides the nearest comparison. They both possessed equally the gift of simplicity and economy, that of cutting to the bone with grace; and they were equally attentive to trifling details that acquire significance in the proper narrative setting. Yet Chekhov, however discreet, however objective in his style, always noticeably shared in the sufferings of his characters and particularly in their melancholia. He may have been more human, more sympathetic, more poetic than Maupassant; but he was less perfect in his craft.

After Maupassant's departure, this brand of perfection became gradually hollower. This is not to belittle those who are still able to carry on with entertaining skill. Somerset Maugham can be extremely funny in his short stories which express much wisdom and knowledge of the human mind. But Maupassant mirrored his contemporaries as fully as any author could; whilst few would think of seeking a faithful mirror of his contemporaries in Maugham's writing. Nor do I think that Maugham's succinctness, however brilliant, can strike one as having that crystalline economy that distinguished Maupassant at his best. The same applies even more to Maugham's successors.

[1] See footnotes on pp. 93 and 246.

A literary style, like a technological process, may lose its significance without losing its usefulness. Maupassant achieved the utmost that could be achieved with a camera. A Maupassant of our time would not be able to do without either a microscope or a telescope. That microscope would mean a more analytical mind; that telescope a bolder dive into fantasy; and both would require either more direct poetry or more interest in science, politics and the structure of existence and society. On Maupassant's level of art and intelligence, no writer can be non-committed today.

Maupassant left no message, though some *Maupassantiens* are determined to discover one in his works;[1] but he left captivating documents of a fascinating epoch, authentic testimonies of dull and live people, enjoyable stories that do not seem to age. His literary longevity may be irritating to many, quite understandably. It would have particularly irritated his contemporary colleagues, one imagines, could they have witnessed it from the grave. We know what one of his elder protagonists, Edmond de Goncourt, would have said; but his highbrow juniors would have been no less incensed. There was a cavalcade of Angry and Esoteric Young Men in the famous *Enquête*[2] to which Maupassant himself, in practically his last moment of comparative normality, contributed with a hysterical display of his reluctance to 'talk literature'. Gustave Kahn, remembered today as one of the initiators of *vers libre* in France, and an erstwhile comrade of Maupassant in the gang of *La Revue Moderne et Naturaliste*, compared him to a retired businessman strolling about in sports-clothes and writing Norman stories in his spare time. Charles

---

[1] I have already mentioned M. Gérard Delaisement who, in his scholarly and useful Introduction to *Bel-Ami* (Garnier Frères, 1959, p. lxxxiii) argues that this novel is 'une grande œuvre qui joint à ses qualités purement romanesques la valeur d'un prophétique avertissement . . .'. He refers to critics outside France and to François Mauriac amongst his most distinguished countrymen, for support of his admiration. Maupassant *prophétique?* Hardly the *mot juste* I would say. I also find some over-anxiety to appreciate Maupassant as a turgid moral philosopher rather than a clear fact-recorder, in Albert-Marie Schmidt's most carefully documented, pleasantly illustrated but heavily written *Maupassant par lui-même.*

[2] Jules Huret, *Enquête sur l'Evolution littéraire*, 1891.

Morice, a leader of the Symbolist movement, differed from Gustave Kahn only in so far as he thought Maupassant still very active and efficient as a businessman; but 'why doesn't he leave literature in peace and go to the Stock Exchange?' The Beatniks of those days, if so they can be called, dismissed him as he dismissed Feuillet and the rest of that *littérature tarte à la crème*, to be judged as a commodity and not as a work of art. They sneered at Guy de Maupassant as a writer. And that somebody in the 1960s should devote a book to him, calling him one of the greatest writers ever known – the very idea would have produced an explosion of merriment.

I am in full sympathy with those Beatniks of the nineteenth-century Quartier Latin, and do not think that their sneers should be brushed away with the counter-sneers they provoke. There is much to be said for them; there is a blatant unfairness in a posthumous career such as Maupassant's. He lived for the moment and wrote for the contemporary public, he made heaps of money, paraded in luxury, had all the women and could have had all the choicest dishes and drinks and clothes in the world, and never professed to desire anything beyond such earthly goods. He avoided the company of the penniless experimentalists. He flouted the rewards that could not be expressed in cash. He automatically, one would think, waived his claim to perennial laurels, in favour of those struggling and starving for it in their lifetime. Surely there is something wrong in a world order which allows a contemporary entertainer to remain on his pedestal, while the names of his loftier colleagues lapse into oblivion?

To answer that, presumably, neither Gustave Kahn nor Charles Morice was such a giant spirit is no real answer. Nobody really can know. They may or may not have been; very few today would understand all the shades of meaning in what has been preserved of their writings; they belong to the special patrimony of a philological community which may or may not consist of fools by their standard. They may have been forgotten only because their work is not understood, and even if any of them were rediscovered and brought into vogue, it would be due, presumably, to misunderstanding and ignorance.

The more justified their complaint, however, the more it vindicates Maupassant. He not only knew what people were

like, and how to describe them, as he saw them in flesh and
blood but also knew how phoney literary immortality was and,
until the moment of claiming special blood relationship with the
Almighty, refused to be deluded by any of those hopes vested
in a clear-sighted posterity by minds more polished, more
exalted and more gullible than his. With his middle-brow wisdom, with the *je-m'en foutisme* of a 'Norman horse-trader', he
infallibly sensed what it was all about; 'Fame is all chance, the
toss of a coin.' It is Frank Harris who quotes him as saying this,[1]
without adding the original in French, but it does sound so very
like what Maupassant would have said if he had known English,
that, even from Frank Harris, it may be accepted as authentic.

The fashion of belittling Maupassant, sometimes with outright contempt, sometimes with a pitying smile for naïve
foreigners surprisingly bemused by him, has ever since the turn
of the century prevailed in highbrow France.[2] This fashion
should be understood and almost approved, without being aped.
To the French intellectual of, say, 1910, Maupassant must have
stood as the author who had turned out by the dozen the neatly
tailored and slightly *polisson* stories which ever since the *Hepta-
méron* had been so much in the French tradition as to make even
their naughtiness boring, and which later through the tide of the
press had so utterly swamped the market that fastidious minds
longed for something entirely different. Frenchmen for whom
literature meant more than a tickling between two yawns in the
wagon-lit had become glutted by Maupassant, even by what was
best in him, because it seemed indistinguishable at times from the
clever second-rate stuff modelled on it, partly by the grapho-
maniac Maupassant himself. His light touch must have become
almost indistinguishable from superficiality, and this very lightness acted as a shackle on the mind in its search for new shades of

[1] *My Life and Loves*, Vol. 2, Chapter XX; in privately printed
edition, p. 356.
[2] The following paragraphs are to a large extent based on the material
of *Maupassant Criticism in France* by Artine Artinian, King's Crown
Press, New York, 1941. This volume includes in its Appendix the result
of an enquiry made by Professor Artinian amongst well-known contemporary authors some two or three years before the publication, both
in and outside France, of their opinions on Maupassant and his influence
on the literature of their countries.

meaning, in its attempt to look deeper into the 'subconscious' or farther beyond actual surroundings. The titans of German, English, Russian, Scandinavian self-torture and introspection started attracting French authors, at times with catastrophic results; the French, once their taste for misty beauties was awakened, often outstripped their Eastern and Northern inspirers in obscurity. Yet, altogether, it was a necessary and wholesome process, short of which the prose of French *belles-lettres*, most polished in the world, might well have been stranded on the level of *fait-divers* style fiction to which Maupassant had indeed brought it dangerously near. It was good of the French to forget about this craft for a bit whilst foreigners were catching up. This may have been in André Gide's mind when he said that German, English, Russian authors 'étaient riches d'un fonds généreux et manquaient peut-être ce que Maupassant avait à l'excès et pouvait leur apprendre: le *métier*'.

Indeed, it is interesting to see from Professor Artinian's collection how such an unsurpassed master of what can be graceful in heavy prose as Thomas Mann bows in reverence to Maupassant's memory, convinced he would live 'durch die Jahrhunderte als einer de grössten Meister der Novelle', and how his fellow German authors, Heinrich Mann, Zweig, Werfel[1] equally pay high tributes and testify their indebtedness to Maupassant, while their French colleagues divide, broadly speaking, into three categories: the first, apologetic about not liking Maupassant; the second, apologetic about liking Maupassant; the third, proud of not liking Maupassant. Most, however, combine two at least of these three attitudes. Roger Martin du Gard looking for a fair appraisal: 'un de nos grands conteurs-nés' but 'monocorde'; which is true. Gide, typically, finds fault with him because 'he is the same thing to all his readers and does not speak to any of them in secret'; which is hardly true – only in so far as his secret, hid in limpidness, is often more difficult to discover than is secretiveness proper. Simenon, like Maurois, gives the impression of feeling guilt at enjoying Maupassant. Paul Valéry is halfway between apology for, and pride in, lack of interest in such stuff; he is no reader of short stories. Most uninhibitedly proud of his own frigidness is Henry de Montherlant who, one

[1] Actually all of them refugees at that time (1938).

would think, would owe Maupassant a word of thanks for the cult and exhibition of virile strength inherited from him. He has only a smile, not even a pitying one, for Maupassant's reputation abroad.

The same is said, in a more shaded and pertinent way, by M. Jean de La Varende, author of *Grands Normands, études sentimentales* (H. Defontaine, Rouen, 1939), dealing with Barbey d'Aurevilly, Flaubert and Maupassant, a precious book in both senses of the word, originally planned to be called *Deux grands Normands et un petit*. It is a pity perhaps that M. La Varende changed his mind before publishing, because he really has the sense of what was 'petit' in the great Maupassant – the *fait-divers* touch – and it is all the better for such reservations and objections to be made absolutely clear, absolutely explicit, so as to overcome them, as they should be. 'Méfiez-vous!' La Varende teases the foreigners. 'Les Français sont tres fins, avec leurs airs de brouillons.' The French are a very sophisticated lot, he means, however much they look like simpletons. So far so good; but to show off one's sophistication does not mean that one escapes the appearance of a simpleton.

True enough this was written in the late 1930s, and a valuable *Maupassantien* literature has flourished since in France (as well as elsewhere, mainly in the United States), with sympathizers so outstanding, even in France, as François Mauriac. Yet, the general attitude has hardly changed: 'Tout Maupassant, pour une page de Gide', ends a pleasant little essay on Maupassant in a recent collection.[1] There is nothing wrong with it. Stagnation in literary virtues known to be typically French would be much more unpleasing. Instead of this, the French intellectuals are, in the psycho-analyst term, *super-compensating* today for what used to be their one-sidedness some decades ago. They will get over it, one may hope, and come round to appreciating clarity once again, though no longer in that 'simpleton' way the appearance of which M. La Varende is so eager to avoid.

In the meantime, there is no reason why foreigners – I mean mainly writers of the German- and English-speaking worlds – should not try to reteach their French colleagues what they had originally learned from them. They certainly must not be, as

[1] Jose Cabanis, *Plaisirs et lectures*, Gallimard, Paris, 1964.

many doubtless are, abashed by French belittling of a French author whose works impress them. Nor must they, of course, indulge a Maupassant myth in response, and make a habit of rejecting any critical remark about this great writer. To quote once again a French contributor to the American professor's round-table on the French author: Abel Hermant, whilst admitting Maupassant's great talent, confessed to having 'pour ce talent peu de goût', and finding him outdated mainly on account of the poverty of his intellectual equipment. Yes, perhaps; though even this is only true with some qualification. The essays and newspaper articles of Maupassant, and the contemplative paragraphs of his novels, stories, travel diaries, do now and then contain an exceptionally brave and pertinent observation or judgment, thanks to the directness of his approach, his revulsion for self-deception. On the whole, however, they are indeed poor stuff, platitudinous, incoherent, slipshod, often not even elegant. How far all this is from his power to 'conjure' life on to the printed page, 'without second thought', as Pol Neveux said, apparently without any thought at all! The essence of the matter is that he knew far more about rivers, animals, houses and, particularly, people, than about ideas. Can people and ideas thus be divided? Not in the ultimate analysis. The intellectual projection of Maupassant's tragedy may well be taken as a demonstration of the tenet that such division is unfeasible, and that a mind drained of ideas gets swamped by fixed ideas. But until this happened he almost achieved the impossible. He knew the *non plus ultra* that could be known of human beings without always being able to follow them in their thoughts. This was his genius.

CHRONOLOGY

1873 Boating partners: Pinchon, Fontaine, etc. Promoted to salaried clerk in the Directorship of Colonies

1874 Confirmed in his post – Asking his mother to try and find him subjects for short stories – Possible year of contraction of syphilis

1874–5 Agony and death of Jules Maupassant, Guy's grandfather – Guy de Maupassant introduced by Flaubert to Turgenev, Goncourt, Daudet, Zola

1875 His story, *La Main d'écorché* (recalling Swinburne), published in 'L'Almanach de Pont-à-Moisson' – His drama in verse: *La Trahison de la Comtesse de Rhine* – First performance of *A la feuille de rose, Maison turque*

1876 Introduced by Flaubert to *La République des Lettres*, to *La Nation*, to *Le Nouvelliste de Rouen* – Contributions under pen-names: poems, reviews, literary chronicles – Friendship with Catulle Mendès – *Une Répétition*, one-act play in verse – Starting graphomania and heart troubles

1877 Young Naturalists: Alexis, Céard, Hennique, Huysmans, Mirbeau and 'Guy de Valmont' celebrating Flaubert, Goncourt and Zola, *chez Trapp* – Second performance of *Maison turque* – Assisting Flaubert on research for *Bouvard et Pécuchet*

1878 Transfer from the Ministry of the Marine to the Ministry of Education – Melancholia, violent *migraines*

1879 *Histoire du Vieux temps*, comedy in verse – Maupassant introduced to Princess Mathilde – His association with *La Revue Moderne et Naturaliste* – prosecuted for two poems in Etampes – Maupassant hailed by Zola and the young Naturalists for his story, *Boule de Suif* – preparations for the anthology of 'Médan' – Headaches, quivers

1880 *Les Soirées de Médan* (Charpentier) published – *Des Vers* (Charpentier) published – Contributions to *Le Gaulois* – Flaubert's death – Maupassant granted leave without pay, and later resigning from the Ministry – Journey to Corsica – *Les Dimanches d'un bourgeois de Paris* in serial – Eye troubles

1881 Journey to Algeria – The stories: *La Maison Tellier*

and *Mademoiselle Fifi* (about prostitutes); *Histoire d'une fille de ferme* (peasants); *En famille* (clerks – petites gens); *La Femme de Paul* (about Lesbians on the Seine) – Separate volume: *La Maison Tellier* (Havard)

1882 Building *La Guillette* in Etretat – Argument with Taine, Sarcey, Wolff, in defence of his predilection for prostitution and other low-class subjects – Preparing for novels, gradually turning towards upper-class subjects – Amongst short stories: *Ce Cochon de Morin* (cuckold) and *Pierrot* (peasant stinginess, animals' suffering) – Nightmare: stories such as *La Peur* and *Fou?* – Sexual exhibitionism; a Russian journalist staggered by what Harry Alis called his 'superb virility' – Volume published: *Mademoiselle Fifi* (Kistemaeckers, Brussels)

1883 His first novel: *Une Vie* (Havard) – Collection of stories: *Contes de la Bécasse* (Rouveyre) – François Tassart engaged as valet – Portrait of Zola – Portrait of Turgenev – Preface to Maizeroy's novel – Short stories of the year include: *Miss Harriet* (a decent spinster's frustration); *Première Neige* (a decent wife's frustration); *Mon oncle Jules* (fun made of religion, but also of anti-religion); *Décoré!* (the silly cuckold); *Un Sage* (the wise cuckold); *La Ficelle* (peasant stinginess)

1884 Maupassant moves to 10 rue Montchanin, the apartment compared by Goncourt to a pimp's home – Maupassant becoming the 'lion of the Jewish *salons*' – his friendship with Paul Bourget becoming closer – Maupassant one of Countess Potocka's 'Macchabées' – Great essay on Flaubert – Separate volumes of the year: *Au Soleil* (travel diary, Havard); collection of stories: *Clair de Lune* (Monier), *Les Sœurs Rondoli* (Ollendorff), *Miss Harriet* (Havard) – Stories of the year include *La Parure* ('The Necklace'), most typical of the brilliant and snappy Maupassant; also *L'Héritage*; *L'Aveu*; *Le Petit Fût*; *Une Vente*; *Yvette*; *L'Armoire*; *Garçon, un bock!* – Headaches, intestinal-troubles, shower-baths

and other cures, narcotics – Associations, mainly in
Etretat, with Blanche Roosevelt, with Mme Lecomte
du Nouÿ, with 'Clem'

1885   Death of Victor Hugo – Publication of *Bel-Ami*
(Havard) – Soaring sales; arguments about them and
the press – 'Bel-Ami, c'est moi' – Talking 'corpses and
morgue' to Marie Kann and her guests – Signs of
derangement of mind – Anatole France suspects he is
a lunatic – Hallucinations; seeing his *alter ego*; an ether
addict; the stories *Fou* and *Lettre d'un fou* – Preface to
the new edition of *Manon Lescaut*; about the 'femme
d'amour' – Collections of short stories: *Toine*
(Flammarion); *Contes du Jour et de la Nuit* (Marpon
and Flammarion) – Contributions to *Gil Blas* – This
and the previous year peak of his productivity

1886   Courting Geneviève Halévy-Bizet-Straus – In England,
with Blanche Roosevelt, and with the Rothschilds;
allegedly also with Henry James – Labelled by
literary youth a 'notable commerçant' – The story
Le Horla in two versions, 'by a madman' – Separate
volumes: *La Petite Roque* (Havard); *Contes choisies*
(Bibliophiles contemporains); *Monsieur Parent*
(Ollendorff)

1887   His third novel: *Mont-Oriol* (Havard) – Collection of
stories: *Le Horla* (Ollendorff) – Flight on the balloon
'Le Horla' – Conflict with Goncourt on Flaubert
Memorial Committee – Journey to Algeria – Joins
protest against the Eiffel Tower – Developing interest
in psychological novel

1888   His fourth novel: *Pierre et Jean* (Ollendorff) and the
essay 'On the Novel' which served as its Preface –
His crack at '*écriture artiste*' – Goncourt's hatred of
Maupassant grows implacable – Maupassant's quarrel
with *Le Figaro* for mutilating his essay – Launching
of the yacht *Bel-Ami*; cruising in the Mediterranean;
Sur l'Eau (travel diary, Flammarion) – Symptoms of
megalomania

1889   His fifth novel: *Fort comme la Mort* (Ollendorff) –
Hervé's lunacy and death – Collection of stories: *La*

Main gauche (Ollendorff) – Eye troubles becoming serious; forebodings

1890 His sixth and most *mondain* novel: *Notre Cœur* (first published in *La Revue des Deux Mondes*, then by Havard) – Travel diary: *La Vie errante* (Ollendorff) – The story and the volume named after it: *L'Inutile Beauté* (Havard) – Amongst stories of the year: *Mouche*; *Le champ d'Olivier*; *Qui sait?* – His quarrel with Charpentier for publishing his portrait – Writing the play *Musotte* in company with Jacques Normand – Decides to give up writing short stories – The novel *L'Ame étrangère* started and abandoned – His last great literary project: the novel, *L'Angélus*, which he feels will be the *couronnement* of his career

1891 *Musotte* a success in the Gymnase (publ. Ollendorff) – Preface to Swinburne's *Poèmes et Ballades* – Cures in spas in Switzerland – Struggling with *L'Angélus*; 'If in three months' time I have not finished this book I shall kill myself' (he exclaimed in the summer of this year) – Crying over his manuscript – Personal quarrel with God – Consulting Dr Daremberg, Dr Cazalis; instructing the lawyer, M⁰ Jacob – Reads announcements in the press about his insanity; hurries to his mother in Nice

Christmas 1891, New Year 1892 Shuttling between his mother in Nice and his own *Chalet de l'Isère*, Cannes – The mysterious 'two ladies' in Cannes (possibly Marie Kann and her sister) – Maupassant fires at an imaginary enemy through the window; François secretly takes out the bullets from his revolver – 1 January: conflicting reports on Guy's last day with his mother. Return in the evening; to bed – Telegram from the 'lady in grey' – In the small hours of 2 January Maupassant cuts his throat – Farewell to the yacht *Bel-Ami* – By train to Paris; internment in Dr Blanche's *maison de santé* in Passy, 7 January

1892–93 (July) His obsessions: sexomania; money; his urine, jewels; his mother, the mistress of Jesus Christ;

God, in turns his personal enemy and his personal father; talking to imaginary bankers; licking the walls and barking at them – Planting branches: 'Next year, there will be little Maupassants' – Ringing for the straitjacket – His comedy, *La Paix de Ménage*, in the Théâtre Français, March 1893 (publ. Ollendorff)

6–9 July 1893   Death and funeral of Guy de Maupassant; Zola's speech and other tributes

23 August 1893   Death of Adrienne Legay (model of 'Boule de Suif') in Rouen, in utmost penury

1896   Death of Edmond de Goncourt

24 January 1899   Death of Gustave de Maupassant in Sainte-Maxime, Var

1902   Death of Emile Zola

8 December 1904   Death of Laure de Maupassant in Nice

1905–11   Publication of the collection of *Souvenirs* edited by Baron Lumbroso; of the first comprehensive Maupassant biography (by E. Maynial); of Pol Neveux's Preface to the Conard edition of Maupassant's *Œuvres complètes*; of *Souvenirs sur Guy de Maupassant* 'par François [Tassart], son valet'

1924   Death of Anatole France

1935   Death of Paul Bourget

1934–8   The Librairie de France et Grund edition of Maupassant's *Œuvres complètes*, foreword by R. Dumesnil

1949   Death of François Tassart

APPENDIXES

1 · (see pp. 69-70)

Fragments published in *Le Cahier d'amour* by 'une Adoratrice de Maupassant', Mlle X— (Gisèle d'Estoc), prefaced by Pierre Borel, 'Les Œuvres Libres' (Librairie A. Fayard, Paris), No. 216, June 1939.(Cf. Appendix 8.)

J'avais treize ans. Ce jour-là, sous la grange,
Je m'étais endormi par hasard dans un coin

. . . .

Jean, le valet, tenant dans ses bras notre bonne,
Ils étaient enlacés je ne sais trop comment,
Et leurs derrières nus s'agitatient vivement,
Je compris qu'ils faisaient une chose très bonne.

. . . .
. . . .
. . . .

Elle serra mes reins autant qu'elle était forte,
Un grand feu de bonheur nous tordit jusqu'aux os,
Elle criait: 'assez, assez!' et sur le dos
Elle tomba, les yeux fermés, comme une masse.

. . . .

Hélas! depuis ce temps, j'ai tenu dans mon lit
Bien de corps différents, des ventres et des cuisses,
Des flancs si bien tournés, des seins tellement lisses
Qu'on les eut dit taillés dans l'ivoire poli.
Toute femme m'a plu: j'ai joui sur chacune;
Sur la blonde qu'un soir on baise au clair de lune,
Auprès d'un ver luisant, avec des mots très doux;
Sur la brune qui râle et vous brûle de fièvres,
Vous étrangle et vous boit avec ses quatre lèvres,
Et vous pince et vous b—, et vous s— à genoux;

Sur la molle géante et la femme velue
Comme un ours, et qui sent le bouc, et qui vous mord,
Vous chevauche au galop toute la nuit, goulue
Du v—, et vous laisse exsangue comme un mort;
Sur l'épouse d'un autre, et sur la jeune fille
Qui pleure et dit: 'Encor' d'une façon gentille.
Eh bien! malgré cela je n'ai point oublié
Et tout mon souvenir à Jeanne est lié.
Je la revois toujours, mignonne, fraîche et blonde,
Qui s'en va devant moi, montrant sa croupe ronde.

2 · (*see p.* 79)

Dieu, cet être inconnu dont nul n'a vu la face,
Roi qui commande au rois et règne dans l'espace,
Las d'être toujours seul, lui dont l'infinité
De l'univers sans bornes emplit l'immensité,
Et d'embrasser toujours, seul, par sa plénitude
De l'espace et des temps la sombre solitude,
De rester toujours tel qu'il a toujours été,
Solitaire et puissant durant l'Eternité,
Portant de sa grandeur la marque indélébile,
D'être seul pour qui le temps soit immobile,
Pour qui tout le passé reste sans souvenir
Et qui n'attend rien de l'immense avenir;
Qui de la nuit des temps perce l'ombre profonde;
Pour qui tout soit égal, pour qui tout se confonde
Dans l'éternel ennui d'un éternel présent,
Solitaire et puissant et pourtant impuissant
A changer son destin dont il n'est pas le maître,
Le grand Dieu qui peut tout ne peut pas ne pas être!

3 · (see p. 87)

I am taking this interpretation of Marx's attitude from the book on the Paris Commune (*A párisi Kommün*, Pantheon, Budapest, 1932) by the late Andor Németh, a most accomplished literary essayist and author of several biographies more or less *romancées*. Knowing Németh's foible for paradoxes, I was first rather sceptical about this; but then, he showed me his subsequent correspondence with some of his Communist friends who were at that time refugees in the U.S.S.R., the well-known and extremely intelligent Hungarian author, the late Andor Gábor amongst them. The latter reproached Németh for crediting Marx with ingenious and deliberate myth-making, but was unable to rebut any of the factual statements on which Németh's hypothesis was based. I have learned from another source that the publication of Németh's book in German was considered at that time but the publisher dropped the idea on the unfavourable reader's report by George Lukács.

About the development of Marx's attitude towards the Commune from 1871 till 1881, see *Marxism* by George Lichtheim, pp. 112–21 (Routledge, 1961).

4 · (see p. 89)

Goncourt's *Journal*, Vol. IV, p. 533. In the same entry and, in greater detail, in a former one, Vol. IV, p. 382, recorded in April 1893, on the grounds of his conversation with Léon Hennique, Goncourt recalls another episode of Maupassant's sexual exhibitionism in his later, prosperous years. According to this, when the Russian writer, Bobukin, was in Paris, Maupassant said, 'I must stagger [épater] the Muscovite!', took a girl from the Folies Bergères, and, in the presence of the Russian, had intercourse six times with this woman and, soon after, three times in the neighbouring room with another woman.

Numbering of volumes and pages according to the unexpurgated full edition of the *Journal des Goncourt*, edited by Robert Ricatte, published by Pasquelle and Flammarion, Paris, 1956, printed in Monaco.

5 · (see p. 181)

5 · (see p. 181)

Paul Morand, in his *Vie de Guy de Maupassant*, writes: 'Les salons juifs exercèrent de 1880 à 1914 une très grande influence sur les littérateurs français; on y coudoyait tous les mondes et c'est là que les écrivains rencontraient les aristocrates qu'ils n'auraient pas vus ailleurs. . . . "Les écrivains de l'époque," écrit Albert Thibaudet dans ses *Réflexions sur la Littérature*, "étaient loin de posséder dans le monde la situation où ils sont parvenus depuis. Il y entraient surtout par les salons israélites ou grands bourgeois métèques" . . .' M. Morand seems to think this should be held *against* those Jews and *métèques*.

6 · (see p. 223)

6 · (see p. 223)

M. Fernand Lemoine, in his useful and intelligent booklet, *Guy de Maupassant*, in the series 'Classiques du XIXᵉ Siècle', Editions Universitaires, Paris, 1957, p. 37, writes:

> De Boule de Suif à Michèle de Burne, de la prostituée à la femme du monde, il [Maupassant] décrit la gamme de celles qu'il a connues: demi-mondaines, midinettes, femmes mariées, jeunes filles. Chacune d'elles correspond à un moment de son existence. Toutes, dans sa vie comme dans son œuvre, ont un trait commun: elles sont blondes.
>
> Any de Guilleroy (1), Michèle de Burne (2), Mme Roland (3), Christiane Andermatt (4): rien que des blondes. Penchant marqué de Maupassant: 'Elle était charmante, blonde d'un blond tendre et chaud, faite pour les caresses,' écrit-il déjà dans *Bel-Ami*.
>
> (1) *Fort comme la Mort.*   (2) *Notre Cœur.*
> (3) *Pierre et Jean.*   (4) *Mont-Oriol.*

This is not absolutely so. In his life, he was perfectly eclectic; no particular shade of hair seems to have deterred him. In his writings, his preference for the blonde was only prevalent when he described women from Northern provinces, or aristocratic types. Even this, with notable exceptions; Boule de Suif with her 'yeux noirs magnifiques' is more likely to have been a brunette, and Countess de Mascaret, in *l'Inutile Beauté*, had black hair 'comme une nuit'. I agree, however, that the clause quoted from *Bel-Ami* is most typical of his vision.

Speaking of Maupassant's mistresses, it would be ungrateful to forget about 'Clem': Clémence Brun-Chaban, a 'chestnut-haired' girl as François saw her, young widow of a coffee merchant, who, though apparently quite well off, acted for a while as Maupassant's secretary. She was an impish but charitable person who turned up in Etretat as a voluntary nurse not only for Maupassant but also for Mme Lecomte du Nouÿ when their failing healths required. She took it for granted that she was but one of many mistresses, and also that she should become invisible when her lover entertained the chic world. She was, however, most popular with Maupassant's intimates who would refer to her as the 'Gamine de Paris'. With her easy ways and bawdy tongue, she is supposed to have been the model of the charming brunette, Mme Clotilde de Marelle, or Clo, in *Bel-Ami*; but, in addition, she was a professional help to her lover, and made Maupassant dictate to her when his bad eyesight disabled him from writing. So much modesty and self-sacrifice was too much for Maupassant; one day he fled her, on his yacht. She did not intrude on him any longer; but turned up at his burial, in the funeral procession. (Cf. Charles Lapierre, 'Souvenirs Intimes', *Journal des Débats*, 10 August 1893, reprinted in *Souvenirs sur Maupassant*, ed. Lumbroso.)

7 · (see p. 224)

7 · (see p. 224)

Souvenirs sur Maupassant, compiled and partly written by Albert Lumbroso (Rocca, Roma, 1905) is conspicuous for its unselective but precious material on this as well as other matters relating to Maupassant; it includes Mme de Maupassant's statements which, though far from unbiased, should certainly not be disregarded. Tassart's *Souvenirs* contains no less valuable material, presented, of course, with no more medical expert knowledge. The first to publish a comprehensive medical study on the matter was M. Louis Thomas, in his book *La maladie et la mort de Guy de Maupassant*, Arthur Herbert, Bruges, 1906. Of the psycho-pathological studies, *Guy de Maupassant, étude de psychologie pathologique*, by Charles Ladame, in *Revue Romande*, Lausanne, 1919, has had a noteworthy influence on literary historians. *La Fin de Maupassant* by Georges Normandy (Albin Michel, Paris, 1927) contains fascinating and horrifying material of Maupassant's lethal melodrama.

8 · (see pp. 81, 217, 227–229 and Appendix 1)

Maupassant had already been dead for about half a century when a new name was added to the register of his conspicuous mistresses: Gisèle d'Estoc. She was introduced to the readers by the Maupassant biographer, Pierre Borel, who had been in close touch with one of Maupassant's erstwhile boating partners, Léon Fontaine ('Petit Bleu'). In 1927, M. Borel based on Fontaine's recollections his book, *Le destin tragique de Guy de Maupassant* (Editions de France), but his most dramatic revelations of Maupassant's love-life only followed later.

In 1939, the periodical *Les Œuvres Libres* (Librairie Arthème Fayard, Paris) in its No. 216, published *Le Cahier d'Amour*, written by someone referred to at this juncture as 'Mlle X—, une adoratrice de Maupassant', and annotated by its discoverer, Pierre Borel.

The *Cahier* is an erotic diary, written with skill, sense of rhythm and cheap elegance. If the authoress is to be believed, its place of origin was mainly Bezons on the Seine where she used to live with Maupassant as his lover and intimate. The entries are not dated, but the references to events make it clear that they were spread over several years, including 1886 which may perhaps be termed as the moment of Maupassant's transition from glory to madness.

The atmosphere the *Cahier* conveys is a constant orgy of the senses, and an intellectual complicity based on it. Maupassant emerges in these pages not only as the prince of writing and, which is even less surprising, of love-making but also as the most brilliant of conversationalists. The diarist adores him. What unites them may not be love in the ordinary or romantic way; but it is deeper than that: '. . . Cette fusion du couple, l'extase du sexe . . . plus fort que l'amour, bien plus violent . . .' Monogamy does not come into it, on the contrary. Their idylls are adorned by other women, seduced by her as a Lesbian and then recruited by her for him to be seduced; seduced to share in the pleasures of sex and ether. A tragic and violent pleasure-seeking lust permeates the *Cahier*; 'Puisque le bonheur m'est défendu, je prendrai ma revanche dans le plaisir,' Guy said. And as she understood him so perfectly, he came round to loving her in spite of all his (and her) vows to keep themselves free of the shackles of love. 'Je n'ai jamais aimé aucune femme,' he told her, 'mais toi, je t'aime furieusement.' And she believed him; and Borel believed *her*. He claimed that this up to then unknown woman had been 'la plus aimée' of Guy de Maupassant.

Most of the *Maupassantiens*, however, were most sceptical about the whole affair. Some thought the diary a fake; the very existence of its alleged authoress was doubted. A long-drawn inter-philologist war flared up and, in the course of the years passed since, M. Borel has disclosed, in a considerable number of publications, more and more about both his heroine in general and her links with Maupassant in particular. The publications included long letters from their correspondence. The way M. Borel had got hold of these letters was not always made clear, but he did emphasize that his initial source of information on the matter was Léon Fontaine who had told him in full confidence about this one great and secret love of his illustrious friend. She was known under the name Gisèle d'Estoc.

The most important writings or publications by Pierre Borel on the matter (besides the *Cahier*) were these: *Maupassant et l'Androgyne* (Editions du Livre Moderne, 1944); *Le vrai Maupassant* (Cailler, Genève, 1951); *Une amoureuse inconnue de Maupassant* (1959), and *Guy de Maupassant et Gisèle d'Estoc* (1962), both published in *Les Œuvres Libres*. Most emphatic in their doubts about the whole story were Auriant who questioned the authenticity of the *Cahier* (in *Mercure de France*, 15 July

1939; to which M. Borel replied in the same periodical, (one month later), and the American Professor A. Artinian who in his *Maupassant and Gisèle d'Estoc: A Warning* questioned the authenticity of the letters attributed by Borel to Maupassant. Perhaps the only *Maupassantien* actively to take up Borel's case was the associate editor ('rédacteur en chef') of *Les Œuvres Libres*, M. Armand Lanoux who made enquiries in French provincial archives about the woman who may have been identified as Gisèle d'Estoc, and succeeded in this way in verifying some at least of M. Borel's allegations. Readers interested in the controversy may be referred to the scholarly Introduction, by Dr Pierre Cogny, to the 1962 edition of *Notre Cœur* (Librairie Marcel Didier, Paris) which on pp. IX–XVII contains a summing-up. Yet I should like to ask the reader's permission to tell him in my own words about: (*a*) the essence of Pierre Borel's (and partly Armand Lanoux's) findings or allegations; (*b*) the way the *Maupassantien* world reacted to them; and (*c*) what I myself feel to be true.

(*a*) *Borel's findings:* I am afraid I shall have to be somewhat vague about these because – as I shall come to explain it under (*c*) – they are often contradictory. However, these may be regarded as the most important facts.

The woman who in literary and artistic life figured as Gisèle (and some time even as Gysel) d'Estoc was called in legal documents Marie-Elise, or Marie-Paula, Courbe; and later also Madame Desbarres. She was born in Nancy, in 1863; and died, when forty-four, of leprosy, in Nice, where she had spent quite a few years.

She was an authoress and sculptress of considerable courage and originality, and a woman of captivating appearance, with a Diana-like figure. Manet painted her.

She was energetic, impulsive, enterprising, ambitious. In a self-introductory letter to Maupassant she described herself as an *androgyne*. She often dressed up as a man, partly for fun, partly as a challenge to conventions. She felt that 'a third sex' was being born, and she was its representative. She was attracted to men and women of genius who struck her as typical, in one way or another, of that inter-sex state which she felt was much more interesting than to be simply male or female. She raved about the homosexual visions of Michelangelo, in the Sistine chapel. And her fellow-countrywoman, Jeanne d'Arc, was her favourite. She wrote (so M. Borel termed it) 'une monographie intuitive' of her. She saw in her the embodiment of the domineering, virile woman, virile in brains and strength of character though ravishing as a female; not neutralized, as it were, but rather like having two active sexes.

As society in those days did not offer much chance to women of such inclinations, Gisèle turned to the social revolutionaries in her theoretical sympathies; she was interested in Blanqui and Proudhon, and their doctrines.

Her love affairs with men were unhappy, or rather dull, meaningless; 'arriviste, Gisèle finit par avoir de l'amour une idée arrêtée: *ne jamais se donner, jouir*' . . . Anyway, she felt about women more passionately, and met her punishment from their hands: 'Si notre héroïne a toujours été cruelle pour les hommes, c'est par les femmes qu'elle sera punie . . .' She fell in love with a young 'femme de lettre . . . dans le goût de Barbey d'Aurevilly et d'Edgar Poe', and this woman deserted her. Then, in what was the stormiest drama of her life, she started an affair with the beautiful blonde, Emma Bouer, trapeze artist of the Cirque Medrane, also painted by Manet. When Emma, too, failed to comply with her demands, she (Gisèle) stabbed her, but Emma survived and forgave.

Apparently, it was in the course of such an inter-sex imbroglio that Gisèle fell out with the writer Laurent Tailhade. In 1894 this name was well known to the French audience, less for his literary work than on account of a police scandal in which he almost lost his life. Anarchist attempts were then quite frequent, and after one with fatal consequences Tailhade was noted to have exclaimed, 'Qu'importe les victimes si le geste est beau!' Very much *fin du siècle*, we may add, though akin to what any 'rebel without a cause' in any epoch, including our own, may have said in comparable circumstances. Poor man, he got his retribution, or almost; as he was in the Café Foyot, he was wounded by an exploding bomb. Everybody thought that that bomb had been planted by the anarchists; but the police officer Ernest Reynaud, who was a symbolist poet, had another idea. He knew that only some hours before the explosion, Gisèle had sworn in anger to 'settle her accounts' with Tailhade, and she tried.

There was but one man, according to Pierre Borel, to whom Gisèle really could 'give herself', and this was Maupassant. Her initial feeling of affinity with him was to some extent intellectual; in his writings, she sensed the man who had become aware of the *tiers sexe*. He, in his turn, was attracted by her unconventional wit and her concoction of homo- and hetero-sexuality; from his short story, of his early thirties, *La femme de Paul*, dealing with Lesbians on the Seine, until his last finished novel, *Notre Cœur*, with a sensual and sophisticated heroine who also betrays such inclinations,[1] he always searched for this sort of partner. In Gisèle, he found it – though this partnership was not to last for ever either.

(*b*) M. Borel got harsh treatment from his colleagues. I mentioned some outright attacks; to these may be added snubs such as that coming from M. Vial who in the bibliography of his *Guy de Maupassant et l'Art du Roman* emphatically warns the reader against trusting M. Borel's information, on the occultism of Maupassant's ancestors as well as on his love affairs. As the friend of the late Léon Fontaine, as the editor of a considerable part of Maupassant's correspondence, Pierre Borel's name was quoted, but with undisguised reluctance. As to Gisèle d'Estoc, she has been completely ignored in most of the scholarly books on Maupassant, including the biographies by Dumesnil and Steegmuller (though the latter treats his hero's sex life at some length and touches also on his 'Lesbos' complex).

How far is this attitude justified? To some extent, Borel no doubt invites it. His narrative, with paragraphs such as

> A la porte, Guy se penche et dépose sur la main de Gisèle un long baiser qui tremble.
> Dans la rue, la jeune femme se hâte, envahie par un affreux pressentiment. Elle voudrait se retourner pour revoir encore

---

[1] Dr Cogny writes: 'Michèle [de Burne] était plus nettement lesbienne dans la version primitive [du roman *Notre Coeur*]. A la page 193 du manuscrit, Michèle et la princesse Malten s'embrassent sur la bouche, ce qui fait dire à Mariolle: *Toutes ces femmes-là finiront par s'aimer entre elles*' (op. cit., p. xxxvii). This just in support of M. Borel's conjecture.

une fois la maison où si souvent elle a été heureuse. Elle n'ose
pas . . .

is certainly unlikely to rank with the pieces of highest standing
in literary history writing. What he says, occasionally smacks
of penny-paper spiritualism; more often, of woman's magazine
eroticism; and consistency about dates is not one of his merits.
But this is no reason to dismiss all his findings either as a fake or
as irrelevant. My feeling is that his trade has on the whole been
a bit unfair to him.

(c) In this trial, there can be no final judgment passed to acquit
him of all suspicions because, as his defender, M. Lanoux says:[1]

> Tout laisse à penser que le *Cahier d'Amour*, les lettres de
> Guy de Maupassant à Gisèle d'Estoc, les originaux photo-
> graphiques qui les accompagnaient sont actuellement aux
> U.S.A., entre les mains des collectionneurs américains. On
> peut espérer que le hasard les mettant en présence de ces
> lignes, ils feraient connaître le lieu où se trouvent ces pièces,
> leur déscription et leur inventaire. . . .

Which boils down to the fact that 'one can hope' if one insists on
certainty. I, personally, cannot imagine, however, that the
essential part of the documents presented by M. Borel should be
forged.

The existence of an authoress with the name or pen-name
Gisèle d'Estoc in the late nineteenth century is ascertainable in
the Bibliothèque Nationale, Paris. Of her *Psychologie de Jeanne
d'Arc*, only a mutilated copy is available, but this is sufficient to
show her as the sort of fuss-maker about the virile genius in the
female flesh that one guesses from M. Borel's descriptions she
must have been. The booklet contains what one guesses was a
doctored portrait of the authoress, a cropped hair girl, with large
and brave eyes, and the cross of Lorraine on her neck. Even more
typical perhaps is her sort of satirical novel of 1887, *La Vierge-
Réclame*, in the series 'Les Gloires malsaines', with frolicsome
illustrations; on the title page, a woman in circus tights, hitting
the drum and cymbals. This book contains guesses and anec-

[1] *Les Œuvres Libres*, August 1962, p. 137. (Introducing P. Borel's
publication.)

dotes round the 'virginité problématique' of a girl who, when twenty, 'publia un livre sans précédent: *L'Homme-Vénus*'. I am now unable to make out of my notes jotted down in the Bibliothèque, whether it was the Virgin of Orléans or the 'Réclame' Virgin at whose birth Gisèle d'Estoc imagined this dialogue could have taken place:

> — C'est une fille!
> — Elle mourra de n'être point assez fille.

This woman, 'femme par les sentiments, virile par la pensée', committed 'le crime de lèse-banalité'. In both these writings by Gisèle d'Estoc, one comes across the facetious self-pity of a woman who fornicates in protest against the social order. As a type, a link between George Sand and Simone de Beauvoir. Surely it would be beyond Pierre Borel to *invent* anything like that!

And the *Cahier*. Very much by the same authoress if in a panting and musing, not to say orgasm-ridden, mood. Full of inaccuracies, no doubt; but these strike me as evidence of their genuineness rather than a reason to doubt that. Let me just illustrate it by one example, this entry (p. 74):

> Guy était très superstitieux comme le sont souvent les grands esprits. Il me dit un jour: 'Cette nuit, j'ai rêvé que Harry Allis se noyait. J'ai peur qu'il lui soit arrivé un malheur.' Le soir du même jour, on venait lui annoncer la mort de son ami.

This could not possibly refer to anybody else than Maupassant's old pal, erstwhile editor of *La Revue Moderne et Naturaliste*, Hippolyte Percher, known under his pen-name Harry Alis (not A*ll*is); but, factually, it is wrong. Harry Alis lived longer than Maupassant, and was killed, on 3 January 1895, in a duel. His death was recorded amongst other places, in *The Times*: in his own country, of course, it was a matter of common knowledge. So Gisèle must have muddled him up with another friend, or worked up a minor accident into a fatal one in her memory, or mis-remembered a third and fourth detail as she mis-remembered the spelling; but surely a literary forger would avoid such pitfalls with ease? Why would he think at all of bringing in the misdated death of a man so completely forgotten as was Harry Alis by the 1930s? Only to make the reader attribute the lapse in memory to the hysterical phantasmagories of a super-excitable 'androgyne'? Too subtle to be true. We are on safer ground by assuming that the *Cahier* is genuine, and so are the mistakes in it.

Gisèle d'Estoc was only human (or feminine? or androgynous?) when she grossly overrated her own importance in her lover's life; and M. Borel, too, was as human as any historian, journalist, research scholar and scoop-hunter can be in his eagerness to establish his authority in the subject-matter he had chosen, and to outmanoeuvre his competitors by attributing to his own findings more decisive interest than to those of others. This may not be *chic*, but such are women, such are men and such are authors.

I do not suggest one should *believe* M. Borel. In fact, it is impossible to believe *everything* he wrote; his vagueness about dates and sources acts as a deterrent, and his description of the love affair published in 1962 differs considerably from that published in 1959 . . . My impression is that he was often unable to resist the temptation to pad his material with the products of his imagination, and was reluctant to make this clear – even to himself perhaps – when some new document got hold of by him threw a different light on the subject. Apart from these conflicting details, it seems clear that Gisèle was not, to use M. Borel's term, 'la *plus* aimée' of Maupassant; *prima inter pares* in that impressive cavalcade was doubtless Marie Kann. It is certain, however, that Gisèle d'Estoc did exist; more than likely that she did have an affair with Maupassant; and that some facets of his personality became manifest in the course of this love affair more than they did in any other male or female company. His pan-sexualism, conspicuous in his excitement about Lesbian love, and his hunt after killing *drogues* and tragic pleasures, in a mood inherited from his uncle, Alfred, received an outlet in the temporary partnership with a woman who shared these passions and added to them the posture of a prophetess. My own guess is that it was this posture which first mesmerized Maupassant and then got on his nerves.

9 · (see p. 243)

Harry Alis (Chapter 30; and Appendix 8) as quoted by Auriant, *Mercure de France*, 1 May 1931, p. 610, noted as a matter of common knowledge amongst the friends of Guy de Maupassant that

> un journaliste dont je mutile peut-être le nom bicornu, Boborygine, venu pour demander au poète des chroniques mondaines ... s'enfui épouvanté de cette virilité superbe.

This seems to be the same performance as the one mentioned by Goncourt on pp. 382 and 533, Vol. IV, of his *Journal* (cf. Appendix 4); and is likely to have taken place in 1882, when Maupassant was thirty-two. But, apparently, neither his potency nor his exhibitionism slackened until his physical collapse; or else, he made up in exhibitionism what he was losing in potency, and could carry on noticeably unabated. Frank Harris's chapter on Maupassant (Vol. II, Chapter XX in *My Life and Loves*, quoted on other matters on p. 247, Chapter 48 of this book) supplies very interesting material from this point of view. I have no illusions about Harris's reliability; and even this chapter is full of factual inaccuracies and psychological absurdities, too trivial to enumerate. But there is no reason to doubt that Maupassant liked to boast, as Harris describes him, of being able to produce erection whenever he wished. (Some readers may know the relevant paragraph from Steegmuller's book in which it was quoted verbatim). I found, however, most interesting his inadvertent admission of the fact that he was often but pretending. After boasting, a bit like the Marseillais in his *Maison turque*, that 'I have counted twenty and more ...' he told Harris: 'Surely you know that in two or three times you exhaust your stock of semen, so that you can go on afterwards without further loss.' In other words, vanity made him go on with a nerve-exhausting exercise without even hoping to get the pleasure of orgasm out of it. Similar feats – erection without ejaculation – were practised by some exotic sects as part of a flagellant and ascetic discipline. Maupassant practised them as a dedicated pleasure-seeker. *Les extrêmes se touchent.*

INDEX OF PERSONS

INDEX OF WORKS
BY MAUPASSANT